THOUGHTS FOR TODAY

A COMPILATION OF DEVOTIONAL THOUGHTS FOR EACH
DAY OFFERED WITH THE HOPE THAT EACH ONE WILL
DRAW THE READER INTO A MORE INTIMATE RELATION-
SHIP WITH THE AUTHOR OF THE BIBLE, THE HOLY SPIRIT,
AND THE LORD OF GLORY, JESUS THE CHRIST OF GOD.

BY

GEORGE M. STOVER JR., D.MIN., TH.D., PH.D.

"... But we have the mind of Christ (the Messiah) and do hold the thoughts (feelings and purposes) of His heart"
1 Corinthians 2:16 (AMP)

Thoughts For Today

by
George M. Stover Jr., Ph.D.

Thoughts For Today
by George M. Stover Jr., D.Min., Th.D., Ph.D.

Printed in the United States of America

ISBN 978-0985512811

Published by
Wellspring Publishing
4870 Janell Drive
Las Vegas, Nevada 89149
USA
For further information:
(702) 631-5027
wecan@wellspringministries.com
www.wellspringlv.com

DEDICATION

THIS BOOK IS DEDICATED TO THE HOLY SPIRIT; WITHOUT WHOM I WOULD HAVE NOTHING TO WRITE, MY LOVELY WIFE, SHARON, WHO REVIEWED THE LAYOUT AND TEXT, AND ENCOURAGED ME ALONG THE WAY WHILE ALLOWING ME THE TIME TO COMPLETE THE WORK.

I COULD NOT HAVE GONE TO PRINT WITHOUT MY DEAR FRIENDS, REV. CAMILLE BECKER, TH.M., DR. LOU GRILLO, D.C.ED., AND DR. JOHN ONYEMA, M.D., TAKING THE TIME TO EDIT THE TEXT.

THANK YOU, TOO, TO THE MANY FOLLOWERS OF MY BLOG WHO REQUESTED THESE THOUGHTS IN BOOK FORM.

TABLE OF CONTENTS

JANUARY

January 01 - Investments Return

Give, and it shall be given unto you; good measure, pressed down, and shaken together, and running over, shall men give into your bosom. For with the same measure that ye mete withal it shall be measured to you again.
Luke 6:38 (KJV)

Giving something away, without thought of return, is not generally practiced by self-serving people. Oh, a bribe or a gift to garner favor, is a normal practice for those who deal under the delusion that, "the end justifies the means." Even Christians, immature or imitators, find themselves giving to get from God.

But, you might say, "Isn't that what this verse is saying? If I give then I will receive?" Ah, my friend, the answer is both, "Yes," and, "No."

Yes, liberal, glad to do it, giving that is intended to bless the recipient does result in a lavish return. This is at the heart of God, who does everything to benefit the object of His love. Even those things that the devil or other people mean for evil, He will turn for good.

No, stingy, self-seeking people will not realize the benefit and power that this verse is speaking of. The key to understanding this verse is found in the last sentence, "For with the same measure that ye mete withal it shall be measured to you again."

The words translated, the same measure, **autos metron**, convey the thought of, not only of a container size or type, but that of the rule or standard of judgment that produces the giving. This, then, is speaking of the standard of giving rather than the amount of the thing given. We are speaking of giving that is due and fit for the occasion. We could call this kind of giving, righteous. This giving flows from the heart of God through the giver to the recipient.

It is the regard for, the high esteem or opinion of, the recipient of the gift that determines the value of its return and resultant multiplication. That which is given in, and due to, the love of God will return with the unfailing abundant provision of the love of God.

January 02 - Fulness Received

And of his fulness have all we received, and grace for
grace. For the law was given by Moses, but grace and truth
came by Jesus Christ. John 1:16-17 (KJV)

How many Christians do you think have received the fulness
of God? Do you consider yourself to have received God's
fulness? For years I had not and would not have were it not for
a revelation of the grace of God.

Pleroma, is the Greek word translated, fulness. It with the
idea of a ship inasmuch as it is filled (i.e. manned) with sailors,
rowers, and soldiers. In the New Testament we understand it
to mean, the body of believers, as that which is filled with the
presence, power, agency, and riches of God and of Christ. It also
speaks of being fulfilled or satisfied. Our verse says that we all
received this fulness, "and grace for grace."

Herein is the key to our experiencing the fulness that "all
we received." We read, "and grace for grace." Grace, *charis,* for,
anti, Grace, *charis*. This word, *anti*, implies being over against or
opposite to. It also means to replace something with something
else or, for this cause.

The merciful kindness of God, grace, *charis,* was displayed
under the law to a certain extent (Mat. 5:45 (KJV) ". . . [H]e
maketh his sun to rise on the evil and on the good, and sendeth
rain on the just and on the unjust.". But to the believer, He
replaces limited grace with unlimited grace, favor and blessing.

John 8:32 (KJV) says, "And ye shall know the truth, *alethes*,
and the truth shall make you free, *eleutheroo*, set you at liberty
from the dominion of sin". The law exposes sin but cannot
deliver from it. Only New Testament grace, *charis*, can deliver
one from the power of sin.

It is the truth of the Good News that unmerited, unearned,
unlimited, lavish grace has replaced the limited grace of the law
that sets the believer free from sin's power.

The love of God is now shed abroad in their hearts and love
cannot fail in its work of faith.

Receive the grace, *charis,* that only the Son of God can give
to His own. It will change the rest of your life!

January 03 - Should Races Blend?

Be ye not unequally yoked together with unbelievers: for what fellowship hath righteousness with unrighteousness? and what communion hath light with darkness? And what concord hath Christ with Belial? or what part hath he that believeth with an infidel? 2 Corinthians 6:14-15 (KJV)

Did the title of today's "Thought for Today" cause your hackles to rise? That was my intention.

Let me clarify: There are only two races of people; the sons of Satan and the sons of God. God only deals with covenant people and the lost. He recognizes no other people groups on earth.

Our verse today sets in place a principle that should never, never, never be ignored: "Be ye not unequally yoked together with unbelievers" (those of the lost race). The reasoning of God is flawless in this matter, as in all matters. Righteousness cannot coexist with unrighteousness anymore than oil can successfully mix with water.

For the saved and the unsaved to marry each other or to be partners in a business only brings confusion and every evil work. The anointing of the Anointed One (Christ Jesus) and the darkness of the devil controlled world are incompatible and cannot agree. They cannot have communion any more than light and darkness can exist in the same place at the same time.

During my years of pastoral ministry, my experience is that these unequal covenants never work well. In marriage, each individual naturally desires that their spouse be a part of what they are interested in and enjoy. This is especially true of a believer who desires to share their intimate relationship with the Lord with their soul mate.

In business there is usually a great deal of friction that develops over integrity issues. A lost person and a Christian have diametrically opposed views on how business should be conducted, the rules by which they operate and how profits will be handled.

Neither can unregenerate politicians properly serve a Christian community. Such can be seen in America's condition at present.

January 04 - Agreeing With God

And what agreement hath the temple of God with idols? for ye are the temple of the living God; as God hath said, I will dwell in them, and walk in them; and I will be their God, and they shall be my people. Wherefore come out from among them, and be ye separate, saith the Lord, and touch not the unclean thing; and I will receive you, And will be a Father unto you, and ye shall be my sons and daughters, saith the Lord Almighty.
2 Corinthians 6:16-18 (KJV)

Whoever you agree with brings its own reward. Agreeing with demonic forces, represented by idols, will bring you loss, death and destruction. Agreeing with God holds great promise.

The thief cometh not, but for to steal, and to kill, and to destroy: I am come that they might have life, and that they might have it more abundantly. John 10:10 (KJV)

Our text above tells us that there are seven promises that are ours if we agree with God. They are promises that allow us to have life and life more abundantly. Politically speaking, "life, liberty, and the pursuit of happiness."

When we receive Jesus the Christ, the Anointed One of God, as our Savior, we become the recipients of all the blessing that is included in the family of God. We have been adopted into the family!

What are those seven promises? Well, look at this: the Almighty says,

(1) I will dwell in them. (2) I will walk in them,
(3) I will be their God, (4) You shall be My people,
(5) I will receive you, (6) I will be a Father unto you, and
(7) You shall be My sons and daughters.

Imagine, God, the Creator of all that there is, living inside of you. No wonder the Bible says, "greater is he that is in you, than he that is in the world" (1 Jn 4:4 KJV).

God, Himself, is present within you at all times, walking in you and affirming you as His own and working out His plans for your good.

January 05 - Agreeing With God (Continued)

He has said that,

The steps of a good man are ordered by the LORD: and he delighteth in his way. Psalms 37:23 (KJV).

By "a Christian" I mean someone who has become born again by receiving Jesus the Christ as Lord and Savior. Jesus, Himself, said that we must be born again:

Jesus answered and said unto him, Verily, verily, I say unto thee, Except a man be born again, he cannot see the kingdom of God. John 3:3 (KJV)

Way too many "Christians" have never really become Christians. They go to church. They may even tithe, teach Sunday School or serve the Church in some way, but they have never really made the connection that only comes by repentance, confession and acceptance.

Then Peter said unto them, Repent, and be baptized every one of you in the name of Jesus Christ for the remission of sins, and ye shall receive the gift of the Holy Ghost. Acts 2:38 (KJV)

That if thou shalt confess with thy mouth the Lord Jesus, and shalt believe in thine heart that God hath raised him from the dead, thou shalt be saved. For with the heart man believeth unto righteousness; and with the mouth confession is made unto salvation. Romans 10:9-10 (KJV)

Once you have received the Lord Jesus you will experience the reality, "that he which hath begun a good work in you will perform it." Your confidence level will soar and the seemingly impossible will become possible.

And Jesus said unto them, Because of your unbelief: for verily I say unto you, If ye have faith as a grain of mustard seed, ye shall say unto this mountain, Remove hence to yonder place; and it shall remove; and nothing shall be impossible unto you. Matthew 17:20 (KJV)

For with God nothing shall be impossible. Luke 1:37 (KJV)

And he said, The things which are impossible with men are possible with God. Luke 18:27 (KJV) - *Selah*

January 06 - God will not fail you

Being confident of this very thing, that he which hath begun a good work in you will perform it until the day of Jesus Christ: Philippians 1:6 (KJV)

Over the years I have found many people who are lacking confidence in their ability to succeed in life. They allow situations and circumstances, or what they hear, press them to become something less than what they are actually capable of. National fear mongering coupled with drug use is causing a wave of self-destructive behavior that is becoming a crisis of national scope.

A Christian should never allow themselves to be convinced by the devil, demons or people used by them that they cannot be, or do, anything. God, who cannot lie, has said that we should say, "I can do all things through Christ which strengtheneth me" Philippians 4:13 (KJV), believe it and act on it.

God will not fail you! He gave His Word so that you could speak it in faith. He has promised that if you will believe and speak His Word you will receive what you say:

And Jesus, replying, said to them, Have faith in God [constantly]. Truly I tell you, whoever says to this mountain, Be lifted up and thrown into the sea! and does not doubt at all in his heart but believes that what he says will take place, it will be done for him. For this reason I am telling you, whatever you ask for in prayer, believe (trust and be confident) that it is granted to you, and you will [get it]. And whenever you stand praying, if you have anything against anyone, forgive him and let it drop (leave it, let it go), in order that your Father Who is in heaven may also forgive you your [own] failings and shortcomings and let them drop. Mark 11:22-25 (AMP)

Your God, who cannot lie, has told you to lay hold of His faith, stand against doubt, believe and speak, and you will have whatsoever you ask for. He will not fail you!

Don't fail yourself by refusing to let go of every wrong done or word spoken against you. Yes, unforgiveness will separate you from every covenant promise that you should be enjoying.

Don't fail yourself. God will never fail you.

January 07 - There is a Spirit in Man

But there is a spirit in man: and the inspiration of the Almighty giveth them understanding. Great men are not always wise: neither do the aged understand judgment. Job 32:8-9 (KJV)

Those who we deem to be "great men" are not necessarily wise men nor, because of age, does mankind understand righteousness, **mishpat**, that is, righteous judgement. In fact, thanks to our educational system, many have grown old with ideas imparted to them by atheists and agnostics, socialists and Marxists.

Rather than learning to read, write and relate to God's creation through a scriptural education, they have been taught that knowledge has nothing to do with God and that evolution is the answer to our origin and that science, so called, is supreme. This long term deconstruction of Christian thought is being felt in ever increasing changes in our society and will, unchecked, lead to our ultimate destruction.

The Book of Mark records the following:

And Jesus answering said unto them, Do ye not therefore err, because ye know not the scriptures, neither the power of God? Mark 12:24 (KJV)

Take heart. "There is a spirit in man," born again humanity that is able to yield to "the inspiration of the Almighty" and receive "understanding" that can only come from God through His Word and His Spirit.

The fear of the LORD is the beginning of wisdom: and the knowledge of the holy is understanding. Proverbs 9:10 (KJV)

The inspiration I'm speaking of is the, **neshamah**, or, breath of God. The very life of God imparted into the spirit and soul of man:

For who hath known the mind of the Lord, that he may instruct him? But, we have the mind of Christ. 1 Corinthians 2:16 (KJV).

This, and this alone, gives the understanding, **biyn**, that is, the discernment, knowledge and understanding necessary to become truly "great men" who "understand judgement."

January 08 - God has a Soul

But he is in one mind, and who can turn him? and what his soul desireth, even that he doeth. Job 23:13 (KJV)

Have you ever considered that God has a soul? That should be a thrilling revelation if you have not considered it before.

Man is a tripartite being, much like God.

And the very God of peace sanctify you wholly; and I pray God your whole spirit and soul and body be preserved blameless unto the coming of our Lord Jesus Christ. 1 Thessalonians 5:23 (KJV),

In John 4:24 we find that, "God is a Spirit." This Spirit Being has a soul. The soul consists of the will, intellect and emotions. Scripture is full of examples of God displaying will, intellect and emotion.

What God the Father does not have is a flesh and blood nor a flesh and bone body. Now, however, God (Father, Son and Holy Spirit) does have a body of flesh and bone because the resurrected Jesus has a body. There is now a Man in heaven.

Behold my hands and my feet, that it is I myself: handle me, and see; for a spirit hath not flesh and bones, as ye see me have. Luke 24:39 (KJV)

The Godhead (Father, Son and Holy Ghost) is One: "Hear, O Israel: The LORD our God is one LORD" Deut. 6:4 (KJV). The One LORD, **YHWH**, "is in one, *'echad*, mind." This Hebrew word, *'echad*, means: one after another, once for all, one by one. This confirms our understanding of the Triune God, *'elohiym*, which translates as: Gods [plural intensive-singular] or, the true triune God.

The Father and the Holy Ghost are Spirit and the Son is Spirit with a body. The Eternal Godhead is inseparable and of "one mind, and who can turn Him?"

Because God has a soul, He can love you, cherish you, think thoughts of good toward you, make plans for you, determine to bless you, and speak to you. That is a wonderful revelation to consider today!

For I know the thoughts and plans that I have for you, says the Lord, thoughts and plans for welfare and peace and not for evil, to give you hope in your final outcome. Jeremiah 29:11 (AMP)

January 09 - Concerning the Wicked

Though he heap up silver as the dust, and prepare raiment as the clay; He may prepare it, but the just shall put it on, and the innocent shall divide the silver.
Job 27:16-17 (KJV)

If we are not careful we can begin to accuse God of not providing for us properly. We look at what the wealthy non-Christian has and wonder why we don't have it. This, Beloved, is a trap of the devil, the lying accuser. His tactics have not changed since he spoke to Eve in the garden saying, "Hath God said?" (Gen. 3:1, 3). He always tries to instill doubt in the mind of those who serve the Lord.

We are told to, "Rest in the LORD, and wait patiently for him: fret not thyself because of him who prospereth in his way, because of the man who bringeth wicked devices to pass" (Psa. 37:7 KJV), and we are assured that, "A little that a righteous man hath is better than the riches of many wicked" (Psa. 37:16 KJV).

Our God has said that it is His will that we, "prosper and be in good health, even as our soul prospers" (3 Jn. 2). He has also told us that it gives Him pleasure to prosper us (Psa. 35:27).

If God, who cannot lie, has given us these promises, how can we but believe. This is the stuff faith is made of: Trusting the Lord to do what He has promised.

Oh, don't forget Proverbs 13:22, ". . . the wealth of the sinner is laid up for the just." Or, how about Job 27:16, 17, "Though he heap up silver as the dust, and prepare raiment as the clay; He may prepare it, but the just shall put it on, and the innocent shall divide the silver." There is more. Read Isaiah 23:18; Proverbs 28:8, or Ecclesiastes 2:26. The promise is the same. The lost "may prepare it, but the just shall put it on." We learn from Haggai 2:8 that the silver and gold of the earth belongs to the Lord: "The silver is mine, and the gold is mine, saith the LORD of hosts".

Our God will give it to whom He will. Don't be covetous but rejoice in His goodness toward you. Then you will see the transfer of wealth that so many are speaking of.

What our God is about to do is marvelous in our eyes.

January 10 - Trouble Makers or Problem Solvers?

Where no wood is, there the fire goeth out: so where there is no talebearer, the strife ceaseth. As coals are to burning coals, and wood to fire; so is a contentious man to kindle strife. Proverbs 26:20-21 (KJV)

I'm sure that we all know people who have a knack for getting right to the root of a problem. They can come into a situation and almost immediately see how to fix it. My wife, Sharon, is like that. There is a spiritual discerning and a gift of insight that work together in her life. Pastor Glenn Foster, a prophet, once told her, "You are God's plumber. You will go in and find the clog in the pipe and know exactly how to unclog it."

Then, there are others who seem to make a problem out of nothing and then offer themselves as the fixer of the problem. They, then, become the hero of the day and gain a certain amount of control. Perhaps you know someone like this. Unfortunately, many are manipulated (which is witchcraft) by subtle suggestions or passionate pleas for righting perceived wrongs or offenses. Heavy doses of guilt pour from such a one.

By innuendo the "contentious man" kindles strife. The Hebrew word for strife, **reeb**, means to cause controversy and contention which leads to strife. It means, a contest without real cause; a slanderer. It is simply a power play on the part of the contentious one.

The word, contentious, **nirgān**, comes from an unused root meaning, to roll to pieces. By constant innuendo, something that is good can be rolled to pieces until it looks like something broken, bad, evil or wicked.

Beloved, beware of such and put them out of your circle of influence until they can see their wicked way and repent. If you don't, they will tear up your relationships, destroy your church or organization and then wonder what went wrong while saying, "Trouble seems to always find me," and in pride saying, "or am I sent to trouble to fix it?"

January 11 - What Are You Worth?

Forasmuch as ye know that ye were not redeemed
with corruptible things, as silver and gold, from your vain
conversation received by tradition from your fathers;
1 Peter 1:18 (KJV)

Today, I would like to talk to you about what you are worth.
It is vitally important that you come to understand your value.
If you are not convinced of your inestimable worth then you
may sell yourself short.

If you watch the Antique Road Show program you will soon
realize that many of the folks you see with extremely valuable
pictures, vases, art work, or other memorabilia, found them at
little or no cost on someone else's trash heap or garage sale. The
previous owner did not know the value of what they had.

Satan will do anything to get you to believe that you are
worthless or worth very little. If he can deceive you in this area
you will sell out for almost any price.

The truth, however, is that you are priceless. Your value has
been established by God Almighty Himself.

But with the precious blood of Christ, as of a lamb
without blemish and without spot: 1 Peter 1:19 (KJV)

He paid the highest price of heaven for you. You are one-
of-a-kind and worth everything to Him. He gave His only
begotten Son, His most prized possession, for you. Don't sell
yourself short.

You are so important to Him that He chose to live in you
(1 Cor. 3:16; 2 Cor. 6:16). He made you a king and priest (Rev.
1:6; 5;10).

There is not a man or woman on earth that can pay what
you are worth. Don't sell your body, your integrity, your ministry,
your anointing, for any amount of money. You are worth more
than that. Besides you are not your own.

For ye are bought with a price: therefore glorify God
in your body, and in your spirit, which are God's.
1 Corinthians 6:20 (KJV); [also, 7:23].

January 12 - The Shout Of A King

He hath not beheld iniquity in Jacob, neither hath he seen perverseness in Israel: the LORD his God is with him, and the shout of a king is among them.
Numbers 23:21 (KJV)

For those who live a life cleansed by the blood of Jesus, for those who shun iniquity and perverseness, there is the promise of the LORD's continual presence. This makes them more than conquerors and over-comers in His sight. The shout of the King is among them.

Much of the Christian community has thrown off the idea of holiness as an attainable life style, yet, this is still the call of heaven to those that are the King's.

Sanctify yourselves therefore, and be ye holy: for I am the LORD your God. Leviticus 20:7 (KJV)

And ye shall be holy unto me: for I the LORD am holy, and have severed you from other people, that ye should be mine. Leviticus 20:26 (KJV)

But as he which hath called you is holy, so be ye holy in all manner of conversation; Because it is written, Be ye holy; for I am holy. 1 Peter 1:15-16 (KJV)

As you can see, the call to holiness is both in the Old Testament and the New. Our God is holy and His Spirit within us is holy.

If we are born-again Christians we are new creations, our spirit is new, pure and holy, and commingled together with the Holy Spirit of God Himself. He superimposed Himself upon our spirit. We are one with Him.

The Victor of the Cross, the King of Glory, is within us and He utters "the shout of a king" to declare the victory over sin is won and that those that are His own are cleansed from all unrighteousness by His blood. Every enemy arrayed against us trembles in terror at the sound of His voice.

Darkness has fled and light has come. The iniquity of the old man [Jacob] is not seen any more and perverseness is not found in the princes [Israel] of God.
Selah

January 13 - New Testament Tithing

> Woe unto you, scribes and Pharisees, hypocrites! for ye pay tithe of mint and anise and cummin, and have omitted the weightier matters of the law, judgment, mercy, and faith: these ought ye to have done, and not to leave the other undone. Matthew 23:23 (KJV)

It has been said that tithing is not mentioned in the New Testament and that our verse for today referred to the law so it does not apply to New Testament times. This, Beloved, is the spirit of stinginess, poverty, and lack that holds the Church back from achieving its mandate to reach the world with the Gospel.

The simple truth of Scripture is easily understood when one allows scripture to explain and expand upon Scripture. The following verse reveals Jesus speaking concerning this same issue; comparing the works of the Pharisee's and Sadducee's with those of the Christian.

> For I say unto you, That except your righteousness shall exceed the righteousness of the scribes and Pharisees, ye shall in no case enter into the kingdom of heaven. Matthew 5:20 (KJV)

If we are honest and open to the Word of God Himself, we see that the "tithe," which means 10%, is a requirement of the law. But the Christian is bound by a higher law that calls for a righteousness that exceeds that of the law. In other words, the Christian minimum "tithe" is at least 11%, but actually limited only by the heart and spirit of giving that is found in the character and nature of God.

> For God so loved the world, that he gave his only begotten Son, that whosoever believeth in him should not perish, but have everlasting life. John 3:16 (KJV)

Christians are to be unlimited givers that make the law seem totally inconsequential. Their reward is seen below:

> Give, and it shall be given unto you; good measure, pressed down, and shaken together, and running over, shall men give into your bosom. For with the same measure that ye mete withal it shall be measured to you again. Luke 6:38 (KJV)

January 14 - Every Tongue Against Thee

No weapon that is formed against thee shall prosper; and every tongue that shall rise against thee in judgment thou shalt condemn. This is the heritage of the servants of the LORD, and their righteousness is of me, saith the LORD. Isaiah 54:17 (KJV)

I bring this much quoted verse to you once again so that you can benefit from the richness of its treasure.

There is nothing meant for your harm that can prosper. The weapon, *kaliy*, can be a thing, person or that which issues from a thing or person. It's being formed, *yatsar*, can be something conceived, planned or born of human or spirit activity or purpose. God has put an end to such things that are planned, purposed or devised against you; whether spiritual, mental, emotional or physical.

Today, I want you to see that this verse contains the eternally established promise of your healing. God has promised that "no weapon that is formed against you will prosper." This is the once-and-for-all promise of our Father.

If we understand that God has given you and I dominion authority on this earth, then we can see the secret of maintaining our divine health contained in the next part of this verse.

Any tongue, *lashown*, language, speaker or talker that shall arise, *quwm*, come on the scene and stand, or speak, or, perform an act, or pronounce a case or diagnosis, *mishpat*, a judgment or sentence against you, you shall, *rasha',* declare to be wicked, unethical and against the promise of God.

In other words, when you are given a diagnosis of sickness or disease, which is in absolute contradiction to the promise of God, you will speak words of judgement against it. Your confession, or profession of faith in God's Word will be:

He sent his word, and healed [me], and delivered [me] from their destructions. Psalms 107:20 (KJV)

Who his own self bare our sins in his own body on the tree, that we, being dead to sins, should live unto righteousness: by whose stripes ye were healed. 1 Peter 2:24 (KJV)

January 15 - Honoring Your Sons

> Why then do you kick [trample upon, treat with contempt] My sacrifice and My offering which I commanded, and honor your sons above Me by fattening yourselves upon the choicest part of every offering of My people Israel? 1 Samuel 2:29 (AMP)

Great care must be taken that we, as parents, do not begin to idolize our children and refuse to train or correct them. Our society has been immersed in a sea of unrestrained gluttony wherein it is believed that our children will be harmed if they can't have what they want immediately. Great debt is incurred and legitimate bills are not paid to satiate the insatiable desire for the latest technological gadgets.

I ask, where is it written that a child will die if they do not have a cell phone with texting capabilities? Since when are children capable of making mature decisions about their faith, how much internet access they should be allowed, who they should hang out with, and what they should watch or listen to?

The priest Eli knew what his sons were doing and ignored their folly. They took the best of the gifts brought to the Lord in order to satisfy their own lust. They became demanding, abusive and perverse, yet, he would not discipline them. As a result, he and his sons lost the privilege and honor of the priesthood. This brought a curse upon Eli and all of his descendants: "there shall not be an old man in thine house . . . all the increase of thine house shall die in the flower of their age" (1 Sam. 2:31-33 KJV).

We are to "train up a child in the way he should go . . ." and love our children enough to discipline them:

> He that spareth his rod hateth his son: but he that loveth him chasteneth him. Proverbs 13:24; 22:6 (KJV)

Whether we have natural children or spiritual sons and daughters, we must guide and instruct them in the ways of righteousness. This includes teaching them how to obey authority, respect privileges and serve at their own expense.

Jesus, Himself, ". . . made himself of no reputation, and took upon him the form of a servant" (Phil. 2:7). Should we do less?

27

January 16 - Taste and See

O taste and see that the LORD is good: blessed is the man that trusteth in him. Psalms 34:8 (KJV)

Have you ever sat down for dinner as a guest in someone's home and had them serve something that you weren't sure you wanted to eat? If you have ever traveled to other countries and allowed yourself to enter their culture you have. I've been there and have found that sometimes looks are deceiving. The very thing that I didn't think I would like turned out to be absolutely delicious and I couldn't get enough of it.

The things of God are similar in that they don't always sound or look as good as they are. This, no doubt, is why the Word of God encourages us to "taste and see."

The word, "taste," is the Hebrew word, **ta'am**, which simply means to taste, to eat, and, interestingly enough, to perceive.

See, **ra'ah**, not only means, to look at, or behold, but also carries the meaning of "perceive." There is a strength to this Hebrew word which causes one to give it more weight than our English understanding normally calls for. We are to, learn about, find out about, give attention to and look intently at, the fact that, "the LORD is good." **YHWH**, the Existing One, is, **towb**, good, precious, prosperity, wealth, excellent, becoming, pleasant, valuable in estimation , kind, benign, right (ethical), absolutely moral and right.

The man that realizes this and is willing to trust Him enough to "taste and see" will be blessed, **'esher**. This person will find himself filled with happiness and overcome by God's favor and protection. This word, **'esher**, also means that he will find himself to be made holy.

So, don't push the plate away. Dive in and "taste and see that the LORD is good." Once you do, you will be back for more and more and more even though every "bite" completely satisfies. Enjoy the table of the LORD and His goodness, excellence, wealth and prosperity. Receive by faith in the mighty name of Jesus, the Christ of God, our Lord and Savior.

January 17 - Fear the LORD

Fear the LORD, ye his saints: for there is no want to them that fear him. The young lions do lack, and suffer hunger: but they that seek the LORD shall not want any good thing. Psalms 34:9-10 (KJV)

Are you a saint of God? Indeed you are if in fact you have received Jesus the Christ of God as your Lord and Savior.

Why, then, is the church suffering from hunger and lack? Perhaps we "saints" have lost the fear of the LORD. I believe that the Church is in the condition it is in due to a lack of fearing God. We have come into the revelation of Him as our Loving Father, as our Provision and Healing, and as our Wonderful Counselor. We know Him as our Peace and Protection, our Wisdom and Knowledge, and our Savior.

In these precious and powerful truths, however, we have lost all fear of Him. I'm afraid that it is the old adage come to pass: "familiarity breeds contempt." It is the malady of the children today that have made their parent their peer. May God have mercy on the parent that allows such disrespectful foolishness.

Fear, is the Hebrew word, *yare'*, and it means just what you think it means and more. Yes, it means, to be afraid of, to stand in awe of, to honor and respect, to dread the judgement of, and, to be terrified of being on the wrong side of.

Let us not be so familiar with God as our loving Father that we forget that He is also the Righteous Judge. He is able to give and take life, lift up and take down both leaders and nations. He is our Creator and He is the Sovereign of all that there is or ever will be.

With the right balance of fearing Him and basking in His loving grace, we find complete safety and provision. They that fear Him and seek Him shall have no want of any good thing. The word translated, seek, *darash*, brings to mind more than a casual looking for. Here is a seeking with care, a frequent consulting and enquiring of in prayer and worship. This is a seeking out and following after Him whom we require.

Then, we "shall not want any good thing."

January 18 - A Sun and Shield

> For the LORD God is a sun and shield: the LORD will give grace and glory: no good thing will he withhold from them that walk uprightly. Psalms 84:11 (KJV)

In our verse for today we see, once again, the wonderful promise that "no good thing will he withhold from them that walk uprightly" and that the man who trusts in Him is blessed. How assuring are these promises as they are repeated over and over in scripture by Him who is our sun and shield, giver of grace and glory.

Jehovah, the One God in three Persons, *elohiym*, is a sun and shield. This word, sun, *shemesh*, can be interpreted to mean that He is our battlement and glittering or shining shield. His presence will blind every enemy because of His, *shekinah,* glory. Then, we see that this statement is followed by the word, *magen*, which is interpreted, shield. This reinforces the idea of Jehovah God being our armed defense, a buckler and glittering shield in time of battle.

We will also be given grace and glory by Him with Whom we have to do. The word, give, is, *nathan*. It states more than, give. It refers to something being bestowed upon, assigned to, or provided for, someone. This, giving, is accomplished by an utterance. God is here speaking a blessing of grace and glory that we are being entrusted with.

Grace, *chen*, is, as in the New Testament, unmerited favor and acceptance. It says that the one receiving grace is well favored. The glory spoken of is none other than, *kabowd*, which is glory, honor, abundance, riches, splendor, dignity and reputation. This is the heavy weighting of the glorious anointing of the Almighty upon a mortal life.

There is absolutely nothing, no good thing, *towb*, that the Lord will deny or refrain from giving to those in covenant with Him. This does include, but is not limited to, prosperity, wealth, favor, joy, happiness, health, pleasantness, agreeableness, what is excellent, valuable in estimation, appropriate, becoming, or anything else that pertains to a fulfilling, spirit-led life.

January 19 - Blessed

O LORD of hosts, blessed is the man that trusteth in thee. Psalms 84:12 (KJV)

Do you continually put your trust and confidence in the Lord? Trust, **batach**, also carries the thought of being secure, because of having confidence in, and, being bold because of feeling safe with, the Lord. If you are able to trust Him, and feel secure in His presence, then you are truly blessed.

This blessedness, **'esher**, brings happiness. This is the result of being blessed. Each of us is happy when we are feeling safe, secure and free from fear of harm. Such is the condition of a true believer.

When we receive Jesus the Christ as our Lord and Savior, repenting of our sin and accepting Gods forgiveness in and through the blood of the cross of Calvary, we come under the protection of all of heavens host.

The LORD, **YHWH**, The Existing One, God Himself, is the Supreme leader of the hosts of heaven. **Tsaba'**, means, army, host of an organized army, all who go out to war or to serve at the direction of the Spirit of God. This is a great company of those who serve and war in heaven.

You could only experience an example of this kind of security if your natural father were the ruler of the whole earth and all of the military were loyal, and completely obedient, to him. Especially if he assigned all of those under his command to watch over and protect you.

This is exactly what has taken place in all of creation when you accept God's invitation to enter into covenant with Him through the sacrificial work of His Son, Jesus the Christ. From that moment the angels of God were commissioned to watch over and protect you. As it is written in Hebrews 1:14 (KJV), "Are they not all ministering spirits, sent forth to minister for them who shall be heirs of salvation?" and in Psalms 34:7 (KJV), "The angel of the LORD encampeth round about them that fear him, and delivereth them."

You are safe and secure in the everlasting covenant of the Lord who has redeemed you out of men. You are His Beloved child and He will instruct and guide you. (Psa. 32:8 KJV)

31

January 20 - Magnified Thy Word

I will worship toward thy holy temple, and praise thy name for thy loving kindness and for thy truth: for thou hast magnified thy word above all thy name. In the day when I cried thou answeredst me, and strengthenedst me with strength in my soul. Psalms 138:2-3 (KJV)

I have always enjoyed using a magnifying glass so that I could see what was hidden from the natural eye. As I age, it seems to be more and more necessary than it was when I was young. Be that as it may, I remember ants becoming huge when viewed through a magnifying lens. Feathers and flowers became items of great intrigue as the tiny intricacies of their make up became visible. Textures and hues unseen before now became discernable. Binoculars and telescopes serve the same purpose for things at distances small and great. Thank God for them!

The word translated, magnified, is the Hebrew word, *gadal.* It not only means magnify, in the sense of making larger, but it also means to become great or important, to promote, make powerful and greater.

His Word tells us that He regards His Word as being more important, greater and more powerful than His name. His Word has been promoted above His name.

This is intriguing to me in that His name has been lost. All we have left is the Tetragrammaton. This the name of God with the vowels removed. Thus, we are left with, *YHWH.* We have the name of His Son, Jesus, who is the Logos, or Word:

In the beginning was the Word, and the Word was with God, and the Word was God. John 1:1 (KJV)

Scripture teaches us that it is the revelation of Jesus, that Jesus is the focus of its every word, and that it is a living text.

For the word of God is quick, and powerful, and sharper than any twoedged sword, piercing even to the dividing asunder of soul and spirit, and of the joints and marrow, and is a discerner of the thoughts and intents of the heart. Hebrews 4:12 (KJV)

There is nothing more important or powerful on earth than the living Word spoken by our lips. - *Selah*

January 21 - I Was In The Spirit

John the Revelator said, "I was in the Spirit - rapt in His power - on the Lord's day, and I heard behind me a great voice like the calling of a war trumpet," Revelation 1:10 (AMP)

What, exactly does he mean, "in the Spirit?" We know that to be "born again" is to be in the Spirit and that if we will continue to "walk in the Spirit that we will not fulfill the lust of the flesh. [Romans 8:9; Galatians 3:3; 5:25]

Also, there is a language of the Spirit in which we are told to pray and worship. [1 Corinthians 14:2; Ephesians 6:18; John 4:23-24; Philippians 3:3]

None of these things, as wonderfully profound as they are, seem to touch what John is trying to convey to those who seek to know Jesus and the things of God more perfectly.

So then, What exactly does the term "in the Spirit" mean within the context of Revelation 1:10? Is there something that we need to know about this experience? What should we expect to happen when we are in the Spirit?

I believe the answer is found in the book of Revelation.

After this I looked, and, behold, a door was opened in heaven: and the first voice which I heard was as it were of a trumpet talking with me; which said, Come up hither, and I will shew thee things which must be hereafter. Revelation 4:1 (KJV)

The Apostle John saw, "looked," paid attention to, "behold," listened, "heard," entered, "Come up hither," and received revelation, "I will shew thee things which must be hereafter." Being "in the Spirit," therefore, should allow us to connect with heaven through an open portal.

One thing is for sure, we should desire to know more perfectly all that Jesus secured for us as He "was manifest in the flesh, justified in the Spirit and received into glory" (1 Tim. 3:16 KJV).

January 22 - Hear, See, Move

According to Revelation 1:10 and 4:1, 2 John heard. We can expect to hear when we are in the Spirit. This is not natural hearing but supernatural. We will hear the Voice of God. This is that same Voice that walked in the Garden with Adam.

There is also a supernatural sense of being able to see. Revelation 4:2 recounts that John saw "a throne" and One sitting "on the throne." The grace (gift) of Discerning of spirits includes the seeing of various things in supernatural realms. Many are the Scriptural accounts of such occurrences of supernatural sight. Many times these experiences are so clear that one does not know if the seeing is natural or supernatural. Other times it is as if one is superimposed over the other. Either way, it is a marvelous experience that leaves one knowing that they have met with the Lord.

Ezekiel 37:1; Revelation 17:3 and 21:10 also reveal to us that we may expect to move in the Spirit. Each records that the person involved was carried away in the spirit to another place (realm) where certain things were seen and/or heard.

Might we still have these experiences today? Yes! Yes! Yes! I'm still looking forward to flying "Phillip Air" one of these days. Remember, he baptized the Ethiopian Treasurer and came up out of the water in a different city.

We are safe in the Spirit. There is absolutely no reason to fear the supernatural when we are in the everlasting arms of God. What is most important is that we seek Him and not the experiences.

Seek Him with all that you are. Then hold on as He draws you into the realms of God and reveals to you the hidden things.

January 23 - Do Not Forbid

Wherefore, brethren, covet to prophesy, and forbid not to speak with tongues. 1 Corinthians 14:39 (KJV)

Every Bible translation I have read says the same thing:
"DO NOT FORBID OR HINDER speaking in [unknown] TONGUES." 1 Corinthians 14:39 (AMP)
That seems fairly clear to me. How about you?
How can one build themselves up if they do not allow themselves to do what is required to accomplish the task. The book of Jude says,

But you, beloved, building yourselves up on your most holy faith, praying in the Holy Spirit, Jude 1:20 (KJV).

To me it is fairly obvious that we need the power of God more than ever before. These are days of gross darkness and it is only in the supernatural strength of Jesus Christ, the Anointed One, and His anointing that we will run the race, reach the mark, and win the crown promised the overcomer. [Jam 1:12; 1 Pet 5:4; Rev. 2:10; Rev. 3:11;]

... Not by might, nor by power, but by my spirit, saith the Lord of hosts. Zechariah 4:6 (KJV)

Let this be a time of setting aside the traditions of men and the leaven of religious form without power. Let this be a time of seeking the Lord and of receiving ALL that He shed His blood and died to purchase for us.

Followers of Jesus, the Christ of God, received a command from Him to receive this enduement of power:

And, being assembled together with them, commanded them that they should not depart from Jerusalem, but wait for the promise of the Father, which, saith he, ye have heard of me. Acts 1:4 (KJV)

Beloved, can't you see that what Jesus did was to command His followers to wait for and receive the "promise of the Father?"

And, behold, I send the promise of my Father upon you: but tarry ye in the city of Jerusalem, until ye be endued with power from on high. Luke 24:49 (KJV)

What was the "promise of the Father?" According to Acts 1:8 (KJV) it was that you would "receive power, after that the Holy Ghost is come upon you: . . .".

January 24 - Gathering to Give

For God giveth to a man that is good in his sight wisdom, and knowledge, and joy: but to the sinner he giveth travail, to gather and to heap up, that he may give to him that is good before God. This also is vanity and vexation of spirit. Ecclesiastes 2:26 (KJV)

What could be more futile than amassing a fortune, only to leave it to someone you don't even know? This is the "vanity and vexation of spirit" spoken of by the "Preacher" in the book of Ecclesiastes.

He was said to be the wisest natural man that ever lived. His views are worth considering especially when you consider that most people on earth are greedily accumulating all the worlds goods that they can. They never can have enough to feel secure. No wonder, in that the only real security is in the One true God and His Son, our Lord, Jesus the Christ.

If, under the Old Testament, the principle of the unjust gathering up riches for the just was in place; how much more would this principle be working for the sanctified saints of God under the New Covenant of grace?

Those who are "good in his sight" are His born-again, blood bought, sons of God in Christ. It is to them that He has promised to give "wisdom, and knowledge, and joy" as well as the benefit of the sinner's labor. Wisdom and knowledge make one to know that everything about God is that of giving. He so loved us He gave! God is love and love gives at its own expense for the benefit of another. Wisdom and knowledge reveals that our strength is in our joy of the Lord. We have joy when we give because our Father gave. We recognize that all we have comes from Him and are eager to return to Him what is His (the tithe) and to freely give of His blessing to further His cause.

We are blessed to be a blessing. We have received so that we can give. It all comes from Him.

January 25 - A Shining Light

But the path of the just is as the shining light, that shineth more and more unto the perfect day.
Proverbs 4:18 (KJV)

The word, path, *'orach*, can be translated, the way of living or the passing of life. Both ideas are caught in our text for today.

The way of the just, **tsaddiyq**, a just, lawful and righteous man, is as the, **nogahh**, brightness or bright light, **'owr**, of the face of God, the Light of life, prosperity and instruction.

The just one is one who has ceased to live in and of himself but now Christ lives in and through him. His life is then governmentally righteous as justified and vindicated by God Himself. What he does is right, correct and lawful and he backs God's righteous cause.

Such a man will prosper on earth, even as his soul prospers under the instruction of the Word of God. Like Jesus, he will do what he sees the Father do and hears the Father speak. He lives in the face of God, the Light of life, and enjoys the fellowship and guidance of the Good Shepherd.

The end of such a man is that he will, shineth,**'owr**, be illuminated and give illumination more and more, **halak**, as he walks about, dying to self and leading others out of the darkness of sins shadow. His journey is taking him to the perfect day, **kuwn**, when he will, like Paul, say, "I have fought a good fight, I have finished my course, I have kept the faith" (2 Tim. 4:7 KJV).

This the day set up and established in the heart, mind and plan of God. It is a securely determined, fixed, arranged and settled day in which God establishes, accomplishes and makes firm the completion of His plan and purpose.

As the just walks out his earthly course he is assured of being changed from glory to glory as God transforms him into the very image of His own dear Son.

As this just one finishes his course on earth and steps out of his body of flesh he is welcomed into the place set in order, especially arranged, established and waiting for him.

Such is the goodness and grace of our loving, all powerful, all gracious and all merciful God.

January 26 - A Great Light

The people that walked in darkness have seen a great light: they that dwell in the land of the shadow of death, upon them hath the light shined. Isaiah 9:2 (KJV)

The Amplified Bible renders this verse this way:

The people who walked in darkness have seen a great Light; those who dwelt in the land of intense darkness and the shadow of death, upon them has the Light shined. Isaiah 9:2 (AMP)

The people spoken of by the prophet are those of the nation of Israel in a time when even the religious children of God were estranged from God by their stiff necked rebellion and selfish ambition, God sent His only begotten Son to call them to Himself.

The "land of the shadow of death" being spoken of was specifically the nation of Israel and could be understood today as any nation in the same condition today.

For God so loved the world, that he gave his only begotten Son, that whosoever believeth in him should not perish, but have everlasting life. John 3:16 (KJV)

To them, the Light Himself came to, *nagahh*, illuminate them. He came to reveal Himself in and through His son.

Today He has sent His Holy Spirit to convict of sin and, through every believer, to call whosoever will unto Himself. His call is not just to the Jew as at the first but to both Jew and Gentile the world over.

I say then, Have they stumbled that they should fall? God forbid: but rather through their fall salvation is come unto the Gentiles, for to provoke them to jealousy. Romans 11:11 (KJV)

The way to salvation is now open in Christ Jesus to all who call upon His name. The Light has come. Let us welcome Him.

For God sent not his Son into the world to condemn the world; but that the world through him might be saved. He that believeth on him is not condemned: but he that believeth not is condemned already, because he hath not believed in the name of the only begotten Son of God. John 3:17-18 (KJV)

January 27 - Cover Me In War

O GOD the Lord, the strength of my salvation, thou hast covered my head in the day of battle.
Psalms 140:7 (KJV)

There is a covering that overshadows us when we are in the midst of battle. Some call this covering, "the anointing." Whatever you may call it, is the, guiding and power of the Holy Ghost when the battle rages in our lives.

Whether on the field of battle, the business marketplace or the attacks of the enemy on you and your ministry, the covering will guide, keep and protect you. You will not be consumed! You will not fail! You will not lose!

There is a holy unction that teaches you as you go.

Blessed be the LORD my strength, which teacheth my hands to war, and my fingers to fight: Psalms 144:1 (KJV).

There is also the promise that no matter what weapon is fashioned and used against you will not harm you.

No weapon that is formed against thee shall prosper; and every tongue that shall rise against thee in judgment thou shalt condemn. This is the heritage of the servants of the LORD, and their righteousness is of me, saith the LORD. Isaiah 54:17 (KJV)

You see, Beloved, the Lord God Almighty is a Man of War and He is on your side (Exo. 13:3). Just as David, the champion of God who slew Goliath, took men who were in distress, in debt and discontented, He took you and I, right where we were, and has made us to be more than conquerors (Rom. 8:37 KJV).

His very Presence, which is Love, overshadows us with unfailing ability and might that makes it impossible for us to fail (1 Joh. 4:16; 1 Co. 13:8).

His covering, His anointing, overshadows us and hides us in His secret place as we call out to Him in our time of trouble.

Thou calledst in trouble, and I delivered thee; I answered thee in the secret place of thunder: I proved thee at the waters of Meribah. Selah. Psalms 81:7 (KJV)

He that dwelleth in the secret place of the most High shall abide under the shadow of the Almighty.
Psalms 91:1 (KJV)

January 28 - Dare Any of You

Dare any of you, having a matter against another, go to law before the unjust, and not before the saints?
1 Corinthians 6:1 (KJV)

One of the most disturbing things that I see happening within the Body of Christ is believers suing other believers. The justification is always the same, "If they were 'real believers' then I wouldn't sue them, but . . ." There always follows a list of wrongs done and more justification of why their particular law suit is acceptable. What happened to Jesus admonition to yield to the one who despitefully uses you?

And if any man will sue thee at the law, and take away thy coat, let him have thy cloke also. And whosoever shall compel thee to go a mile, go with him twain. Give to him that asketh thee, and from him that would borrow of thee turn not thou away. Ye have heard that it hath been said, Thou shalt love thy neighbour, and hate thine enemy. But I say unto you, Love your enemies, bless them that curse you, do good to them that hate you, and pray for them which despitefully use you, and persecute you;
Matthew 4:40-44 (KJV)

I was in business for years before I was saved and for several years after I received Christ. Many were the occasions that warranted a law suit to recover the costs of labor and materials not paid for. Once a Christian, I could not, in good conscience, sue a "brother." Who was I to determine who was a "real brother" or not? If they said they were saved, I figured that they must be saved whether they acted like it or not.

But brother goeth to law with brother, and that before the unbelievers. Now therefore there is utterly a fault among you, because ye go to law one with another. Why do ye not rather take wrong? why do ye not rather suffer yourselves to be defrauded? 1 Corinthians 6:6-7 (KJV)

What I learned was that when someone takes from you by fraud or thievery, the Lord will make the devil pay it back. If you are slandered the Lord will vindicate you. Whatever the case, God has promised to make right the wrongs done. Forgiveness is the key that releases the provision of God.

January 29 - Seek To Excel

> Even so ye, forasmuch as ye are zealous of spiritual gifts, seek that ye may excel to the edifying of the church.
> 1 Corinthians 14:12 (KJV)

Everything that God does is in the highest and best interest of those who are His sons and daughters of faith. So, too, it must be that we develop this same character, nature and mind. Everything we do should be done with the highest and best interest of the Body of Christ and men and women everywhere.

Many "Christians" are intrigued, fascinated by, and caught up with the operation of spiritual gifts. But, I wonder, how many are zealous, *zelotes*? That is, how many are, burning with zeal, jealous of the things of the spirit, and most eagerly desirous to understand and use them properly. How many are willing to die to self to acquire this gift.

The Greek language is not saying, spiritual gifts, when it uses the word, *pneuma*. The Apostle Paul is saying, "you are burning with a desire to know the Holy Ghost, the Spirit of God Himself, the Breath of Life." "You are zealous to become intimately acquainted with the third person of the triune God, the Holy Spirit, coequal, coeternal with the Father and the Son."

He then calls for each one who is zealous to know the Holy Spirit and His ways to seek to excel for the purpose of building up the church. The words used are, *perisseuo*, which is translated, excel. It means to overflow unto the abundance that exceeds the natural and outstrips the casual seeker. Next is the word, edifying, *oikodomer,* which means to build up, encourage and strengthen. The object of the verse is the church, the *ekklesia.* These are the called out ones, those chosen and sent by God.

Imagine the Church of today, if each member in particular would esteem the other members the same way that bodily organs and members support the health and well being of each other part. If every member would work in harmony with the intention of bringing the highest and best of God to each and every one born of His Spirit and washed in the Blood. Let this be your quest today.

January 30 - The Fig Tree

He spake also this parable; A certain man had a fig tree planted in his vineyard; and he came and sought fruit thereon, and found none. Luke 13:6 (KJV)

Why would a man plant a fig tree in a vineyard?

For the workers The Fig Tree was several things: (1. It provided shade from the heat of day. (2. It Provided a healing poultice. (3. It offered nourishment. (4. It's trunk was a place to lean on while sitting and resting. This was a "Resting Place." (5. It was a place to have fellowship; to talk about and share life.

The Fig Tree is a type of: The Church. It is planted "in the vineyard" which is the Harvest Field of God. The Fig Tree is God's provision to man through man.

The owner [God - Jesus] came to take what was his just due. It has been said that, The Jewish owners would make a very potent Fig Wine out of the Figs and Only The Owner was allowed to drink it! Imagine that, Fig Wine!

This is what God receives from the Church! He drinks the worship and praise that is given "in spirit and in truth." This is also why pastors tend the flock, work the field, and preach; just to get a taste of that "Figgy Wine!"

Then said he unto the dresser of his vineyard, Behold, these three years I come seeking fruit on this fig tree, and find none: cut it down; why cumbereth it the ground? Luke 13:7 (KJV)

If you remember, Jesus Ministry lasted just over 3 years. He came seeking fruit on the "Fig Tree" [Israel - the Church of that hour] and found none. This is why the Old was "cut down" and the New "planted." This is why Jesus cursed the Fig Tree - in Mark 11:13-21.

It was a type of the Church that was bearing no fruit, no wine, for the owner. He cursed it to it's roots - and it withered and died!

We can also see the Son coming to check out the Church in Rev 1:12,13,20; 2:1, where He is seen in the midst of the Lampstand [The Church - Rev 1:13].

January 31 - The Fig Tree Revisited

He spake also this parable; A certain man had a fig tree planted in his vineyard; and he came and sought fruit thereon, and found none. Luke 13:6 (KJV)

The local church that you and I belong to is to be a fruit bearing Fig Tree.

We are to be a church of worth. Our church is to be a place that produces what is needed for the laborer and provides for the owner.

Laborer's are to be "under the fig tree" - In The Church!

And the eyes of them both were opened, and they knew that they were naked; and they sewed fig leaves together, and made themselves aprons. Genesis 3:7 (KJV)

Most likely Adam and Eve used the leaves of the Tree of Knowledge of Good and Evil to cover their newly perceived nakedness. It was here they sinned and it was here that they became aware of both natural and spiritual nakedness.

It appears that the Fig Tree was the Tree of Knowledge of Good and Evil. Their Eyes were opened = EYES = Eye [fig. or lit.]; Fountain; Knowledge,

They MADE THEMSELVES APRONS. In other words, they Entrusted themselves to themselves, Furnished themselves, Yielded themselves to, Their own Covering [armor]. They Girded Themselves.

The Church is where humanity comes to receive the "Knowledge of Good & Evil." If this is merely an intellectual pursuit it is vanity and an abomination of God. We come together to meet with God in His Garden.

The Church today must not become it's own covering. The church must be the place where God is. We come to the Church to meet with Him and to sit with Him under His Fig Tree and to walk with Him in His Garden.

FEBRUARY

February 01 - Stand Fast

Watch ye, stand fast in the faith, quit you like men, be strong. 1 Corinthians 16:13 (KJV)

As I open the Word of God each morning I thrill to "Watch" and see what the Lord will show me. This Greek word, *gregoreuo*, to stay awake, to be vigilant, wake, to be watchful. A soldier on guard duty at night must take care to stay awake and to be vigilant or he endangers his charge as well as himself. We, who watch over the souls of men, must be like minded. Revelation breaks upon us when we are attentive and watchful and our soul is fed, strengthened and encouraged. The watchful are given the ability to stand fast in the faith that only comes by hearing the Word of God.

We stand fast, *steko*, that is, persevere and persist in the faith, *pistis*, that was acquired supernaturally and is maintained by consistent watching in the Word. Oh, granted that there will be many opportunities for faith to be exercised, but don't think for a moment that you are building your faith as a natural act of the will. When circumstance and situation demand the exercise of your faith, it will be available in its power to the degree that it has been fed and strengthened by daily watching in the Word during the first watch of the day.

For each of us to make a man of ourselves or to make, or show ourselves to be brave, *andrizomai*, quit you like men, is only possible when we are strengthened with His might. You and I are, "Strengthened with all might, according to his glorious power, unto all patience and longsuffering with joyfulness" (Col. 1:11 - KJV).

Our soul is refreshed and strength comes as we are filled with the very life of God that comes as we faithfully watch.

But if the Spirit of him that raised up Jesus from the, dead dwell in you, he that raised up Christ from the dead shall also quicken your mortal bodies by his Spirit that dwelleth in you. Romans 8:11 (KJV)

Then, watching for Him in the Book, will we increase in strength, *krataioo*.

February 02 - Attend To My Words

My son, attend to my words; incline thine ear unto my sayings. Let them not depart from thine eyes; keep them in the midst of thine heart. For they are life unto those that find them, and health to all their flesh. Keep thy heart with all diligence; for out of it are the issues of life.
Proverbs 4:20-23 (KJV)

When the Lord says, "Let Me have your attention," it should make us stop everything we are doing and direct our attention and focus on His words. The importance of what is being said has been magnified by His insistence that we pay attention and listen carefully.

We are drawn to a heightened awareness of the importance of continual communion with the Word of God that cause His words to find permanent residence in our hearts. As a son or daughter of God we have a special responsibility to honor our Father and His words. Verse 20 begins, **ben,** My sons (translated as such 2978 times), or My children (translated as such 1568 times). This makes what is being said personal and exclusive to those who are in the family as children of God.

The Father is talking to His child and giving important instruction concerning the issues of life. The word translated, issues, is the Hebrew word, **towtsa'ah**, which, besides, going forth, means, the source, of life. It also carries the thought of, escape from death. As the children of God we are being taught one of life's most important lessons: Our life flows out of the Word of God, which is the source of life, and our escape from eternal death is held in its words.

Nothing is more important to our well-being than the Word of God. Nothing has such weight and value to the human spirit, soul and body. Is it any wonder, then, that our loving Father would encourage us to keep His Word in the midst of our heart?

The "heart" spoken of here is the inner man of the soul, the seat of our understanding. This word, **lebab**, refers to the seat of our will, our inclinations and the seat of our appetites, emotions, passions and courage. No wonder that we are to keep the Word in the midst of our heart . For something to be in the midst, **tavek**, is for it to be fully permeated by and held in the center as prominent and dominant. May we be saturated with His life giving words today.

February 03 - Receive My Sayings

Hear, O my son, and receive my sayings; and the years of thy life shall be many. Proverbs 4:10 (KJV)

How well do we hear, **shama'**, the instructions of our Father?

Shama', is a word that has many shades of meaning. It is not only speaking of hearing an audible sound but of comprehending and embracing the concepts conveyed by that sound. The willingness to obey what is heard and understood is also a part of the full meaning of this word, "Hear."

Not only are we, as believers, given the power to "have ears to hear," (Eze. 12:2; Matt. 11:15, 13:9) where the heathen and rebellious do not, we have the ability to hear with attentiveness and interest. We "hear" and actually listen to what we hear with the ear. This is supernatural in its origin; for, as Romans 10:17 (KJV) says, "So then faith cometh by hearing, and hearing by the word of God."

When our Father says, "Hear," He gives His own the ability to obey. He causes His words to be heard, **shama'**. There is also given the supernatural ability to understand the language of God and to discern the meaning as if hearing the case in a court of law. So, we see, that we are given the ability to "receive" the sayings of God by the supernaturally given ability to "hear."

The word translated "receive" is, **laqach**, which implies becoming one with; as in being married to it, as though we take His words to wife. When we receive the words of God we are taking possession of them and making them a part of who we are. More accurately, we become what we have heard spoken by the mouth of our God and King.

This Hebrew word, **laqach**, also gives us the sense of being captured and taken away by what we have heard. The Word strikes our innermost being and understanding like lightning flashing about within.

Have you ever experienced this kind of revelation breaking upon you? If you have, then you know the joy that comes with knowing that God has spoken to you personally. If not, you are about to experience the thrill of a life-time as you ponder the sayings of His matchless living Word.

49

February 04 - Living A Longer Life

And if thou wilt walk in my ways, to keep my statutes and my commandments, as thy father David did walk, then I will lengthen thy days. 1 Kings 3:14 (KJV)

The Lord told King Solomon that the way to a long and healthy life was for him to walk in His ways and to keep His statutes and commandments. We know that this is not a legalistic walk of death in the letter of the law but a walk of loving regard for God and His Word. This can be seen by the phrase, "as thy father David did walk." David made many mistakes, big ones, but still was a man after God's own heart (Acts 13:22).

Too many Christians ignore the ways of God in favor of the acts of God. They chase signs, wonders and miracles, or popularity, position and promotion rather than chasing after God Himself. Many are the books purchased in order to learn how to perform the acts rather than those that call one to heartfelt repentance and a life of holiness marked by character and integrity. Church growth seminars are much more willingly attended than times of prayer.

To walk, *yalak*, is to live a manner of life that has died to self and lives in Christ. The word, ways, *derek*, refers to the course of life, manner, habit, or way of moral character. Statutes, *choq*, speaks of the prescribed actions expected of oneself while, commandments, *mitsvah*, establishes the code of wisdom commanded by God. Thus, we gather that if one is to experience the supernatural addition of years to their life, they must have a heart like King David.

As a lover of God, you will, from the heart, learn the Lord's code of wisdom and what is expected of you as you develop the moral character that will guide the course of your life. With a deep, heartfelt desire to please the Lord, you will live a crucified life in Christ based upon His Word. As such, you will find resurrection life flowing in your spirit, soul and body. You will have the mind and the anointing of Christ, the wisdom and understanding of God manifest by the Spirit of Holiness and the benefit of that peace that passes all understanding.

This is not law but grace, the outworking of unfailing divine love.

February 05 - A Tree Of Life

The fruit of the righteous is a tree of life; and he that winneth souls is wise. Proverbs 11:30 (KJV)

Wisdom compels one to win souls if, for no other reason, than that it strengthens society and protects upcoming generations by providing righteous leadership. This assures righteousness, peace, joy and prosperity in the land.

When the righteous are in authority, the people rejoice: but when the wicked beareth rule, the people mourn. Proverbs 29:2 (KJV)

The birthing and nurturing of righteous seed is the call of God to humanity. It has been so since the beginning.

And God blessed them, and God said unto them, Be fruitful, and multiply, and replenish the earth, and subdue it: and have dominion over the fish of the sea, and over the fowl of the air, and over every living thing that moveth upon the earth. Genesis 1:28 (KJV)

The righteous seed of man was to have been in authority for the benefit of Gods creation. This is the "fruit of the righteous." So, then, what is meant by "the fruit of the righteous is a tree of life"?

A spiritual son or daughter has eaten the fruit of the tree of life [Christ at the Cross of Calvary] and become a partaker of eternal life in Him. When this child of God duplicates himself, he has produced "fruit" that will mature into a "tree of life" for others. This what is meant where we read in Obadiah 1:21 (KJV), "And saviours shall come up on mount Zion to judge the mount of Esau; and the kingdom shall be the LORD'S."

This fruit will remain throughout eternity:

Ye have not chosen me, but I have chosen you, and ordained you, that ye should go and bring forth fruit, and that your fruit should remain: that whatsoever ye shall ask of the Father in my name, he may give it you. John 15:16 (KJV)

This fruit will be "eaten" by multitudes that cannot be numbered any more than the stars of the sky nor the sands of the sea and God will receive eternal praise and thanksgiving because of it.

February 06 - Spirit Filled ???

This is a most interesting hour. Many who call themselves "Spirit filled" Christians deny the most basic and elementary teachings of Scripture as concerns the graces [gifts] of the Spirit of God. They maintain that "tongues aren't for everyone" or that "tongues don't belong in a church gathering - because we don't want to offend anyone." This kind of teaching is typical of Satan's deceits in that it gives great pride to those who have "the gift" and also reveals Satan's fear of tongues - the least of the gifts - in its power to arrest the attention of the unbeliever and to strengthen the believer.

Wherefore tongues are for a sign, not to them that believe, but to them that believe not: 1 Corinthians 14:22

He that speaketh in an unknown tongue edifieth himself; 1 Corinthians 14:4 (KJV)

Doesn't it seem a bit odd to think that Jesus would command all of his followers to receive the promise of the Father and then change His mind as it relates to the Church of today. Would He Who is the same yesterday, today, and forever, give the early Church power and authority and then with-hold that same power and authority from the believer of today? That God has become a "respecter of persons" or has now decided that there is a "difference" so that one can be more, or have more, than another is inconceivable to me! Take the time to read: (Act 1:4,5,8; Luk 24:49; Joh 7:37-39) (Act 10:34; 15:8-9)

We are admonished by God's Holy Word to move past the traditions set in place by men and:

Study to shew thyself approved unto God, a workman that needeth not to be ashamed, rightly dividing the word of truth. 2 Timothy 2:15 (KJV)

For God shows no partiality [undue favor or unfairness; with Him one man is not different from another]. Romans 2:11 (AMP)

The gifts of the Spirit are for all believers, regardless of denominational affiliation, so that they can be witnesses with signs, wonders and miracles working in their lives as they reach out to a lost and dying world.

February 07 - By a Prophet

And by a prophet the LORD brought Israel out of Egypt, and by a prophet was he preserved.
Hosea 12:13 (KJV)

You may ask, "Are there really prophets in the land today?" Oh yes, Beloved, there are men and women who hear the voice of the Lord and speak truly. Men and women of high moral excellence and character; people of integrity.

The problem is that they are in the minority and seldom recognized because of the promotional hype of false prophets of perverse character and connection.

But, let us not "throw out the baby with the bath." We must never disavow the things of God because there is a counterfeiter moving about. Phoney money only can be passed off as the real because there is the real.

The devil would love for you and I to begin to distrust the prophets of God because by means of a prophet people are liberated and kept safe. Just as the counterfeit leads into darkness and danger, far from Christ, the true prophet of God contends for the flock and leads them beside green pastures and still waters. With the rod of his mouth, the words of the Living God flow forth with direction, guidance, warning, protection and creative power.

And they rose early in the morning, and went forth into the wilderness of Tekoa: and as they went forth, Jehoshaphat stood and said, Hear me, O Judah, and ye inhabitants of Jerusalem; Believe in the LORD your God, so shall ye be established; believe his prophets, so shall ye prosper. 2 Chronicles 20:20 (KJV)

The prophet holds your prosperity in his mouth! He will speak God words of provision, protection, prosperity, and promotion into your life.

You might ask, "Who is my prophet?" You shouldn't have to look very far. Your Pastor is a good place to look. He'll speak words of life into you every Sunday.

February 08 - Anyone

I assure you, most solemnly I tell you, if anyone steadfastly believes in Me, he will himself be able to do the things that I do; and he will do even greater things than these, because I go to the Father. 1 John 14:12 (AMP)

Anyone can do the works of Jesus if they will yield to the Holy Spirit:

Anyone! Any 1.

And they were all filled (each one was filled) with the Holy Spirit and began to speak in other (supernatural) languages (tongues), as the Spirit kept giving them clear and loud expression [in each tongue in appropriate words]. Acts 2:4 (AMP + gms)

This releases the power spoken of in Acts 1:

But you shall receive power (ability, efficiency, and might) when the Holy Spirit has come upon you, and you shall be My witnesses in Jerusalem and all Judea and Samaria and to the ends (the very bounds) of the earth. Acts 1:8 (AMP)

This is the power given to anyone who asks:

And He said to them,

Go into all the world and preach and publish openly the good news (the Gospel) to every creature [of the whole human race]. Mark 16:15 (AMP)

And these attesting signs will accompany those who believe: in My name they will drive out demons; they will speak in new languages; They will pick up serpents; and [even] if they drink anything deadly, it will not hurt them; they will lay their hands on the sick, and they will get well. Mark 16:17-18 (AMP)

And they went out and preached everywhere, while the Lord kept working with them and confirming the message by the attesting signs and miracles that closely accompanied [it]. Amen (so be it). Mark 16:20 (AMP)

It's time for you to become the "anyone" spoken of in our verse for today and begin to move in the things of the Spirit of God.

February 09 - We Shall Be Saved

Turn us again, O God, and cause thy face to shine; and we shall be saved. Psalms 80:3 (KJV)

Turn us again, **shuwb**, is also correctly rendered as, restore us to the spiritual relationship we once had, or, deliver us from our separation from You by paying our fine. This concept should ring a loud bell to those who have received the sacrifice of God's Son for their sin.

The importance of this thought is emphasized by the fact that practically the same words are used three times in the same Psalm. Could it be a reference to the Godhead, *'elohiym*. *'Elohiym* is the plural intensive-singular meaning word used in the Book of Genesis to convey the concept of God being "Three in One." God the Father and God the Holy Spirit being evidenced and God the Son, present but not presented (as seen in John 1:1-3); that is, not being revealed in Scripture until later.

Turn us again, O God of hosts, and cause thy face to shine; and we shall be saved. Psalms 80:7 (KJV)

Now, **YHWH**, Yehovah the God , *'elohiym*, of hosts, **tsaba'**, which is, by many, understood to be (a theophany) God the Son.

Turn us again, O LORD God of hosts, cause thy face to shine; and we shall be saved. Psalms 80:19 (KJV)

The Psalmist ends his song with the same phraseology as the second. Consider with me, John 14:9 as we read Jesus saying, "Have I been so long time with you, . . he that hath seen me hath seen the Father."

What I see here is a cry to, firstly, the Holy Spirit, secondly the Father, and thirdly the Son. This is not to suggest three Gods but a prophetic heartfelt cry to the full nature and character of the Godhead.

The revelation, *'owr* , shining, of seeing Him face to face, **paniym,** His faces, presence or person, of the One True God, Father, Son and Holy Ghost, is what is needed to receive the benefit of the price paid at Calvary's tree for our sin. So shall "we be saved, **yasha**"!

February 10 - In The Beginning

In the beginning God created the heaven and the earth. Genesis 1:1 (KJV)

The beginning, *re'shiyth*, is the firstfruits of God's Word spoken, the beginning of the chiefest, the choicest part, and the best. God had you in mind when He created everything that it would take to support your life and the lives of the rest of creation. The creation which, in fact, was made to bless mankind.

God, *'elohiym*, (plural intensive-singular meaning = One God in three Persons, Him whom we call the Holy Trinity). He declares Himself without explanation or apology. He would continue to unveil Himself in His dealings with mankind as is recorded in scripture.

Created, *bara'*, created, shaped or formed, chose, made or dispatched, fashioned (always with God as subject) the heaven, *shamayim*, visible heavens, the sky as the abode of the stars; the visible universe, the sky, atmosphere, etc., and the earth, *'erets*, the firm, earth or world.

Today, there is a tremendous move of the spirit of anti-Christ among otherwise well meaning people to repudiate, or simply ignore, the biblical account of creation. Even scholarly ministers of the Gospel, such as the respected Finnis Dake, promoted the "gap theory" with scriptural juggling of the most agile sort. Wanting to defend the authority and accuracy of the scriptural record of creation by trying to "help" by making the Word of God fit with "science," so called.

Evolutionary thought was anything but scientific. It was purely speculative from an anti-God anti-biblical point of view. There was never any allowance for a Creator who created. Creationist thinking accepts the truth of there being a God to whom one must answer.

Herein lies the problem. Those who oppose God and all He stands for must embrace the lie of evolution. On the other hand; If one has no problem with there being a God who created, then science can become pure, that is, logical, observable, provable and sustainable.

The Word of God has been proven over and over and so it stands incontestable. Pure science always proves that which God has declared to be so. May our conceptualizing do likewise.

February 11 - How Long Is a Day?

>And God called the light Day, and the darkness he called Night. And the evening and the morning were the first day. Genesis 1:5 (KJV)

When questioned about the creation account in The First Book of Moses, Genesis, Christians who are unsure of the authority of scripture will say some interesting things.

For instance: When asked how long it took for God to create everything they will say something like, "We're not sure. It could have been thousands of years. After all the Scripture says, ". . . one day is with the Lord as a thousand years, and a thousand years as one day" (2 Pet. 3:8 KJV).

Can we actually interpret this quote from Peter as a literal answer to that question or should we understand it as a figure of speech that reveals the eternal dwelling of God. What would you say? The scripture also records the Psalmist saying, "For a thousand years in thy sight are but as yesterday when it is past, and as a watch in the night" Psalms 90:4 (KJV). Well now, a watch in the night is only four hours long. So, is a thousand years a "watch in the night," a "day," or "as yesterday?"

Why is it so difficult to believe that God knew what He was saying when He "called the light Day, and the darkness He called Night. And the evening and the morning were the first day" (Gen. 1:5). The word day, *yowm*, simply means "day:" a twenty four hour period of time that includes light and darkness (day and night). How difficult is that to understand?

Those who practice true science understand that it is the earth's rotation that causes night and day as it faces or turns away from the sun. Its rotation has been consistent since its creation. It rotates at the perfect speed to sustain life. There never was a time when the earth only rotated once every thousand years!

Beloved, we do not need to defend the Bible. Science must defend its findings by being present at an event, recording and observing the many facets of the event. That is why God asked Job: "Where wast thou when I laid the foundations of the earth? declare, if thou hast understanding" Job 38:4 (KJV).

Only God, Himself, can prove or disprove, scientifically, how the earth was created and how long it took. He said "six days."

February 12 - What About the "Evidence"?

> And, behold, I, even I, do bring a flood of waters upon the earth, to destroy all flesh, wherein is the breath of life, from under heaven; and every thing that is in the earth shall die. Genesis 6:17 (KJV)

Every child that has ever attended Sabbath or Sunday School knows the story of the great Flood. The question is, Do they really believe it? Actually, many of the teachers of those children do not believe the story because of what "science" says in today's educational system. Their unbelief passes to the students quite easily.

Evolutionary "scientists" of all disciplines point to the "fossil record" to show how the layers of dead things trapped in the soil prove that the earth has been here for "millions of years." Carbon dating is used to intimidate and "prove" the age of many of these fossils and rocks.

Let's face it, if you put a pressure gauge on a tank that is pressurized at 20 psi and your gauge needle is out of whack and points at 20,000 psi, you could "prove" that the tank pressure was 20000 psi. If you, then, build all gauges to read 20,000 psi at 20 psi, you would have set a standard of measurement that was always going to be false. A 100 psi tank would always read 1,000,000 psi.

This is basically what has happened to the carbon dating process. It has been altered to benefit the evolutionist anti-creationist theory. Along with "missing links" that are not "missing" at all; a fantasy world of ever evolving animals crawls from the goo to you by way of the zoo. The highest creation of God, mankind, is now lowered to "just another animal" status.

This makes him expendable if he is perceived to threaten the rest of the world and its creatures and allows him to gratify his basest of "instincts" as would any other animal.

The "fossil record" is simply the result of a world wide flood as recorded in the Bible. Caves were filled with dead things (which fossilized), sediment settled in layers with dead things (which fossilized) and we have the record, not of millions of years of sedimentation, but of the sedimentation resulting from a world wide flood.

February 13 - Set Me On Fire Once More . . .

The Lord is saying:

It was not that there was a bush burning in the wilderness that drew such great attention for the man that God had chosen. It was that the bush was not consumed.

"Hearken unto the voice of the Lord your God, for you shall not be consumed in the burning. Fear not to draw close unto Him. Stand not afar off in your own tent but come unto the tent of meeting. Come unto the bed chamber, the bridal chamber. Let the purging fire of the Holy Ghost come upon you and consume all that is not like Him.

You fear that there will be nothing left; but My beloved, you have no idea, you have not eyes to see how much of Me is in you already. How much I have imparted of Myself within your being. Within you is the Holy One. Yes, birthed within you is the image and likeness of Mine own Self! I watch over to keep and protect, to nurture and guard. Yes, it has even grown since the day of your conception says your Lord.

For I have purposed to have me a people and have reached unto you and have drawn you close unto me.

From out of the bed of affliction. From out of the natal blood. I have found you and washed you and salted you and cleansed you and drawn you unto Myself. I have said, You My beloved, are Mine own and there is neither height nor depth, nor anything above nor beneath, nor on the surface of the sea, nor on any land, nor in any realm that can separate you from My love.

I have purposed to have you as My own bride and I Am a jealous God.

So, say not, I am not worthy. For Jesus blood was shed and that separated you unto Me, cleansed you, made you holy, and set you apart unto My love."

February 14 - Does a lover see?

The Lord spoke to me concerning you:

"Does a lover see the imperfections of the one loved? Nay, I say unto you, There are none visible, there are none considered. But, even so, who, other than Myself can do away with all imperfections? Is it not written, be you perfect even as I Am perfect? Would I tease you, mock, and make sport of you to speak unto you that which cannot be done? Is anything too hard for Me?

I have purposed to cleanse and perfect you. You are being brought to perfection even as you stand perfected. It is a mystery and yet it is as sure and fixed as My Word. It is more sure than the rising of the sun or any other natural order.

I hear you cry. I hear you murmur. I hear you complain. I hear you say you can not.

I say unto you, You can!

Oh child, speak what I have said. Consider yourself as I consider you. See yourself as I see you. Run to Me and see if I will not forgive and heal your wound.

It is not My desire to harm you. It is not within Me to do you ill. I have planned good. I have planned blessing. I have spoken concerning you and it shall come to pass.

Let the life of this word flow within you. Yield to the swelling of the wave that is coming for it is My love and it will not fail. It is the word of power within you to perform all that I say.

I chastise you whom I love, that you be not snared, for I see the fowler setting his net and, yea, some have fluttered, yes, fallen into his trap. But I say unto you this day, Once again I tear the net and set you free!

Choose this day. Choose this day. Choose this day to be free! For I have purposed for you to be free!"

February 15 - The Life is in the Blood

For the life of the flesh is in the blood: and I have given it to you upon the altar to make an atonement for your souls: for it is the blood that maketh an atonement for the soul. Leviticus 17:11 (KJV)

The life, *nephesh*, that which breathes, the breathing substance or being, soul, the inner being of a creature or man. A living being; the man himself, person or creature. This *nephesh* of the creature (man or beast) is in the, *basar,* flesh, of the body, of humans, animals or all living things as that which gives it life. This life is in the blood, *dam*.

After creating all that was necessary to sustain living things, God created the creatures of the sea and the fowl of the air on the fifth (24 hour) day. Then, on the sixth day, the animals (living creatures) were created "after his kind." This is key. Each animal "kind" was a unique, special creation that would reproduce "after his kind." Dogs reproduce dogs, cattle reproduce cattle, cats reproduce cats and yes, monkeys reproduce monkeys.

It was not until the sixth literal day that God said, "Let Us make man in our image, after our likeness" (Gen. 1:26), and "created mankind in his image, in the image of God created he him; male and female created he them" (Gen. 1:27).

Each creation was distinct and the "life (blood)" was distinctly suited to each creation. There are similarities as one would expect from there being a common Creator but attempts to mix the blood ("life") of one with another have failed completely. The "life of the flesh" is perfectly suited to its "kind."

Even in the act of atonement, it was necessary that the cleansing blood be of the same "kind" than the covering blood of animal sacrifice. For it is not possible that the blood of bulls and of goats should take away sins. Hebrews 10:4 (KJV) For mankind to be cleansed and separated from the infection of sin, it would take the blood of a Man; the Man, Christ Jesus. But with the precious blood of Christ, as of a lamb without blemish and without spot: 1 Peter 1:19 (KJV)

So Christ was once offered to bear the sins of many; and unto them that look for him shall he appear the second time without sin unto salvation. Hebrews 9:28 (KJV)

February 16 - When Everything Comes Crashing Down

And whosoever shall fall on this stone shall be broken: but on whomsoever it shall fall, it will grind him to powder. Matthew 21:44 (KJV)

When everything around you comes crashing down, when nothing seems to be working out, when chaos appears to be overwhelming the peace of God within; what can you do?

When people revile you, lie about you, use and abuse you; what can you do?

Whatever comes against you, whatever presses you beyond your limit, whatever words are spoken to slander and demean you; fall on the Rock.

You may say, "You don't understand how they have hurt me." I may not, but I have had enough betrayal in my life to know that it took my being broken to rise above the pain of those betrayals.

We, dear Christian, have a mandate from God to forgive; not to justify or defend. In Mark 11:25-26 (KJV) we read, "And when ye stand praying, forgive, if ye have ought against any: that your Father also which is in heaven may forgive you your trespasses. But if ye do not forgive, neither will your Father which is in heaven forgive your trespasses."

It seems so unfair until it is compared with the betrayal of the Son of God who only went about doing good and healing all that were oppressed of the devil.

We can see Him falling on the rock in the Garden of Gethsemane until He sweat great drops of blood and yielded to the horrors of the Cross. He fell on the stone until He was broken and was enabled to endure the betrayal of friends, the mocking of the crowds, the jeering of the religious leaders puffed up with religious pride, and even the moment when His Father looked away from Him while He hung on the Cross, bearing the sin of all mankind.

Dear One, Fall on the Rock, Christ Jesus. Humble yourself before the Cross of His (and your) victory until you are broken enough to let Christ live in you to the degree that you, too, can say with complete joy, "Father, forgive them; for they know not what they do." (Gal. 2:20; Luke 23:34 KJV)

February 17 - Does It Edify?

All things are lawful for me, but all things are not expedient: all things are lawful for me, but all things edify not. 1 Corinthians 10:23 (KJV)

Let no man seek his own, but every man another's wealth. 1 Corinthians 10:24 (KJV)

Conscience, I say, not thine own, but of the other: for why is my liberty judged of another man's conscience? 1 Corinthians 10:29 (KJV)

Even as I please all men in all things, not seeking mine own profit [well being], but the profit [well being] of many, that they may be saved. 1 Corinthians 10:33 (KJV)

Saved, *sozo*, a primary contraction that means "safe." So, the liberty we give ourselves should reflect our, *agapao*, love for others and not our own desire to gratify our flesh. We are our brothers keeper and responsible to keep them safe and sound, and to rescue them from danger or destruction. This is the law of love that Jesus taught.

A pet peeve of mine is that ministers today take such liberty to show the grace of God by living life-styles that are like bear traps to the flock of God. Let me tell you a story to illustrate the danger:

While attending a home Bible study a guest teacher brought bread and wine to administer communion. The owner of the home asked him to use grape juice instead of wine and he agreed. He put his bottle of wine in their refrigerator, meaning to take it with him when he left. Well, as would have it, he left after the meeting and forgot his bottle of wine.

Living in the home with the family was the wife's mother. She had been an alcoholic for years and had now been dry for over three years. She was wont to get up in the night and go to the refrigerator to get a snack and go back to sleep. This night, however, she found a bottle of wine beckoning to her and she went on a ten year binge.

Her problem, you may say. No, not at all. The law of love dictates that we not put a stumbling block in the way of the weak. This was an unintentional accident, but what of the Pastor I just saw at the Olive Garden guzzling down a bottle of wine? *Selah.*

February 18 - The Hand of Our God

For I was ashamed to require of the king a band of soldiers and horsemen to help us against the enemy in the way: because we had spoken unto the king, saying, The hand of our God is upon all them for good that seek him; but his power and his wrath is against all them that forsake him. Ezra 8:22 (KJV)

We, the Christian Church, do not need the protection and help of the government to "help us against the enemy in the way." In fact the letter written by Thomas Jefferson to a concerned Baptist church stated that there would always be a "separation between the Church and State." This, in its context, was meant to insure the Church that government would never attempt to delve into the affairs of the church nor attempt to impose its will upon the church.

This letter has been twisted and turned by the enemies of Christ to mean that the Church should stay out of Government. No, Beloved, it meant, and means, that the Government should stay out of the Church. There is to be "freedom of religion," not, "freedom from religion."

Ezra 7:24 shows us the proper esteem the government and people should have for the leaders of the Church: "Also we certify you, that touching any of the priests and Levites, singers, porters, Nethinims, or ministers of this house of God, it shall not be lawful to impose toll, tribute, or custom, upon them." My how things have changed along the way.

"What can I do," you may ask? Remember that it is, "In God We Trust" and not a government that thinks it should take care of each of our wants and needs. Become familiar with the Constitution of the United States and the Bill of Rights and find out just what a government, "by the people and for the people," should look like.

Most of all: Read the Bible and pray. Get to know the Author of the Book of Books, the Holy Spirit, and learn the ways of God.

Look to Him for He has promised to, "supply all our need according to His riches in glory by Christ Jesus" as we become good stewards of His grace.

Find the gifts and talents that God has placed within you and then use them to glorify Him in all that you do. (Mat. 25)

February 19 - So Shall It Come To Pass

The LORD of hosts hath sworn, saying, Surely as I have thought, so shall it come to pass; and as I have purposed, so shall it stand: Isaiah 14:24 (KJV)

Whether for judgement, correction, or in promised blessing, the Word of the Lord is sure. He is ever faithful to bring to pass the thing that He has spoken.

Here we see the Lord speak out of the purpose and abundance of His heart: "as I have thought," and "as I have purposed.." This also reveals His great compassion, for His purpose is to forgive and liberate His people.

"As I have thought," *damah*, devised, imagined or caused to resemble, "so shall it come to pass." "As I have purposed," *ya'ats*, counselled, advised, planned and consulted together in the Godhead, so shall it stand. In other words, His plan and purpose for you will not change.

Remember that Jeremiah 29:11 assures us that God has a prophetically proclaimed divine destiny for those who are His.

For I know the thoughts and plans that I have for you, says the Lord, thoughts and plans for welfare and peace and not for evil, to give you hope in your final outcome. Jeremiah 29:11 (AMP)

Emancipation (liberation) from bondage of all kind is His plan and purpose for you:

That I will break the Assyrian in my land, and upon my mountains tread him under foot: then shall his yoke depart from off them, and his burden depart from off their shoulders. Isaiah 14:25 (KJV)

We learn in Isaiah 10:27 that the anointing is what will decimate every yoke of bondage and lift its control from off the people: "...the yoke shall be destroyed because of the anointing."

Get ready to walk in the liberating joy of the Lord today!

February 20 - Be Glad!

Be glad then, ye children of Zion, and rejoice in the Lord your God: for he hath given you the former rain moderately, and he will cause to come down for you the rain, the former rain, and the latter rain in the first month.
Joel 2:23 (KJV)

This is that:
And it shall come to pass in the last days, saith God, I will pour out of my Spirit upon all flesh: . . .
Acts 2:17-18 (KJV)

Today, I want to look at more of the promise found in the book of Joel; specifically that which is found in Joel 2:23. After two verses commanding us to "fear not," or "be not afraid," we are encouraged to "Be glad!" Because of what is promised in the past two verses, we are to "be glad" and rejoice. God is our God. He is personally the Lord our God.

As He has given the former and latter rains to the just and the unjust in the natural, He now promises a spiritual rain that will fall in the last days in which we are living. On the day of Pentecost the rains began.

The former rain brings forth the fruit of the earth. The spiritual former rain is the Holy Spirit convicting humanity of sin. This rain will fall twice to bring every seeking soul to a place of heartfelt conviction of sin.

Then, the latter rain will fall. This, in the natural, is the final rain before harvest. So, too, in the spiritual realm, the latter rain is the final preparation for harvest. It is the supernatural enabling for the work of the ministry.

This is the beginning of a decade of harvest, the scope of which will pale every outpouring of God that has come before. You and I are living in the days prophesied of 100 years ago by William J. Seymour, pastor of the Azusa Street Mission.

Receive your fresh anointing for the work of the ministry today! Let the "latter rain" of His Spirit fall upon you and prepare you for supernatural ministry to the lost.

February 21 - Empty Vessels Shall Be Filled

And the floors shall be full of wheat, and the fats shall overflow with wine and oil. Joel 2:24 (KJV)

This verse is rich with typology that can only be seen in the original language. Join me as we mine the riches of this text starting with the word "floors.

The "floors," *goren*, are vessels or empty places. Our verse states that these empty vessels will be "full of wheat," *bar*. That is, winnowed, purged and cleansed from the "fats," *yeqeb*, the deep, extreme poverty of man's soul. The result will be that, the deep things of God which are hidden and above man's scrutiny, especially the divine counsels, will be received with wine, *tiyrowsh*, a symbol of joy and celebration and oil, *yitshar*, a symbol of anointing and healing.

e.g. The Good Samaritan on the Jericho Road

And went to him, and bound up his wounds, pouring in oil and wine, and set him on his own beast, and brought him to an inn, and took care of him. Luke 10:34 (KJV)

The promise, here, is that lost individuals who are empty and void of the life of God will be purged and cleansed by the blood of the Lamb slain from the foundation of the world. The deep, extreme poverty of their souls will be replaced with the divine counsels and secrets of God. Supernatural understanding will break upon them in waves of glory.

Each person who receives the Lord and His promised provision will find themselves filled with unspeakable joy and the glory of the Lord God Almighty.

They will live a life of joyful celebration as they find themselves moving in the anointing of Christ the Anointed One.

Healing streams will flow in their lives and restore all that has been stolen by the enemy of their soul.

You and I, Beloved, are partakers of this wonderful promise and are chosen and called to go and tell the good news of God's great desire to bestow His love and mercy to all who will hear.

February 22 - The Lord Reigns!

Beloved, "The Lord reigns . . . He sits enthroned above the cherubim, let the earth quake!"

Each decade brings a greater number of earth quakes of greater magnitude than the previous one. Is it not written in the book of Matthew that "there will be . . . earthquakes in place after place." The increase of these tremblers are "the beginning of the birth pangs".(Matthew 24:7,8)

Every birth is preceded by a time of discomfort, ungainliness, pain, and often travail. These negative aspects of birth are a result of the fall of man in the garden. (Genesis 3:16) Just as in natural birth, so in spiritual birth.

At the end of this age of Grace there will be great travail preceding a great birth! The birth of a new age and a new order! The gestation period is already begun. We are in the "last days".

At the same time, as a necessary preparation, God is birthing a Glorious Church. A Church (a Bride) that will display the Resurrection Power of our risen Lord, Jesus Christ! She is not coming without discomfort, ungainliness, pain, and travail; but she is being delivered. There is no power in heaven or on earth that can stop her moving through the "birth canal".

Her course is set. There is only one way to go. This is no breach baby. Satan cannot abort this one. This is the one destined to inherit the Father's promise. This is the one that Jesus is betrothed to. This is the one that the Holy Spirit is making ready for His coming. This is the one that will do exploits. This is the one that will proclaim to the world.

You Are The Church! Yes, Beloved, it is you who is being birthed in this great hour of visitation. By agency of the Holy Spirit, you are being brought to maturity for just such a day as this. (1 Corinthians 3:16; 12:13,27; Rev. 19:6-8; Esther 4:14)

Will you come forth willingly? Will you entrust your future into The Father's hands? Will you? Will you? Casting all your care upon Him? (1 Peter 5:7; Proverbs 3:5-7)

I know you have, and I know you will. Together we will come forth in power and proclaim Jesus as Lord.

February 23 - A Word for You

It was said of Him, that the Lord has anointed Him, and that the precious oil flowed down upon His head, covered His garment, and flowed even to the footprints left in the sands.

"Know you not, My child, that you are His body, a member in particular, and that the anointing abides upon The Head and runs down to cover, immerse, enfold, and envelope His body, the Church.

As I clothed man in the garden with Light, Life, Anointing, and Glory, so as you draw to Me, I clothe you and the anointing will fall as the dew and as the mist it shall surround you.

Don't you know that as your praise issues from your lips - clouds form and the rains fall - and I come to stand in your midst even, as it were, a cloud and a pillar of fire.

A head cannot be severed from it's body if life is to continue and so we are united. For it is written, that we shall be one even as the Father and the Son are one.

You are the apple of My eye. To harm you is to harm Myself. So shall I keep and guard you.

Feel it now, the anointing oil flowing down upon you. Feel the warmth of its touch, for it is life unto you.

Feel the disorders in your body disappear and fade away. Feel the heart ache melt like snow before the hot coals from off the altar.

Let it caress you, saturate, and permeate your very being.

Breath it in, for it is life unto you this day."

February 24 - Good News

God is speaking very plainly regarding the immediate future of the Church and her part in the great harvest of this hour.

Worship! Worship and high praise is what will usher in this unprecedented move of God. This worship and high praise can only come from those who have put Him first.

Hear this that must be and things to come:

When you put Him in the highest place of your life, far above all the troubles that would distract - When you enthrone Him in glory in your life -You will find yourself in victory - Suddenly! - Because He has the highest place - Enthrone Him today - Lift Him higher - Higher than what you see - Higher than what you feel - Higher than what you have experienced - Lift Him on high - Give in to His dominion - Give in to His authority - Oh, you will never be disappointed.

Look upon the hill of Zion - There's a white horse prancing - Oh, the fire in the Rider's eyes - His hair like wool - The King of Glory, King of Kings, Lord of Lords, Wonderful Counselor, Mighty God, Everlasting Father, Prince of Peace - dressed for battle - the Lord of Hosts is He - You see, the battle is not yours, but it is the Lord's and the outcome was wrought at Calvary!

Assemble! Assemble at the Muster Gate - the house of prayer - the house of worship! - Come and be numbered - Come and be counted as His own.

He will not descend - He will not ride into battle until we've come and gathered around Him - His eye looks to and fro over the face of the earth to see who will rise dressed for battle and go - Who will raise the banner of the redeemed and gather at the gate? It is you! It is you, Beloved. It is you!

He would that none be lost and so He waits for the Father's Voice - Gather to Him while there is yet time and having done all stand - The whole earth will be covered with His glory! Darkness will not triumph - Iniquity will fail - Holiness will prevail - as our King appears in the worshipping congregation!

February 25 - Times of Decision

As I consider you in these critical times of decision I am reassured by my Father and your Father that He is at work to establish and prosper you in ways that you have not experienced before. I heard Him say of you:

"I have caused thee to be planted by the River of life, and your leaves shall not fail, nor shall they wither in the day of dryness. They shall be as leaves of healing for the nations. And under their shadow the multitudes shall come to sit, to be protected, to be shielded from the scorching heat of the hour. Your fruit shall be for nourishment, good to eat; bringing strength and life, encouragement and joy. For you are the planting of the Lord and I have caused you to come and send your roots deep into My provision.

When the stormy winds blow, you will not be uprooted. When the land is parched with dryness, yet you shall be supple and moist. For My River will satisfy you, though on the surface it is not as yet seen, it runs in the depths of the Rock in abundance. Hear its rushing, it is the sound of many waters, the Voice of the Lord your God saying, I AM near.

Settle in, rest and abide while I draw your roots ever deeper into the Rock.

I have caused you to come, I have planted you for this season, I have caused you to drink, and I have caused you to live."

February 26 - They That Wait Upon The Lord

They that wait upon the Lord shall renew their strength ; they shall mount up with wings as eagles; they shall run, and not be weary; and they shall walk, and not faint.
Isaiah 40:22 (KJV)

Whose strength will be renewed? The one who waits.

What does this word "wait" mean? Its strongest meaning is, "To be bound together with."

Be Bound Together With God -

Yet a man is risen to pursue thee, and to seek thy soul: . . . [You] shall be bound in the bundle of life with the LORD thy God; and the souls of thine enemies, them shall he sling out, as out of the middle of a sling.
1 Samuel 25:29 (KJV)

"Wait" upon God. Surely, to be bound together with God will bring His immeasurable strength to bear in every circumstance and situation.

His strength becomes our strength to the degree that we are united with Him.

We must take time out of our busy schedules to "Wait" [be bound together] with God; to become one with Him!

February 27 - Time

Time, as we know it, is moving by so very quickly. God is doing "His act, His strange act." The world is racing toward it's end time fulfillment. All is unfolding as it should.

Do you feel the same stirring within that I do; that thrilling sense of urgency that permeates everything that we are about? What an hour in which to live!

Beloved, the years ahead are going to be years of an open door for the Church. I'm not just talking about opportunities for ministry overseas, in the "mission fields" (although these opportunities will be great!) but right where you live. Walls that have, seemingly, stood against our prayers are coming tumbling down. Schools, Government agencies, sections of Cities, Clubs, Conventions, groups and individuals are going to throw open the door once more!

Your city is one of the greatest harvest fields in the world! The nations have moved next door and are looking for a hand of welcome and encouragement. Jesus would be found moving in their midst, speaking their language, offering hope, pointing them toward the Living God; and such is our calling.

Be strong and very courageous . . . turn not from (your calling) to the right hand or to the left, that you may prosper where ever you go. Do exploits for God in this hour and see them prosper like never before! [Joshua 1:7; Daniel 11:32b].

February 28 - God Is Not A Man

God is not a man that He should lie; neither the son of man, that He should repent; hath He said, and shall He not do it? or hath He spoken, and shall He not make it good? Numbers 23:19 (KJV)

What has God spoken to you?

Think about it. It may have been quite some time since He last spoke to you concerning that special something.

Satan would come, as of old, and ask, "Can it really be that God has said ?"

Hath He Said? -

Don't give any place to such a suggestion! "Resist the devil, and he will flee!" James 4:7 (KJV)

God is not slack concerning His promise; nor has He forgotten you. "For the vision is yet for AN APPOINTED TIME, and IT HASTENS to the end [fulfillment]; IT WILL NOT DECEIVE or disappoint. THOUGH IT TARRY, WAIT [earnestly] for it; BECAUSE IT WILL SURELY COME, it will not be behindhand on its APPOINTED DAY. Habakkuk 2:3 (KJV - emphasis mine)

February 29 - Just Think

Just think, no one else can be what you are for Him. No one has been fashioned in quite the same way. His purpose for you was, and is, unique and special.

Whether you recognize your value or not does not change the plan of God concerning you. Isn't that thrilling to consider? What marvelous love He has for you! He has included you in His strategy to reach the lost multitudes of this age. Beloved, He picked you to publish His name so that the people might ascribe greatness unto Him (Deu. 32:3).

He will provide all that you need to accomplish what He has called you to do.

Whether it is in knowing what, when, or how to do something -

If any of you lack wisdom, let him ask of God, that giveth to all men liberally, and upbraideth not; and it shall be given him. James 1:5 (KJV)

- or whether it is material provision or physical strength to accomplish the appointed task -

Beloved, I wish above all things that thou mayest prosper and be in health, even as thy soul prospereth. 3 John 1:2 (KJV)

- God will supply your every need

But my God shall supply all your need according to his riches in glory by Christ Jesus. Philippians 4:19 (KJV)

MARCH

March 01 - March Already?

March Already? How can it be? Time is moving so swiftly.

Sharon and I trust that you are doing well and that you are pressing in to all that God has for you this year.

This is a year of destiny for many but all will not enter in to what God has prepared unless they be willing to go through to victory.

Going through is the secret. To have victory there must needs be battle. Battle speaks of "the good fight of faith" [1 Tim 6:12; 2 Tim 4:7] and the "good warfare" of those "mighty" in the Spirit. [2 Cor 10:4; 1 Tim 1:18]

"Good" things in the plan and purpose of God concerning us. 1 Peter 1:7 says it this way, "That the trial of your faith, being much more precious than of gold that perisheth, though it be tried with fire, might be found unto praise and honour and glory at the appearing of Jesus Christ:".

Great victory and great reward are ahead for those who will not faint in the battle.

Remember the words of God by the Psalmist, "A thousand shall fall at thy side, and ten thousand at thy right hand; but it shall not come nigh thee. Only with thine eyes shalt thou behold and see the reward of the wicked. Because thou hast made the LORD, which is my refuge, even the most High, thy habitation; There shall no evil befall thee, neither shall any plague come nigh thy dwelling. For he shall give his angels charge over thee, to keep thee in all thy ways" (Psalm 91:7-11 KJV). He will keep you in all your ways!

Beloved, not only will He keep you but he will also manifest Himself as your all sufficient Provider:

> Who goeth a warfare any time at his own charges? who planteth a vineyard, and eateth not of the fruit thereof? or who feedeth a flock, and eateth not of the milk of the flock? 1 Corinthians 9:7 (KJV)

Keep your eyes on Jesus, the Author and Finisher of our faith while He brings you through on your way to - your destiny! - your Victory!

March 02 - Hear The Cry?

Listen!

Listen to the cry of the Nations.

The Romanian people have tasted liberty and are unwilling to let go of what they have tasted.

There is a mighty moving in the breast of the people.

They are not crushed in spirit.

The people in China are not crushed in spirit.

The people in South Africa are not crushed in spirit.

The people in America are not crushed in spirit. World affairs are just a mirror of what is going on in the spiritual realm.

The Spirit of God is stirring, even in the lost, a strong desire for freedom.

It is a yearning that cannot be quenched by military power and political repression.

God has heard the cry of the Church!

The oppressor is about to be taken.

At the cry, Babylon has been taken! the earth shall tremble, and the cry shall be heard among the nations. Thus says the Lord: Behold, I will raise up against Babylon and against those who dwell among those rebelling against Me a destroying wind and spirit;

Jeremiah 50:46-51:1 (AMP)

You may say, 'But can't you see that the end is coming.' Oh yes, I see it. But I also see a great in-gathering that will precede it. There is a promised revival that is sweeping the world! It takes precedence over all else. Beloved, the enemy doesn't win. We do! This is the hour of victory!

March 02 - (Continued)

Hear The Cry?

"He who has an ear, let him hear what the Spirit says . . ." (Rev 3:22 KJV)

God is raising up a destroying wind and spirit that will remove every hindrance to the proclamation of the Gospel to the whole earth!

Beloved, don't look at what you see! Faith can see the unseen. Faith can see what God is doing. Faith can see the enemy fleeing even when it appears that he is winning.

Faith is the substance of things hoped for, the evidence of things not seen. Hebrews 11:1 (KJV).

The time will come for the Great Falling Away. The time will come for the Great Tribulation. Now is NOT that time! Now is the time to Lift up your eyes. "Lift up your eyes, and look on the fields; for they are white already to harvest":

Say not ye, There are yet four months, and then cometh harvest? behold, I say unto you, Lift up your eyes, and look on the fields; for they are white already to harvest. John 4:35 (KJV)

It is Harvest Time! Don't worry about when the end will come. Start reaping the abundant harvest that God has set before you. Continue in the work of God as a good steward should. Jesus told us to "occupy till I come." This means to do business until the moment we see Him (Luk 19:13).

Heed the cry of the Nations!

Listen! They are crying for prayer, encouragement, literature, teachers, and support. Put off indecision! Put off fear!

Hear the cry! Respond in faith! Do Exploits!

March 03 - The Spirit Speaks

I wanted to share this word that came to the congregation with you:

"Oh, at the noising forth of the water spouts, deep cries unto deep and great rivers and floods and torrents of the love of God issue forth. It is for the healing of the Nation and the gathering of a people to the Throne of Grace.

God has issued forth out of His love the infinite, unreachable, unfathomable, depths of His love that surpasses human understanding. Out of the Spirit issues life that is given from the love of God. It is a love that never fails. You have life throughout eternity that does not fail because it is born of the love of God itself. It shall perform what it has been sent to perfect and accomplish in your life. That love will not fail in its working but will bring you unto the fullness of all that God has for you.

Look not at your stumbling and look not at your frailties, but My child, look at the promise of your Father. He has given all things into your hand even as you are submitted to His Son. There is nothing withheld from you, for it is the Father's good pleasure to give you good things. Yes, and glad things, and quiet and peaceful things for your soul.

Oh, the Prince of peace has come unto you! The joy of God is your strength in Him! Take courage! Oh yes, be strong and of good courage, for God has arisen in your behalf." -

Truly Beloved, great days are ahead!

March 04 - Breath In My Words

"It was said of Him, that the Lord has anointed Him, and that the precious oil flowed down upon His head, covered His garment, and flowed even to the footprints left in the sands.

Know you not, My child, that you are His body, a member in particular, and that the anointing abides upon The Head and runs down to cover, immerse, enfold, and envelope His body, the Church.

As I clothed man in the garden with Light, Life, Anointing, and Glory, so as you draw to Me, I clothe you and the anointing will fall as the dew and as the mist it shall surround you.

Don't you know that as your praise issues from your lips - clouds form and the rains fall - and I come to stand in your midst even, as it were, a cloud and a pillar of fire.

A head cannot be severed from it's body if life is to continue and so we are united. For it is written, that we shall be one even as the Father and the Son are one.

You are the apple of My eye. To harm you is to harm Myself. So shall I keep and guard you.

Feel it now, the anointing oil flow down upon you. Feel the warmth of it's touch, for it is life unto you.

Feel the disorders in your body disappear and fade away.

Feel the heart ache melt like snow before the hot coals from off the altar.

Let it caress you, saturate, and permeate your very being.

Breath it in, for it is life unto you this day."

March 05 - Caught Up In Jesus

I'm so caught up in Jesus! Never in my life have I been so aware of His Presence; so completely captivated by what He is speaking.

He has said to me,

"You will not speak to your opposition. You will not speak of your opposition. You will speak of your confirmation and you will speak to your foundation".

Isn't that powerful? Can you grasp this with me?

God has completely taken care of all that has arrayed itself against us! It is as though the enemy does not exist!

He has spoken. He has spoken a word to each of us and we are to abide in it.

Now, we are to speak what He spoke. We are to stir up the memory of the confirmation, the "first fruit", and declare it.

He has executed His Divine plan and nothing can stop its coming into being. The plans have been drawn. The foundation trenches are dug and the reenforcement steel has been put in place. The concrete is poured as we speak concerning the word of the Lord already planted deep within our hearts.

Revelation has taken the cover off the schemes and devices of the enemy. The doubts and concerns of the mind are exposed and recognized as the "fiery darts" of Satan. The shield of faith will stop every one.

So then faith cometh by hearing, and hearing by the word of God. Romans 10:17 (KJV)

Above all, taking the shield of faith, wherewith ye shall be able to quench all the fiery darts of the wicked. Ephesians 6:16 (KJV)

Give thanks for what He has spoken! Give thanks that it is already done! Give thanks that the manifestation is as close as the sound of your voice!

Take heart and know this, Beloved -

"Thus saith the LORD unto you, Be not afraid nor dismayed by reason of this great multitude; for the battle is not yours, but God's" 2 Chronicles 20:15 (KJV).

March 06 - God Is On The Throne

God is on the throne! His Kingdom is an everlasting Kingdom! All rule, authority, dominion, principalities, and powers, are subject to Him! (Ephesians 1:21,22; Colossians 2:10, 15)

There is great increase in darkness but there is greater increase in light! Darkness always flees before the light. Light never gives place to darkness. (1 John 1:5-7)

How often it seems as though darkness has won. How often there appears to be no hope; no way to proceed. You say, I can't go on. You say, I seem to be going in circles. I'm not progressing. I've come to my wit's end.

Dear one of God - Don't give up! Gird yourself with the Word of your Father! He has promised that He "will not leave you as orphans [comfortless, desolate, bereaved, forlorn, helpless]", and has He not said, "I will not in any way fail you nor give you up nor leave you without support. [I will] not, [I will] not, [I will] not in any degree leave you helpless nor forsake nor let [you] down (relax My hold on you)! [Assuredly not!]". (Joh. 14:18; Heb. 13:5; Jos. 1:5)

Don't think it is a strange thing that is happening to you! Your Lord and Saviour has wrought the victory for you! He knew what you would have to go through. He knows your every groaning, your every whisper, your every breath. The vision He has given you will come to pass. Yes, though it tarry, wait for it! It is as a thing done! God spoke it into your heart! Don't stop short of the manifestation! (1 Pet. 4:13,14; 2 Cor. 2:14; Col.2:15) (Hab. 2:3; Heb. 10:36-38)

Know this - Sharon and I are praying for you. We believe God is well able to do exceeding, abundantly, above all that you may ever ask or think! He has purposed you to be a recipient of His precious and exceedingly great promises. (Eph. 3:20; 2 Pet. 1:4)

March 07 - Anyone

I assure you, most solemnly I tell you, if anyone steadfastly believes in Me, he will himself be able to do the things that I do; and he will do even greater things than these, because I go to the Father. 1 John 14:12 (AMP)

Anyone can do the works of Jesus if they will yield to the Holy Spirit:
Anyone! Any One (1).
And they were all filled (each one was filled) with the Holy Spirit and began to speak in other (supernatural) languages (tongues), as the Spirit kept giving them clear and loud expression [in each tongue in appropriate words]. Acts 2:4 (AMP gms)
This releases the power spoken of in Acts 1:
But you shall receive power (ability, efficiency, and might) when the Holy Spirit has come upon you, and you shall be My witnesses in Jerusalem and all Judea and Samaria and to the ends (the very bounds) of the earth. Acts 1:8 (AMP)
This is the power given to anyone who asks:
And He said to them, Go into all the world and preach and publish openly the good news (the Gospel) to every creature [of the whole human race]. Mark 16:15 (AMP)
And these attesting signs will accompany those who believe: in My name they will drive out demons; they will speak in new languages; They will pick up serpents; and [even] if they drink anything deadly, it will not hurt them; they will lay their hands on the sick, and they will get well. Mark 16:17-18 (AMP)

March 08 - Instruction

For the commandment is a lamp; and the law is light; and reproofs of instruction are the way of life:
Proverbs 6:23 (KJV)

The commandment, *mitsvah'*, the commandment of God (God's code of wisdom) is a lamp, *niyr*, glistens and provides light in darkness like a lamp; and the law, *towrah*, direction and instruction found in the body of prophetic teaching concerning God's codes of law, is light, *'owr*, the light of life, prosperity and instruction in the face of God who is Israel's light; and reproofs, *towkechah*, correction and arguments for instruction, *muwcar*, doctrinal discipline and chastisment which illuminate the way, *derek*, the manners, habits and course of moral character of life, *chay*, bringing revival and renewal to the lively activity of man.

Don't be too quick to throw out "the baby with the bath," the values of the law with the legalistic keeping of ritual. Jesus came to fulfill the law, not do away with it.

Grace embraced the fundamental principles of the law and converted them from a list of do's and do not's to want to's that flow from a life of loving obedience.

Too often it is the fleshly nature of mankind striving against godly instruction that screams, "We're under grace, not under the law!" A checkup from the neck up is a good practice every so often.

After all, Jesus said, "If ye love me, keep my commandments" (Joh. 14:15 KJV).

If ye keep my commandments, ye shall abide in my love; even as I have kept my Father's commandments, and abide in his love. John 15:10 (KJV)
Selah

March 09 - Rains of The Spirit

Thou, O God, didst send a plentiful rain, whereby thou didst confirm thine inheritance, when it was weary. Psalm 68:99 (KJV)

Have you ever been so worn out by circumstances and situations that you don't think that you can go on? Have people so disappointed you that you wonder if your calling of God is accomplishing anything? Have you thought of just "throwing in the towel" and moving on to something else? You are not alone. Most of us have at one time or another.

But - as we turn our faces toward heaven and shut ourselves in with God, the Holy Spirit comes and the rains of glory begin to fall. The refreshing downpour begins to fill every dry place in our being and we are confirmed and made to be alive and fruitful once again.

March 10 - A Covenant of Peace

And I will restore [establish a covenant of peace] to you [for] the years that the locust hath eaten, the cankerworm, and the caterpillar, and the palmerworm, my great army which I sent among you. Joel 2:25 (KJV)

There are many "prophets" today who are so focused on world events that they are "prophesying" cataclysmic events that are supposed to be the judgements of God on certain people groups or nations.

I am a strong believer in the prophetic and in God's ability to speak to a man or a people. With this said, I must declare that most doom and gloom "words" are simply the vain imaginings of individuals with underlying character weaknesses that have allowed a spirit of fear to invade their minds.

Does God warn of impending judgement? The answer is a resounding, Yes! When He does, He also gives a call for repentance that will stop the judgement and bring blessing. All one needs do is review the record found in the book of Jonah.

Come to think of it, many of our modern day "prophets" have the same problem that Jonah had. They want the Lord to bring judgement and fail to see the loving kindness of our God and King. Some, like Jonah, actually get mad at God because He is so long suffering, patient and kind.

Let's remember the words of Jesus as He dealt with His companions who were doomsday deliverers:

And when his disciples James and John saw this, they said, Lord, wilt thou that we command fire to come down from heaven, and consume them, even as Elias did? But he turned, and rebuked them, and said, Ye know not what manner of spirit ye are of. For the Son of man is not come to destroy men's lives, but to save them. And they went to another village. Luke 9:54-56 (KJV)

Beloved, be careful of who you listen to and what spirit you expose yourself to. Our Redeemer lives and He is come to bring you into the fulness of all that He is. He has purposed to bring you into all of His heavenly inheritance. He loves you and will not fail you! "Eye hath not seen, nor ear heard, neither have entered into the heart of man" the blessings God has in store for you (1 Cor. 2:9-KJV). *Selah*.

March 11 - Let My People Go!

Like Pharaoh of old, Satan is pursuing those that have left his "Egypt." He has sent forth his demonic army of spirits to demoralize, recapture and destroy the redeemed of the Lord. Deceptive spirits of oppression, depression, and hopelessness have pressed the people of God against the "Red Sea" of despair. Lying spirits have made a frenzied attempt to snare and rebind those that have been set free of mental and emotional weakness by the Spirit of the Living God.

The Almighty has said, "Let my people go!" and has set Himself to lead them to safety with His eye upon them.

> I will instruct thee and teach thee in the way which thou shalt go: I will guide thee with mine eye.
> Psalm 32:8 (KJV)

No power on earth, above nor beneath can stand against the spoken will of God your Redeemer!

> Then said the LORD unto me, . . . I will hasten my word to perform it. Jeremiah 1:12 (KJV)

The word hasten means, to sleeplessly watch over. God who never slumbers nor sleeps is present with us to guarantee that you and I remain free.

> Now the Lord is that Spirit: and where the Spirit of the Lord is, there is liberty. 2 Corinthians 3:17 (KJV)

Where the Spirit of the Lord is - there is Liberty!

Beloved, stretch forth the rod of God, even your faith in Him, and watch the Red Sea situation, the impossible circumstance, the overwhelming odds against you, open before you and allow you to pass through to safety!

The battle is not yours; the battle is the Lord's. The only fight you have is a good fight and God is going to show that He already has drown your adversary in the waters of the crimson red sea of the Blood of Jesus.

> . . . Thus saith the LORD unto you, Be not afraid nor dismayed by reason of this great multitude; for the battle is not yours, but God's (2 Chron. 20:15 KJV).

> Fight the good fight of faith, lay hold on eternal life [Jesus is the Life] . . . (1 Tim. 6:12 KJV).

Your enemy, no matter how powerful, no matter how numerous, no matter how terrifying, is no match for the One who vanquished every foe on Calvary's tree!

> And having spoiled principalities and powers, he made a shew of them openly, triumphing over them in it [the Cross]. Colossians 2:15 (AMP)

March 12 - The Lord Your God Is Mighty!

Know the Lord, your God, in the midst of thee is mighty.

The Lord thy God in the midst of thee is mighty. Able to do exceeding abundantly above all that you can ever ask or think.

He is *Jehovah Rapha*, your healer. The God that stitches you up, binds up your wounds and heals you. He is *Jehovah Shalom*, your peace. Cast, therefore, all your care upon him, for truly He cares for you and He is the prince of peace.

Lean on the breast of your Beloved. Take peace, strength and comfort from Him. He is the Wonderful Comforter, yes, that is come to abide within.

Nothing without. No storm no matter how stout can come and route Him for He is the King of Kings and Lord of Lords. Mighty God is He, Everlasting Father, and He is with you throughout all eternity. He said, I'll never leave thee, I'll never forsake thee, even to the end of the age. Almighty God in the midst of thee.

Mighty! Mightier than cancer. Mightier than depression. Mightier than all of Satan's devices of old. The Lord your God is not created. He is the Creator and all things are subject to Him. Hallelujah! And He has given you authority to speak the name of Jesus. The name that is above every name. Yes, cancer is a name. Aids is a name. Kidney disease; that's a name. Lupus that's a name. Sickle cell anemia, that's a name. He's above every name!

Jesus conquered sin, hell, death, the grave. He's above every name that can be named. Worship Him, watch sickness flee away.

Beloved, Worship Him, watch depression flee. Worship Him, and watch the doubts melt away, faith arise and His enemies scatter. Hallelujah!

March 13 - God Has Set Some

And God hath set some in the church, first apostles, secondarily prophets, thirdly teachers, after that miracles, then gifts of healings, helps, governments, diversities of tongues. 1 Corinthians 12:28 (KJV)

We know that God is a God of order. Is it possible that the Lord has an order of how the "five-fold" ministry gifts work? I believe that our verse for today lays out the pattern of how the Church is to grow and develop.

This verse begins with, "God has set some." The word that I want to look at is the word, set, *tithemi.* It carries the meaning of, to set in place, to appoint, to ordain, establish, and to make (or set) for one's self or for one's use. The word used for, some, is, *men*, which means, surely or truly. So, that being as it may, we see that God ordains and establishes certain people in certain placements to fulfill His own purpose.

It would seem that He sets the Apostle in place to first go and establish the work. The word used for first is, *proton*, which places the Apostle, first in time, rank and place.

Once the Apostle has directions on where and when to go and plant, he will enlist the aid of the Prophet. "Secondarily, *deuteros*, Prophets," would seem to indicate that the Prophet would come after or along side the Apostle to prepare the ground through intercession and prayer and begin to speak life into a people of the region.

Thirdly, *tritos*, comes the need for the Teacher who establish the believers by teaching sound doctrine with revelation concerning Christ and the Cross.

This soul winning, church planting team is not complete without the ministries of the Evangelists who help to gather souls and build the work and the Pastor who, then, watches over and feeds the flock of God.

And he gave some, apostles; and some, prophets; and some, evangelists; and some, pastors and teachers; Ephesians 4:11 (KJV)

The text in the book of Ephesians shows us the whole team in, basically, the same order if understood properly. The Pastor could also have been the Apostle of the work.

One thing is sure. We need the whole working together as set by God.

March 14 - I Shall Not Die

I shall not die, but live, and declare the works of the LORD. Psalms 118:17 (KJV)

Have you ever considered the keeping power of God? You cannot be, killed *muwth*, put to death, die prematurely. When you are doing what God wants you to do, when He wants you to do it, you cannot be cut off before you have accomplished your mission.

I realize that we all have heard stories of people who have given their lives for the sake of the Gospel. Many times we don't understand how that could happen but we must trust God. He knows the beginning from the end. What looks like failure from the outside is actually a resounding victory.

A good example is the Cross of Christ. Many say that Jesus was defeated there. We know that he defeated the devil, his demons and everything arrayed against us in it.

During my many travels to the nations of the world, I have been threatened, attacked, way-laid by road bandits and have driven through dead bodies to go preach the Gospel.

God has protected me every time!

Why am I protected and others, it seems, are not? Only the Lord knows all the details but one thing is sure; neither you nor I can be stopped from completing our course. When our ministry calling is fulfilled, then, and only then, we will die. Not one minute before.

Until my appointed time I will, *chayah*, remain alive, live prosperously and be restored to life or health, from sickness, from discouragement, from faintness and even death, if need be, so that I can declare, *caphar*, show forth, recount and rehearse the, *ma'aseh*, deeds, works of deliverance and judgement of the Lord, *Yahh*, The One True God.

Beloved, you and I are called to be a "muster-officer" for the cause of the Christ of God. Each of us will live until the Lord's purpose for out lives is fulfilled.

No weapon that is formed against thee shall prosper; and every tongue that shall rise against thee in judgment thou shalt condemn. This is the heritage of the servants of the LORD, and their righteousness is of me, saith the LORD. Isaiah 54:17 (KJV)

March 15 - Concerning Spiritual Gifts

> Now concerning spiritual gifts, brethren, I would not have you ignorant. 1 Corinthians 12:1 (KJV)

One of the most precious things that the Lord does for us after we are born-again is to offer us the full equipping of the Holy Spirit. We call this the Baptism in the Holy Spirit with the evidence of speaking in other tongues.

It is so important that the Lord actually commands us to receive this subsequent to salvation infilling (Acts 1:4, 5). This is just the beginning of the empowering of the children of God for the work of propagating the Gospel (Acts 1:8).

Much is said about the "gifts of the Spirit" as enumerated in 1 Corinthians 12:4-11 but not much is said about the connection between them and the "fruit of the Spirit" listed in Galatians 5:22-23.

There are nine gifts of the spirit and nine fruit of the spirit. Each gift is a manifestation of an attribute of the fruit of the spirit. The connection can be first seen in Exodus 39:24-26:

> And they made upon the hems of the robe pomegranates of blue, and purple, and scarlet, and twined linen. And they made bells of pure gold, and put the bells between the pomegranates upon the hem of the robe, round about between the pomegranates; A bell and a pomegranate, a bell and a pomegranate, round about the hem of the robe to minister in; as the LORD commanded Moses. Exodus 39:24-26 (KJV)

The "bell" is mentioned in connection with the "fruit (pomegranate) in 1 Corinthians 13:1 (sounding brass, or a tinkling cymbal). Remember, faith works by love (Gal. 5:6). The "gifts" or "graces" also work by "love." The "fruit of the Spirit is love, joy, peace, longsuffering, gentleness, goodness, faith, meekness and temperance."

Let us administer the "gifts" of God in the "love" of God. We might experience a greater manifestation if we would.

March 16 - The Kingdom of God

> For the kingdom of God is not in word, but in power.
> 1 Corinthians 4:20 (KJV)

Allow me to brag on Jesus and the power of His resurrection for a moment. From the instant that Jesus translated me out of darkness into His marvelous light I have experienced the Word of God as living, powerful and sharper than a two-edged sword.

This walk with Jesus is not just in word, *logos*; not just something written or spoken of, not just a doctrine or saying, but in power, **dunamis**, inherent power, power residing in Christ by virtue of His nature, and which His resurrection exerts and puts forth.

If Christ is in me, and He is in every believer, then there should be a demonstration of resurrection power flowing through each of us.

Can we measure the power that it took to raise Jesus from the dead? Can we measure the power that makes all things new about us and to transform us into a new creature at salvation? I think not. Neither can we measure the power that will open blind eyes, cause the lame to leap and dance, or cleanse the leper.

What we can see and experience, however, is the effect of that power as we minister the Word of God by the Spirit of God.

I have personally been used of God to raise the dead and have been used to create eyes in a blind man who had no retina nor iris present before the power of God was released. I have experienced being used to deliver people from demons and various infirmities and have even been used to raise the dead.

I boast on the unlimited power of my resurrected Savior and claim nothing in and of myself. Jesus still saves, heals and delivers!

Consider the treasure that is within you and begin to allow the Lord to use you to carry the message of salvation and release the power of the Anointed One who is ever present within you.

March 17 - Seeds of Love

Be not deceived; God is not mocked: for whatsoever a man soweth, that shall he also reap. For he that soweth to his flesh shall of the flesh reap corruption; but he that soweth to the Spirit shall of the Spirit reap life everlasting. Galatians 6:7-8 (KJV)

The Word of God teaches us that whatever we sow, we will reap. This principle of the Word of God applies to every area of our lives; not just in our financial area.

Love is the seed that the Spirit of God wants us to sow. Love is always willing to die to itself. The seed that the devil wants us to sow is lust, which is self centered. Self puts ego and agenda first. I heard it said by Dr. Edwin Lewis Cole that, "love gives at its own expense for the benefit of others. Lust takes at another's expense to satisfy self."

All of us go through struggles that are too heavy to bear alone. If we are to bear another's burden, we will have to lay aside our own agenda. This is the heartbeat of God.

The seed of love is simply this:

"Find a need and fill it, find a tear and wipe it; find a wound and heal it, find a yoke and break it, find a burden and carry it, find a shame and cover it."

Perhaps it is time to ask God for crop failure on those times in our lives where we have sown to the flesh.

One thing is sure: the seeds we sow will bring a harvest. Let's take a moment today to recommit to be sowers of the seeds of love. After all, "God so loved that He" sowed the Seed that forever changed our lives.

March 18 - Go Ye

Go ye therefore, and teach all nations, baptizing them in the name of the Father, and of the Son, and of the Holy Ghost: Matthew 28:19 (KJV)

You and I are commissioned to carry the Gospel message to the world. Isn't that exciting? The Word of God assures us that if we will go then Jesus will work with us.

And they went out and preached everywhere, while the Lord kept working with them and confirming the message by the attesting signs and miracles that closely accompanied [it]. Amen (so be it). Mark 16:20 (AMP)

Did you see that? ". . . the Lord kept working with them and confirming the message . . .". He confirms the message spoken by those who are willing to go with "attesting signs and miracles." That means you can be a miracle worker in Christ. Who wouldn't want that?

Jesus said that if we would go and teach the commandments of the Lord that He would always be with us.

Teaching them to observe all things whatsoever I have commanded you: and, lo, I am with you alway, even unto the end of the world. Amen. Matthew 28:20 (KJV)

I have shared the gospel here in the United States and I have gone to the nations and this is what I've found. God is faithful to His Word and signs, wonders and miracles follow me when I preach His Word.

He is no respecter of persons so what He does in and through me He will do in and through you.

And Peter opened his mouth and said: Most certainly and thoroughly I now perceive and understand that God shows no partiality and is no respecter of persons, Acts 10:34 (AMP)

Find out when the next street witnessing team or the next missions trip is planned and go along. It will be the beginning of the greatest blessing of your life.

March 19 - The Man

> Let thy hand be upon the man of thy right hand, upon the son of man whom thou madest strong for thyself.
> Psalm 80:17 (KJV)

Let thy hand, *yad*, strength or power, be upon the man, '*iysh*, servant (the one consecrated) of thy right hand, *yamiyn*, the place of power and authority, *yaw-meen'*, upon the Son of Man (speaking of Christ Jesus who referred to Himself as the Son of Man), *ben 'adam* who thou (God) madest strong, *'amats*, strengthened, made courageous, confirmed and established for thyself (God the Father).

Jesus was born of a woman just like you and me. His Father was God. This set Him apart from all others on earth. His blood was Divine. Yet, He emptied Himself of all that it meant to be God so that He could be a faithful High Priest who had been touched by the feelings of mankind's infirmities and tempted as we.

He walked, as does every believer in Him, dependent upon the strengthening of God. We, like Him, are set at the right hand of power and authority, made courageous, confirmed and established by the will, plan and purpose of God our Father.

> That he would grant you, according to the riches of his glory, to be strengthened with might by his Spirit in the inner man; Ephesians 3:16 (KJV)

This marvelous miraculous work is changing us from glory to glory until we become perfected and arrive at the full measure of the stature of Christ Himself.

> Till we all come in the unity of the faith, and of the knowledge of the Son of God, unto a perfect man, unto the measure of the stature of the fulness of Christ: Ephesians 4:13 (KJV)

March 20 - Dry?

Have you ever had a dry spell in your spiritual life? You read your Bible and pray but it feels like you're just going through the motions? Don't feel alone and don't think for a moment that the Lord has somehow withdrawn from you.

I've had seasons like that and when I do I've come to realize that it is simply an opportunity to refortify my faith. The first time it happened I thought I had blasphemed the Holy Spirit. It was early in my Christian walk and I was so used to physical sensations accompanying the anointing of His Presence that when it stopped I was beside myself.

Fortunately, I had been taught to not go by feelings but by every word of God. I dove into the Bible even though I felt like I was getting nothing out of it. Once, after a year-and-a-half the feelings returned and I asked the Lord what had happened. I heard Him as clear as day when He said, "My son, you were becoming too dependent upon feelings and I needed you to stand on My Word in faith."

Since then I've learned that the best way to get through the dry times is to read the Bible more and spend more time praying in the Holy Spirit. The life giving river that flows from God's throne makes even the dry seasons fruitful seasons. The refreshing rains of the Spirit will fall and fresh revelation will flow again and again.

Just let the River flow and water the written Word that is being planted in the depths of your soul and spirit.

He who believes in Me [who cleaves to and trusts in and relies on Me] as the Scripture has said, From his innermost being shall flow [continuously] springs and rivers of living water. John 7:38 (AMP)

March 21 - He Alone Is Worthy

Thou art worthy, O Lord, to receive glory and honour and power: for thou hast created all things, and for thy pleasure they are and were created. Revelation 4:11 (KJV)

This verse gave birth to one of the great old hymns of the Church; and no wonder. It declares the majesty of our Lord's being and declares His mighty works. It speaks of the Omnipotent (all powerful), Omniscient (all knowing), Omnipresent (present everywhere at once) God without Whom nothing that exists could, or would, exist.

The book of Revelation, which draws on the whole Bible for its content, is filled with the glory of our risen Lord and Savior, Jesus the Christ. He, and He alone, was able to break the seals off of the scroll of heaven:

And [now] they sing a new song, saying, You are worthy to take the scroll and to break the seals that are on it, for You were slain (sacrificed), and with Your blood You purchased men unto God from every tribe and language and people and nation. Revelation 5:9 (AMP)

Salvation's door was opened, in Him, "for every tribe and language and people and nation."

Saying in a loud voice, Deserving is the Lamb, Who was sacrificed, to receive all the power and riches and wisdom and might and honor and majesty (glory, splendor) and blessing! Revelation 5:12 (AMP)

This glorious Lamb who is revealed in the Scripture is the Lamb slain from the foundation of the world.

And all the inhabitants of the earth will fall down in adoration and pay him homage, everyone whose name has not been recorded in the Book of Life of the Lamb that was slain [in sacrifice] from the foundation of the world. Revelation 13:8 (AMP)

This majestic Savior not only gave His life and shed His blood to redeem those out of mankind that would receive His atoning work but is also able to keep those who are His.

... I am [positively] persuaded that He is able to guard and keep that which has been entrusted to me and which I have committed [to Him] until that day. 2 Timothy 1:12 (AMP)

March 22 - If You Have Been Raised

IF THEN you have been raised with Christ [to a new life, thus sharing His resurrection from the dead], aim at and seek the [rich, eternal treasures] that are above, where Christ is, seated at the right hand of God.
Colossians 3:1 (AMP)

The tragedy of this hour is that most Christians are earth bound. They are chained to the sense realm of the five natural senses (sight, smell, sound, taste, & touch) unaware that they also have the same senses in the spirit.

Beloved, you and I were designed to "seek those things which are above" where Christ Jesus rules from the right hand of God the Father.

When we became born-again we were positioned in Him and He in us. When He arose from the grave, we arose with (in) Him. When He sat down at the right hand of God, we sat down with (in) Him.

Is it any wonder, then, that the next verse encourages us to "set our affection on things above" rather than "on the things of the earth?"

And set your minds and keep them set on what is above (the higher things), not on the things that are on the earth. Colossians 3:2 (AMP)

Beloved, the Anointed One and His anointing is in you! You are filled with resurrection power.

And if the Spirit of Him Who raised up Jesus from the dead dwells in you, [then] He Who raised up Christ Jesus from the dead will also restore to life your mortal (short-lived, perishable) bodies through His Spirit Who dwells in you. Romans 8:11 (AMP)

March 23 - The Lord Bless Thee

For the LORD thy God blesseth thee, as he promised thee: and thou shalt lend unto many nations, but thou shalt not borrow; and thou shalt reign over many nations, but they shall not reign over thee. Deuteronomy 15:6 (KJV)

The concept of God's children being blessed is not just a New Testament principle. Almighty God has always purposed to lift His own up above all other peoples on the earth. Today, I pray that you will grasp the reality of this desire of God's to do good to you whom He loves.

The LORD, **Y hovah**, The Existing One, thy God, **'elohiym**, One true God, blesseth thee, **barak**, praises, salutes and blesses you, as He promised thee, **dabar,** declared, commanded and spoken concerning you: and thou shalt lend unto many nations, **'abat rab gowy**, take a pledge of multitudes that they become indebted to you, a people more numerous than yourself of the peoples outside of the covenant. You shall be their chief.

But you shall not borrow, **'abat**, give a pledge for a debt; and thou shalt reign over many nations, **mashal,** have dominion over and be governor of multitudes more numerous than yourself of the peoples outside of the covenant. You shall be their chief, but they shall not have dominion authority over you.

In Christ you and I rule and reign with the authority of Almighty God Himself. This promise is given to those who obey the covenant agreement between God and man in Christ Jesus just as assuredly as it was given to those who kept the commandments of God during the Old Covenant.

March 24 - Ask Of The Lord Rain

Ask ye of the LORD rain in the time of the latter rain; so the LORD shall make bright clouds, and give them showers of rain, to every one grass in the field. Zechariah 10:1 (KJV)

We are told that if we do not ask of the Lord we will not receive of the Lord. It is also written that if we ask to satisfy our own personal lust [greed] we will not receive that for which we ask.

Ye lust, and have not: ye kill, and desire to have, and cannot obtain: ye fight and war, yet ye have not, because ye ask not. Ye ask, and receive not, because ye ask amiss, that ye may consume it upon your lusts. James 4:2-3 (KJV)

While our verse in Zechariah is literally speaking of the time of natural harvest, we can also apply it to the spiritual. The Lord of the Harvest has told us that we should ask for the harvest of lost souls because they are our inheritance.

Ask of me, and I shall give thee the heathen for thine inheritance, and the uttermost parts of the earth for thy possession. Psalm 2:8 (KJV)

If we ask for the lost in prayer we will find that we have great success in reaching the lost with our action of sharing the good news of the gospel.

Remember, you and I cannot save anyone; only the Holy Spirit can convict of sin and reveal Jesus to the unbeliever. We are just the messengers, the voice of God, if you will, that bring the message of faith to hungry hearts. Souls are saved through the foolishness of preaching and the word of our testimony as we work together with the Holy Spirit.

The "latter rain" was the rain that brought the harvest to the point of readiness for the reapers. When we ask the Lord will send the clouds of glory and showers of the Spirit's blessing to produce fruitfulness. Then we will have lasting fruit.

Ye have not chosen me, but I have chosen you, and ordained you, that ye should go and bring forth fruit, and that your fruit should remain: that whatsoever ye shall ask of the Father in my name, he may give it you. John 15:16 (KJV)

Ask today and see if the Lord will not answer you.

March 25 - Spirit of the Lord

And the spirit of the LORD shall rest upon him, the spirit of wisdom and understanding, the spirit of counsel and might, the spirit of knowledge and of the fear of the LORD; 3 And shall make him of quick understanding in the fear of the LORD: and he shall not judge after the sight of his eyes, neither reprove after the hearing of his ears: Isaiah 11:2-3 (KJV)

Don't you know that the Spirit of the Lord is resting, in, and upon you because Christ is in you?

Know ye not that ye are the temple of God, and that the Spirit of God dwelleth in you?
1 Corinthians 3:16 (KJV)

What? know ye not that your body is the temple of the Holy Ghost which is in you, which ye have of God, and ye are not your own? 1 Corinthians 6:19 (KJV)

You, as a believer, need to be assured that Christ abides within you and makes you one with Him.

To whom God would make known what is the riches of the glory of this mystery among the Gentiles; which is Christ in you, the hope of glory: Colossians 1:27 (KJV)

That they all may be one; as thou, Father, art in me, and I in thee, that they also may be one in us: that the world may believe that thou hast sent me. And the glory which thou gavest me I have given them; that they may be one, even as we are one: John 17:21-22 (KJV)

Beloved, you and I were destined to be adopted into the family of God and filled with the fulness of Christ Himself.

Till we all come in the unity of the faith, and of the knowledge of the Son of God, unto a perfect man, unto the measure of the stature of the fulness of Christ:
Ephesians 4:13 (KJV)

This fulness of Christ [the Anointed One and His anointing] is given so that we can reach a world steeped in the darkness of sin. Being joined with Him by the Spirit allows us to carry out the "greater works" that Jesus spoke of in John 14:12 (KJV), "He that believeth on me, the works that I do shall he do also; and greater works than these shall he do; because I go unto my Father."

March 26 - Spirit of Wisdom

> And the spirit of the LORD shall rest upon him, the spirit of wisdom and understanding, the spirit of counsel and might, the spirit of knowledge and of the fear of the LORD; 3 And shall make him of quick understanding in the fear of the LORD: and he shall not judge after the sight of his eyes, neither reprove after the hearing of his ears: Isaiah 11:2-3 (KJV)

The Spirit of the Lord rests, **nuwach**, settles down and remains quietly within and upon each believer in Jesus and makes Himself available to impart His wisdom, understanding, counsel, might, knowledge and fear (**yir'ah** = reverence, respect and piety toward God).

Wisdom is the first of His attributes that He reveals to those who are His own. Our first need is to have a revelation of Jesus the Christ who is the power of God and the wisdom of God.

> But unto them which are called, both Jews and Greeks, Christ the power of God, and the wisdom of God. 1 Corinthians 1:24 (KJV)

The deep and passionate cry in every true Christian's heart is this:

> That I may know him, and the power of his resurrection, and the fellowship of his sufferings, being made conformable unto his death; Philippians 3:10 (KJV)

To fear, **yir'ah**, Him is the beginning of Wisdom but to know Him in the three-fold way mentioned in Philippians is it's culmination. One's total yieldedness to being made conformable to the image of Christ brings the power of Almighty God to bear on the affairs of earth. This conformability is what brings the fulness promised in Ephesians 4:13.

The more you and I allow ourselves to die that He might live is the degree to which the power of God is released into and through our lives.

> I am crucified with Christ: nevertheless I live; yet not I, but Christ liveth in me: and the life which I now live in the flesh I live by the faith of the Son of God, who loved me, and gave himself for me. Galatians 2:20 (KJV)

Our unsurpassing victory is found only in our allowing the Spirit of God to settle down and rest within.

March 27 - Spirit of Understanding

>And the spirit of the LORD shall rest upon him, the spirit of wisdom and understanding, . . . Isaiah 11:2-3 (KJV)

The Spirit of the Lord brings understanding, *biynah*, and discernment. This is supernatural understanding like that which is spoken of in Hebrews 11:3 where it says:

>By faith we understand that the worlds [during the successive ages] were framed (fashioned, put in order, and equipped for their intended purpose) by the word of God, so that what we see was not made out of things which are visible. Hebrews 11:3 (AMP)

There is a "seeing" and an understanding of the Word of God that only comes by faith. The faith I am speaking of is not natural faith such as the faith we have that a chair will support us when we sit in it or in an airplane that it will leave the ground and land safely at our intended destination. No, the faith spoken of is supernaturally given by God through His Word (the Bible):

>So then faith cometh by hearing, and hearing by the word of God. Romans 10:17 (KJV)

>The entrance of thy words giveth light; it giveth understanding unto the simple. Psalm 119:130 (KJV)

It is the Word of God, as taught by the Spirit of God, that brings supernatural understanding and the clear operation of discerning of spirits given to those baptized in the Holy Spirit with the evidence of speaking with other tongues. These graces of the Spirit, or gifts, are given to enable the believer to have supernatural insight into the realm of the spirit. Supernatural abilities are what gives the believer in Christ the power to move in the things of God to save, heal and deliver those in bondage to sin, sickness and death.

No wonder, then, that it is impossible to please God without this God given faith and understanding.

>But without faith it is impossible to please him: for he that cometh to God must believe that he is, and that he is a rewarder of them that diligently seek him. Hebrews 11:6 (KJV)

March 28 - Spirit of Counsel

And the spirit of the LORD shall rest upon him, the spirit of wisdom and understanding, the spirit of counsel and might, . . . Isaiah 11:2-3 (KJV)

The Spirit of the Lord is also the Spirit of Counsel. He is the Wonderful Counsellor of Isaiah:

For unto us a child is born, unto us a son is given: and the government shall be upon his shoulder: and his name shall be called Wonderful, Counsellor, The mighty God, The everlasting Father, The Prince of Peace. Isaiah 9:6 (KJV)

When we do not know what to do we can ask of God and He will counsel us through His Word and by His Spirit. When the Word of God (the law of Love) is in our hearts we are counselled how to live by the indwelling Spirit of Counsel.

The law of his God is in his heart; none of his steps shall slide. Psalm 37:31 (KJV)

It is the covenant right and privilege of every believer to be led by the Spirit who is our counsellor, teacher, and guide.

For as many as are led by the Spirit of God, they are the sons of God. Romans 8:14 (KJV)

The Spirit of Counsel brings the thoughts and purposes of the Almighty, our Father to our consciousness so that we can say what God would say and do what God would do.

Thou . . . the Great, the Mighty God, the LORD of hosts, . . . Great in counsel, and mighty in work: for thine eyes are open upon all the ways of the sons of men: to give every one according to his ways, and according to the fruit of his doings: Jeremiah 32:18-19 (KJV)

The Holy Spirit only says what He hears the Father say:

Howbeit when he, the Spirit of truth, is come, he will guide you into all truth: for he shall not speak of himself; but whatsoever he shall hear, that shall he speak: and he will shew you [counsel you concerning] things to come. John 16:13 (KJV)

March 29 - Spirit of Might

And the spirit of the LORD shall rest upon him, the spirit of wisdom and understanding, the spirit of counsel and might, . . . Isaiah 11:2-3 (KJV)

The Spirit of Might, *g'buwrah*, is within and for you. The unlimited power of the Almighty is yours. By the Spirit of God you are endued with resurrection power.

But if the Spirit of him that raised up Jesus from the dead dwell in you, he that raised up Christ from the dead shall also quicken your mortal bodies by his Spirit that dwelleth in you. Romans 8:11 (KJV)

This, Beloved, is how you can raise the dead, cleanse the leper, heal the sick and deliver the possessed. Maybe you've never allowed God to use you in this way but this is the normal Christian life that the Lord has enabled you to live.

And these signs shall follow them that believe; In my name shall they cast out devils; they shall speak with new tongues; They shall take up serpents; and if they drink any deadly thing, it shall not hurt them; they shall lay hands on the sick, and they shall recover. Mark 16:17-18 (KJV)

Are you a believer? Then you can cast out devils, speak with new tongues, forcibly cast out and run off that old serpent, the devil himself. You can enjoy Divine protection when you eat or drink and you can heal the sick. This is what God had in mind for you when He sent His Son to redeem you and His Spirit to abide within you.

Nothing can really be accomplished in this life without the supernatural enabling of the Spirit of the Lord. Nothing of real value is wrought by the might of man but by the might of the Spirit of the Lord.

Zechariah, a prophet of God said it this way, ". . . Not by might, nor by power, but by My Spirit [of Whom the oil is a symbol], says the Lord of hosts. Zechariah 4:6 (AMP). When you are facing a battle of any kind you can have victory in the Lord through the Spirit of Might.

Who is the King of glory? The Lord strong and mighty, the Lord mighty in battle. Psalm 24:8 (AMP)

March 30 - Spirit of Knowledge

And the spirit of the LORD shall rest upon him, the spirit of wisdom and understanding, the spirit of counsel and might, the spirit of knowledge . . . Isaiah 11:2-3 (KJV)

The Spirit of Knowledge, *da'ath*, is the Spirit of perception, skill and discernment. The people of God are destroyed because of false perceptions, a lack of skill in using the Word of God and discerning the good from the vile according to it. Accurate knowledge depends upon perceptions that are based in truth.

The sum of Your word is truth [the total of the full meaning of all Your individual precepts]; and every one of Your righteous decrees endures forever. Psalm 119:160 (AMP)

Being skillful in the Word of God demands knowledge of the whole counsel of God as given in the Bible. I pray that you are not one of those Christians that only reads your favorite passages of scripture or that lives on the words of others. If you are, you are headed for destruction.

My people are destroyed for lack of knowledge; because you [the priestly nation] have rejected knowledge, I will also reject you that you shall be no priest to Me; seeing you have forgotten the law of your God, I will also forget your children. Hosea 4:6 (AMP)

In order for the Spirit of Knowledge to impart the knowledge of God and His Christ, Jesus, you must let Him teach you out of the pages of The Book He wrote.

Every Scripture is God-breathed (given by His inspiration) and profitable for instruction, for reproof and conviction of sin, for correction of error and discipline in obedience, [and] for training in righteousness (in holy living, in conformity to God's will in thought, purpose, and action), 2 Timothy 3:16 (AMP)

No one will have the knowledge of God and the things of God without the Spirit of Knowledge.

Howbeit when he, the Spirit of truth, is come, he will guide you into all truth: . . . John 16:13a (KJV)

March 31 - Spirit of Quick Understanding

And the spirit of the LORD shall rest upon him, the spirit of wisdom and understanding, the spirit of counsel and might, the spirit of knowledge and of the fear of the LORD; 3 And shall make him of quick understanding in the fear of the LORD: and he shall not judge after the sight of his eyes, neither reprove after the hearing of his ears: Isaiah 11:2-3 (KJV)

Understanding is a wonderful thing. My dilemma used to be that I might understand something important but not until it was too late to be of any benefit. To be of "quick understanding" is what God has in mind for you and I. Without it we can make decisions or determinations that are made without all the facts necessary to make them correctly.

What is interesting in this verse is that the word for quick is the word, *ruwach,* which is the same as the word for Spirit. It also means to be alive, therefore, to have a living, or quickened, inspired, revelatory understanding.

This kind of understanding also will give us a proper understanding of the fear of the Lord which is vital to a beleivers having a proper relationship with God.

The fear, *phobos*, of the Lord, *kurios*, can be translated as follows: The reverence for ones husband to whom I am committed and belong to. Now, doesn't that sound different than what the word "fear" normally brings to mind?

The fear of the LORD is the beginning of wisdom: Psalm 111:10 (KJV)

The fear of the LORD is the instruction of wisdom; Proverbs 15:33 (KJV)

The fear of the LORD tendeth to life: and he that hath it shall abide satisfied; he shall not be visited with evil. Proverbs 19:23 (KJV)

March Bonus - Spirit of Judgement

And the spirit of the LORD shall rest upon him, the spirit of wisdom and understanding, the spirit of counsel and might, the spirit of knowledge and of the fear of the LORD; 3 And shall make him of quick understanding in the fear of the LORD: and he shall not judge after the sight of his eyes, neither reprove after the hearing of his ears: Isaiah 11:2-3 (KJV)

Each of us makes judgements about a great deal of things during any given day. If we are not careful we form strong opinions about things based upon natural thinking. The Spirit of Judgement, *ruwach shaphat*, causes us to move outside of ourselves so that we can consider things based upon the Word of God (the mind of Christ - *nous Christos*) rather than what we see or hear.

For who hath known the mind of the Lord, that he may instruct him? But we have the mind of Christ. 1 Corinthians 2:16 (KJV)

Our spirit man has the same senses as the natural man. We can see in the spirit, hear in the spirit, taste in the spirit and touch in the spirit, etc. Unfortunately, most are not in tune with the realm of the spirit where the Holy Spirit operates. Jesus taught us that we should only say what we hear the Father say and only do what we see the Father do.

For I have not spoken of myself; but the Father which sent me, he gave me a commandment, what I should say, and what I should speak. John 12:49 (KJV)

Then answered Jesus and said unto them, Verily, verily, I say unto you, The Son can do nothing of himself, but what he seeth the Father do: for what things soever he doeth, these also doeth the Son likewise. John 5:19 (KJV)

Herein is the Spirit of Judgement operating properly.

APRIL

April 01 - Limiting God

Yea, they turned back and tempted God, and limited the Holy One of Israel. Psalms 78:41 (KJV)

Can God be limited? Oh, Yes. You can be assured that the Sovereign, Himself, has limited Himself by our attitudes and actions.

Our attitude must be one of a believer. You may say, "I believe in Jesus." That's great! It is just not enough.

Do you believe that Jesus died to provide you with total acceptance by the Father. Do you believe that Jesus brought you into the family of God? Do you believe, then, that, in Christ, you are the adopted child of God? Do you believe that you have all the rights and privileges of a son? Do you believe that every resource of heaven is at your disposal. Do you believe that God is for you and not against you? - All the time? If not, then you are limiting what God will do for, in and through you.

But, if you are a believer then you will be a speaker:

We having the same spirit of faith, according as it is written, I believed, and therefore have I spoken; we also believe, and therefore speak; 2 Corinthians 4:13 (KJV)

What will you speak? Speak what God says in His Word.

You will speak of what is promised. You will speak of being the Father's child. You will speak as one who owns all that God owns. You will speak as one who does all that God does. You will speak as one whose home is in heaven. You will speak the Word of God. In other words, you will speak what God speaks, having faith in God who is faithful to perform whatsoever you ask:

And Jesus answering saith unto them, Have faith in God. For verily I say unto you, That whosoever shall say unto this mountain, Be thou removed, and be thou cast into the sea; and shall not doubt in his heart, but shall believe that those things which he saith shall come to pass; he shall have whatsoever he saith. Mark 11:22-23 (KJV)

If you qualify as a "whosoever" then you can have "whatsoever." Do you believe that?

If you do, you are, in fact, a believer.

115

April 02 - Blessed is He that cometh

As Jesus came to Jerusalem riding on a donkey the people cheered and shouted Hosanna! Hosanna in the highest!

The whole city was moved at His coming.

After cleansing the temple we read that the blind and the lame came to Him and He healed them. [Matthew 21]

Blessed is He that cometh . . .

Jesus is come to His Church.

Let us recognize His Presence in and among us.

Let us demonstrate His work in us.

Hosanna ! ! ! !

Hosanna, Hosanna in the highest . . .

Let us greet Him with the words, "Hosanna, Hosanna in the highest!"

When the people of your city can see that Jesus has indeed come to His people the whole city will be moved. Revival fire will sweep into every heart and life.

As we allow Him to cleanse our temple, "Know ye not, ye are the temple" it will become more and more common for the blind and lame to come and be healed.

Jesus is come to His Church!

Let us demonstrate this fact wherever we go and in whatever we do.

April 03 - The Story of Two Colts

One beautiful Spring were two colts born to a mare owned by very kind farmer. One was red and one was brown. They spent their first days learning to walk and then run and then jump and kick in the beautiful fenced field. The spring turned to summer and life was good. It seemed as if the two playing together would never end.

Then, one beautiful summer day the Master came. He beckoned to both of the colts but only the red one would come to him. The other stood far off and neighed his disapproval of his friends yieldedness.

The farmer put a rope around the neck of the red colt and began to train him. He would beckon to the other, but to no avail. The red one spoke and said, come and let him touch you. It really is a touch of love. But the brown one would only glare, snort and run even further away. He thought to himself, I will never be touched or have a rope put around my neck by anyone.

As summer drew on and fall began, the nights became cooler and the leaves changed on the trees. The luscious green grass was turning brown. The Master had been training the red colt and he was growing into a strong and beautiful animal. Every so often the Master would take him into the barn and brush him until he shined. This only incensed the brown stallion who was more rebellious than ever.

Winter came and the Master took the red horse into the barn for the winter. There he talked with him, fed, groomed him and trained him more.

Out in the field the brown horse stood as the first snow began to fall. It was cold and he shivered. He would have to go and stand by a grove of leafless trees to try to stay out of the cold wind. The Master would leave him hay in the field and beckon to him to come. He would even offer him a carrot or an apple to entice him, but to no avail. He really wanted to go into the barn at night but was not willing to be led. So, he stayed outside in the wet and the cold.

Then, one day, the barn door opened wide and out came a beautiful carriage pulled by his red haired friend. It was a magnificent sight as his proud, fulfilled, cherished and lovingly groomed, prancing friend took the Masters family off to church.

He looked so content, so healthy, so well appointed, and so well treated.

What if I had yielded to the Masters hand, thought the lonely, shivering, wet and cold horse?

That night was the coldest night that had ever been in that part of the country - The red horse never saw his old friend again.

Author Unknown

April 04 - Thy Words Were Found

Thy words were found, and I did eat them; and thy word was unto me the joy and rejoicing of mine heart: for I am called by thy name, O LORD God of hosts.
Jeremiah 15:16 (KJV)

Your, *dabar*, sayings were, *matsa'*, discovered and recognized as important and necessary for my spiritual health and my, *'akal*, spirit and soul consumed them; and Your instruction and wisdom and matters of Your heart were, *sasown*, the gladness and rejoicing of my, *lebab*, the inner man of my soul: because I am, *qara'*, called out and commissioned by Your, *shem*, the reputation, fame and glory of your name, *Yehovah 'elohiym tsaba'*, The Eternally Existing One, The Only True God of the multitude of the armies of heaven.

The words of God, the sayings of God, as found in the Bible, are able to transform every circumstance and situation if we will allow them to become who we are. They are not natural words, they are supernatural words endued with tremendous power. This power is released in each believer as they take in the Word and make it their own.

For the Word that God speaks is alive and full of power [making it active, operative, energizing, and effective]; it is sharper than any two-edged sword, penetrating to the dividing line of the breath of life (soul) and [the immortal] spirit, and of joints and marrow [of the deepest parts of our nature], exposing and sifting and analyzing and judging the very thoughts and purposes of the heart. Hebrews 4:12

Open your Bible each day and mine out the great treasures of wisdom, knowledge and insight found within. Within its pages are found the whole counsel of God and everything necessary for life and godliness.

For His divine power has bestowed upon us all things that [are requisite and suited] to life and godliness, through the [full, personal] knowledge of Him Who called us by and to His own glory and excellence. 2 Peter 1:3 (AMP)

God loves you so much that He not only, sent His Only Begotten Son so that you would not perish but have everlasting life, but He gave His Word to so that it could be written; so that you could read it; so that you could speak it; so that you could have life and life more abundantly.

April 05 - When you pray

But thou, when thou prayest, enter into thy closet, and when thou hast shut thy door, pray to thy Father which is in secret; and thy Father which seeth in secret shall reward thee openly. But when ye pray, use not vain repetitions, as the heathen do: for they think that they shall be heard for their much speaking. Be not ye therefore like unto them: for your Father knoweth what things ye have need of, before ye ask him. Matthew 6:6-8 (KJV).

We do not read, "if you pray," we read "when you pray." This is the life flow of a truly transformed individual, One who has been forever translated from darkness to. His marvelous light. It is the very breath of that individual who has "put on the new nature" by being born of the Spirit.

Many there are who call themselves Christian but who do not look, talk, nor live any differently than they did when they "said the sinners prayer." Their desire to spend time with the "lover of their soul" is missing the passion of a heart set on fire with the love of God. Something is definitely missing in the relationship.

Intimacy is meant to be shared in private, not in public view. The call to prayer is a call into the secret place to share what only those in the covenant may share with one another. Our God has called to His beloved to set aside the world and all of its demands to spend some quality time with Him.

He asks that we take off our religious garments and come to Him in transparent fashion so that nothing separates the One from the other. It is not about incessant speaking, but intimate communication that touches the heart in a manner that is similar to the bow of a violin in the hand of the Master.

With such times of prayer there comes a promise of open reward:

But without faith it is impossible to please and be satisfactory to Him. For whoever would come near to God must [necessarily] believe that God exists and that He is the rewarder of those who earnestly and diligently seek Him [out]. Hebrews 11:6 (AMP)

April 06 - When You Fast

Moreover when ye fast, be not, as the hypocrites, of a sad countenance: for they disfigure their faces, that they may appear unto men to fast. Verily I say unto you, They have their reward. But thou, when thou fastest, anoint thine head, and wash thy face; That thou appear not unto men to fast, but unto thy Father which is in secret: and thy Father, which seeth in secret, shall reward thee openly.
Matthew 6:16-18 (KJV)

Again, we do not read, "if you fast," we read, "when you fast." This, too, is the outworking of the divine life flow of the Cross transformed individual. One who has been touched by the blood of Jesus Christ [The Anointed of God] realizes what great need of cleansing there is.

With the prophet, Isaiah, we must say, "Woe is me! for I am undone; because I am a man of unclean lips, and I dwell in the midst of a people of unclean lips: for mine eyes have seen the King, the Lord of hosts" (Isaiah 6:5 KJV).

Fasting, that abstinence from "the king's rich dainties" (Daniel 1:15 Amp), or the doing without all food for a season, will bring "knowledge and skill in all learning and wisdom" and "understanding in all [kinds of] visions and dreams." (Daniel 1:17; Luke 21:15; James 1:5-7).

One would think that, with such great promised gain, everyone would fast at least one day a week. If the subduing of the cravings of the flesh can hone the sensitivity of the spirit to such a grand degree, then surely fasting is a discipline that should be developed in every true believer's life.

Even married couples are encouraged to fast their sexual intimacy for a time.

Do not refuse and deprive and defraud each other [of your due marital rights], except perhaps by mutual consent for a time, so that you may devote yourselves unhindered to prayer. But afterwards resume marital relations, lest Satan tempt you [to sin] through your lack of restraint of sexual desire. 1 Corinthians 7:5 (AMP) (see also: Exodus 19:15).

Some victories cannot be won except by the disciplines of both prayer and fasting:

And He replied to them, This kind cannot be driven out by anything but prayer and fasting. Mark 9:29 (AMP)

April 07 - Public Confession

Therefore, everyone who acknowledges Me before men and confesses Me [out of a state of oneness with Me], I will also acknowledge him before My Father Who is in heaven and confess [that I am abiding in] him. But whoever denies and disowns Me before men, I also will deny and disown him before My Father Who is in heaven
Matthew 10:32-33 (AMP)

When my wife, Sharon, and I became engaged, she and I told everyone we knew. All we talked about was the upcoming wedding. All of our attention was focused on the arrangements and the day of the consummation of our covenant commitment to one another, "in sickness and in health, for richer or for poorer, until death do us part."

Once we were married, we each wore a covenant ring. These rings proclaimed to all that we were no longer available to any other person looking for a spouse. We spoke of each other often when we were with others and never tried to hide the fact that we were married and that we were had "become one flesh" and were "no longer two" (Mark 10:8 AMP).

When a person accepts the Lord's offer of redemption, they must be willing to separate themselves from the world and cleave to God in Christ without reservation. Never should they be ashamed of the relationship that they have committed to. Like the Apostle Paul, we should say boldly,

" . . . I am not ashamed: for I know whom I have believed, and am persuaded that he is able to keep that which I have committed unto him against that day"
(2 Timothy 1:12 KJV; Romans 1:16; 2 Corinthians 7:14).

I am no longer my own, "I am my beloved's, and my beloved is mine . . . and his desire is toward me"
(Song of Solomon 6:3; 7:10 KJV).

For ye are bought with a price: therefore glorify God in your body, and in your spirit, which are God's.
1 Corinthians 6:20 (KJV)

April 08 - Resurrection As A Way of Life

For us, resurrection is a daily theme for we literally live and move in the power of it every moment. "For in Him we live and move and have our being;"(Act 17:28 AMP). We and the church are well and strong! Hallelujah!!!

What a marvelous time we live in! God is speaking and moving with dynamic purpose as He gathers and directs His own. I have heard Him say:

"Oh, My beloved, do not question the path upon which I will take you. Do not look about and say, 'Lord, why are we going this way?' I have purposed a place for you and a path for you to walk on. It will take you into far places and it will take you into seemingly impossible area's. Do not look about and say, 'Lord, is this for me?' for I have prepared you for this time and place. You are chosen to walk in this path. Don't say, 'It is for someone else, not me' for I say it is for you. I have chosen you and appointed you for this time and place, for a work that you do not yet know.

Do not marvel when My mysteries fall about you; and they will. Do not marvel when My Spirit falls about you in a mighty abundance; and He will. Do not marvel at the things that I will bring forth for I have prepared and purposed this thing as I have prepared and purposed you.

Avail yourself, beloved, of all that I am bringing into your life at this time. It will lead you into anointings that you have not yet experienced. As you reach out your hand, healing will flow as never before. As you reach out your hand to heal, the people will fall and cry out 'how may I be saved?'. As you reach out your hand to heal, you will gather your inheritance in great measure for this is the hour of harvest."

Beloved, I am so thrilled and grateful that He has seen fit to knit us together in this great moment of Holy Ghost outpouring.

April 09 - That Which You Hear and See

The blind receive their sight and the lame walk, lepers are cleansed (by healing) and the deaf hear, the dead are raised up and the poor have good news (the Gospel) preached to them Matthew 11:5 (AMP).

Nothing dispels doubt quite like a manifestation of the healing power of God that accompanies the preaching of the gospel.

When John the Baptist was in prison, he began to have doubts about whether he had really heard God. Had he really seen the Holy Ghost descend upon Jesus at the Jordan River? Had he really heard God speak?

Each of us has times when the enemy of our soul will send the fiery darts of doubt our way that we have great difficulty fighting off with the shield of faith and the sword of the Spirit. During these times, we can be strengthened and encouraged by the manifestation of the miraculous.

This is why the working of miracles, gifts of healings, and such, are a part of the arsenal of the Spirit-filled believer. Our faith steps forward and lays hold of the promises of God in Christ Jesus when we preach the good news to the spiritually poor. We know that the kingdom of God is not a distant place, but that it is at hand (Matthew 10:7), and that . . . "faith apart from [good] works is inactive and ineffective and worthless" (James 2:20 AMP).

As we proclaim the good news, our faith will always be met with the encouragement of the demonstration of the closeness and power of God as we, "Cure the sick, raise the dead, cleanse the lepers [and] drive out demons" (Matthew 10:8a AMP). There is no room for doubt or argument as we move in the realm of faith that echoes with the words, "Freely (without pay) you have received, freely (without charge) give" (Mat 10:8b AMP).

April 10 - Repent and Become as a Child

And said, Truly I say to you, unless you repent (change, turn about) and become like little children [trusting, lowly, loving, forgiving], you can never enter the kingdom of heaven [at all]. Matthew 18:3 (AMP)

Nothing is more pleasing to the Lord than to find an individual who has a childlike, "trusting, lowly, loving, forgiving," faith. In fact, this kind of faith is required of every believer who desires to make heaven their home.

A strong faith is the heartfelt demonstration of childlike trust. Trust is a firm belief in the reliability, truthfulness, ability, or strength of someone. Trust accepts truth without evidence or investigation.

One with strong faith is lowly. In other words, faith is found in that person who considers themselves to be crucified with Christ to such degree that they can say, "it is no longer I who live, but Christ (the Messiah) lives in me; and the life I now live in the body I live by faith . . . " (Gal. 2:20 AMP).

Strong faith is the demonstration of great love. "Love never fails [never fades out or becomes obsolete or comes to an end]" (1 Cor. 13:8 AMP). There is nothing impossible with faith because faith is "activated and energized and expressed and working through love" (Gal. 5:6 AMP)

Finally, for faith to operate at its maximum potential, there must be a ready heart to forgive. Unforgiveness has nothing to do with God's kind of love and faith works by God's kind of love: unconditional, unlimited, unending.

We will be found without faith until we repent and begin to live like "little children."

April 11 - What Do You Believe?

You offspring of vipers! How can you speak good things when you are evil (wicked)? For out of the fullness (the overflow, the superabundance) of the heart the mouth speaks. Matthew 12:34 (AMP).

"Belief always drives behavior"- Reggie Joiner

"Behavior betrays belief" - George M. Stover Jr.

A person's behavior will always betray their true beliefs. What a person does is what a person really is. A person is what they believe, and say, about themselves. "out of the fullness (the overflow, the superabundance) of the heart the mouth speaks" (Mat. 12:34b AMP).

There is no way to live in fear and say that you have faith. Fear is negative faith. It believes the worst. Faith, on the other hand believes the best and puts fear out of doors. Faith is an integral part of love and cannot work without it.

There is no fear in love [dread does not exist], but full-grown (complete, perfect) love turns fear out of doors and expels every trace of terror! For fear brings with it the thought of punishment, and [so] he who is afraid has not reached the full maturity of love [is not yet grown into love's complete perfection] 1 John 4:18 (AMP).

April 12 - Superfluous Life

The thief comes only in order to steal and kill and destroy. I came that they may have and enjoy life, and have it in abundance (to the full, till it overflows.
John 10:10 (AMP)

Jesus came that you and I might have life, and more than that, a superfluous life. The Greek word, *perissos*, which is translated abundance [abundantly in the KJV] is full of powerful promise. It tells us that Jesus came to give us life (*zoe* = God life) excessively beyond our human understanding of life. A life that is more "superabundant (in quantity) or superior (in quality)" than anything we could experience in the natural realm of human existence without the indwelling presence of Christ, the Anointed One and His anointing.

Scripture teaches us that this life is exceeding abundantly above what we could know naturally and that it is, in fact, superfluous.

For something to be superfluous, it must be such that it cannot be added to because there is already more than enough. There is just too much to even consider wanting more.

Our God is not enough; He is more than enough. So much so that the true believer is unwilling to accept any attempt by anything, or anyone, to add on to Him (As though one could). As the song says, "He's all I need, He's all I need. Jesus is all I need."

Faith is the only thing that can sound the depths of this place of provision, power, and peace. For faith, and faith alone, can lay hold of what is not seen and enjoy the substance of its reality before it is revealed to the senses.

Now faith is the assurance (the confirmation, the title deed) of the things [we] hope for, being the proof of things [we] do not see and the conviction of their reality [faith perceiving as real fact what is not revealed to the senses].
Hebrews 11:1 (AMP)

April 13 - Zoe Life

In the beginning was the Word, and the Word was with God, and the Word was God. The same was in the beginning with God. All things were made by him; and without him was not any thing made that was made. In him was life; and the life was the light of men. . . .
John 1:1-5 (KJV)

Zoe, What an interesting word. It speaks of the eternal life that lights men.

In this one Divine Person, Jesus the Anointed One, God revealed eternal life to humanity. In fact, He revealed His Eternal Person [nature] to all who accept the Son of God:

And we know that the Son of God is come, and hath given us an understanding, that we may know him that is true, and we are in him that is true, even in his Son Jesus Christ. This is the true God, and eternal life.
1 John 5:20 (KJV)

Satan will do anything to steal the revelation of a superfluous life; kill our desire to press toward the mark of the high calling which will lead us to the superabundant, far over and above, and destroy every remembrance of the omnipotence and all-sufficiency of our God.

Now to Him Who, by (in consequence of) the [action of His] power that is at work within us, is able to [carry out His purpose and] do superabundantly, far over and above all that we [dare] ask or think [infinitely beyond our highest prayers, desires, thoughts, hopes, or dreams]
Ephesians 3:20 (AMP)

Our inheritance is the superfluous life that was purchased by Jesus the Anointed One on Calvary's Tree. "eye has not seen and ear has not heard and has not entered into the heart of man, [all that] God has prepared (made and keeps ready) . . ."
(1 Cor. 2:9 AMP).

April 14 - Anointed Compassion

There are multitudes standing in the valley of decision at this very moment. Jesus looked upon the multitudes and was moved with compassion. This same anointing, an anointing to flow in the compassion of Christ, is going to come upon the servants of the Lord in great measure. It will pour out upon the heads of ministries, churches and organizations. It will flow down to the most unheralded and unseen member, and bring a demonstration of resurrection to the lost and dying world.

I cannot say whether this will be the last great feast of ingathering of all time or not. I do know that this harvest will surpass all that has ever gone before. Soon it will not be said, "The harvest truly is plenteous, but the laborers are few" (Matthew 9:37), for the prayers of those who have asked, "that He would send forth laborers into his harvest" (Luke 10:), will have been answered. There will arise a great company of whom it shall be said, "How beautiful upon the mountains are the feet of [them] that bring good tidings, that publish peace; that bring good tidings of good, that publish salvation" (Isaiah 52:7).

They will move confidently and boldly in their calling because those who have the rule over them (Hebrews 13:7; Hebrews 13:17; Hebrews 13:24;) will have commissioned, anointed and sent them.

And how shall they preach, except they be sent? as it is written, How beautiful are the feet of them that preach the gospel of peace, and bring glad tidings of good things! Romans 10:15 (KJV)

The Lord will position you in His field as you yield to the prompting of His Spirit. There will be changes that take place in your life that you cannot imagine. This will make you ready and able to move in the power of this anointed compassion.

April 15 - Viewing the Impossible

Now at Lystra a man sat who found it impossible to use his feet, for he was a cripple from birth and had never walked. He was listening to Paul as he talked, and [Paul] gazing intently at him and observing that he had faith to be healed, Shouted at him, saying, Stand erect on your feet! And he leaped up and walked. Acts 14:8-10 (AMP)

When was that last time that you came into contact with someone who had been ravaged by polio, a gun accident that left them paralyzed , or who had been born crippled from birth?

What was your reaction? What thoughts went through your mind? Did you consider praying for their healing, or put it out of your mind because it was "a permanent condition" for which there was no hope?

In these few verses we see the words "impossible," "cripple from birth," and "never walked." But, we also see that "he had faith to be healed" and that "he leaped up and walked" when someone was sensitive to perceive his faith to be healed and was willing to say, "Stand erect on your feet," with conviction that God would answer the man's level of faith.

While I am not advocating shouting at every physically challenged individual to do what is impossible in the natural, I am calling for what should be the normal Christian attitude toward the impossible. When the Holy Spirit gives insight into the faith level of an individual, or when we hear the voice of God concerning a matter, we must be willing to instantly obey and speak the miracle into existence.

For with God nothing is ever impossible and no word from God shall be without power or impossible of fulfillment. Luke 1:37 (AMP)

April 16 - Like a Child

And said, Truly I say to you, unless you repent (change, turn about) and become like little children [trusting, lowly, loving, forgiving], you can never enter the kingdom of heaven [at all]. Matthew 18:3 (AMP)

What is it about letting go of our old habit patterns of life? Why do we cling to the old when it was so destructive? How can we be so loyal to a way of life that steals our joy, kills our dreams and destroys our lives?

The people of Jesus' day were no different. They were locked in to their life-styles and had formed a man made religion that had literally forced God out of their presence. Jesus came to restore the lost relationship between God and the people of His love.

Today, the mind set of society is the same as it was then. Self has been enthroned as the ultimate object of worship. God has been reduced to an exalted man, a force, a collective mind, or some other man conceived entity. It is time for a change.

"Repent," is the word that Jesus used to convey the need of humanity. "Become like little children," He said, as He declared it to be the only way a person can enter the kingdom of heaven.

A child is trusting, lowly, loving and forgiving. This is the attitude that one must have to consider repentance. It will take this kind of an attitude for us to humble ourselves to the point that our sinful condition can be admitted as an affront to a holy God. We must lay aside all pride, self-sufficiency and self-protective thinking. We must come to realize that we have dishonored God and counted the gift of His Son as nothing.

Repentance goes further than feeling sorry. It allows that we have grieved the Holy Spirit of grace and are absolutely unwilling to go back to our old ways.

If we say (claim) we have not sinned, we contradict His Word and make Him out to be false and a liar, and His Word is not in us [the divine message of the Gospel is not in our hearts]. 1 John 1:10 (AMP)

April 17 - The Twelve

And as soon as He was alone, those who were around Him, with the Twelve [apostles], began to ask Him about the parables. Mark 4:10 (AMP)

Revelation is for those close enough to Jesus for Him to consider Himself "alone" when they are with Him. Revelation flows freely to those who are in relationship with the Revelator.

The Twelve not only enjoyed His presence but they realized His perception. With them were others who were included in this wonderful inner circle of relational friends.

Jesus, almost always, spoke in parables so that those who treated the things of God as nothing more than a religious curiosity would not be able to understand. These were those mentioned in Isaiah and seen proliferating in the land today:

And He said, Go and tell this people, Hear and hear continually, but understand not; and see and see continually, but do not apprehend with your mind. Isaiah 6:9 (AMP)

The Twelve, and those with them, were the "tenth" that were found faithful in the midst of the "great forsaking" and were called the "holy seed" (Isaiah 6:12, 13). God will always have a remnant people who draw close to Him, love Him and serve Him, and to those He will give the mind of Christ (the wisdom, understanding and insight of Christ).

He said to them, To you it has been given to [come progressively to] know (to recognize and understand more strongly and clearly) the mysteries and secrets of the kingdom of God, but for others they are in parables, so that, [though] looking, they may not see; and hearing, they may not comprehend. Luke 8:10 (AMP)

Don't settle for just going through the motions of religious liturgy. Press in to that ever growing inner circle of relational "friends" that are allowed to "hear" and "see" (John 15:15).

April 18 - Unbelief

And He marveled because of their unbelief (their lack of faith in Him). And He went about among the surrounding villages and continued teaching. And He called to Him the Twelve [apostles] and began to send them out [as His ambassadors] two by two and gave them authority and power over the unclean spirits.
Mark 6:6-7 (AMP)

It is said, "familiarity breeds contempt." So it was with those who knew Jesus as the Carpenter's son. Because they thought they knew Him, they were unable to believe on Him and receive the benefits of that faith so that "He was not able to do even one work of power there, except that He laid His hands on a few sickly people [and] cured them" (Mark 6:5 AMP).

How tragic it is for someone to think that they know Him but are unable to receive the fulness of who He is.

It was to such as these that the Twelve were sent. Their commissioning included the power to confront demonic powers wherever they went. This authority and power over demons is one of the most important things that a Christian must have operating in their life. Without it, their effectiveness as a witness of Christ is greatly hindered.

And these attesting signs will accompany those who believe: in My name they will drive out demons; they will speak in new languages; Mark 16:17 (AMP)

Our nation is filled with people who think they know Christ or think that they know all about Christ, when in truth, they know nothing at all. Some, who desire to know Him, are locked in a powerlessness through the traditional teaching of those who, though proclaimed to be great biblical scholars, are nothing more than "blind guides, filtering out a gnat and gulping down a camel" (Mat. 23:24 AMP)

Determine not to let your traditions keep you from drawing close enough to Jesus to know Him in spirit and in truth.

April 19 - The Blessing of Believing

And blessed (happy, to be envied) is she who believed that there would be a fulfillment of the things that were spoken to her from the Lord. Luke 1:45 (AMP)

And blessed is she that believed: for there shall be a performance of those things which were told her from the Lord. Luke 1:45 (KJV)

Believing that something will happen is entirely different from hoping that something will happen.

The Greek word, *pisteuo* [4100 in Strong's Concordance], that is translated believed in the above text, means to have faith (in, upon, or with respect to, a person or thing), i.e. - to entrust (especially one's spiritual well-being to Christ).

By believing we entrust our whole being to Him. We must be so trusting in God that we know that what He has said will come to pass.

Faith, pistis, is the conviction that activates and empowers, believing when nothing can be seen. Faith gives credence, the evidence and substance, to the thing believed:

Now faith is the assurance (the confirmation, the title deed) of the things [we] hope for, being the proof of things [we] do not see and the conviction of their reality [faith perceiving as real fact what is not revealed to the senses]. Hebrews 11:1 (AMP)

Hope, *elpizo*, is the original expectation regarding a thing. So then, we first hope, then believe in faith, knowing that what we hope for will become reality to us. This is the blessing of believing.

Our steadfast assurance comes in that God, who promised, is Love. Faith works and is empowered by love and love never fails:

Love never fails [never fades out or becomes obsolete or comes to an end]. . . (1 Cor. 13:8 - AMP)

April 20 - With Authority and Power

And they were all amazed and said to one another, What kind of talk is this? For with authority and power He commands the foul spirits and they come out!
Luke 4:36 (AMP)

Luke 4:31-37 tells of a man who was possessed by an unclean spirit. When Jesus came near him the spirit, and those with him, said, "Let us alone . . . have you come to destroy us? I know who you are – the Holy One of God!"

Rest assured, when the Anointed One of God, Jesus, is on the scene, demons know it.

Jesus rebuked the devil and said, "Be silent and come out of him!" and he came out of him. Why should we, then, be amazed when the demonic forces working in the sons of disobedience become agitated in our presence (Ephesians 2:2)? Is not Christ, the Anointed One and His anointing, in you? Don't you know that you are the very residence of the Spirit of Holiness (1 Cor. 3:16; 6:19)? The "Greater One" lives within you (1 Joh. 4:4)! When He comes on the scene, demons cry out and those that are being used by them become extremely agitated.

Don't get confused. There is a war raging between the forces of light and the forces of darkness. It is not a war between mortal human beings. They are simply the agents through which light or darkness are manifest in the land (Eph. 6:12). Our war (wrestling) is not with people, but with the demonic personalities that would seek to steal, kill and destroy those they control.

Use the authority that Christ has given you and deliver the captives. Let the anointing within you open the prison doors and set those locked in free. Even the devil himself is no match for the greater won within you (1 Joh. 4:4).

When you speak, let the people say, "What kind of talk is this?" when you speak.

April 21 - The Crown of Old Men

Children's children are the crown of old men, . . .
Proverbs 17:6 (AMP)

This verse is in harmony with the command given to Adam to be fruitful and multiply (Gen. 1:22, 28). It also speaks of the strength that a large family has in a community. The application is not only natural, but spiritual.

Behold, children are a heritage from the Lord, the fruit of the womb a reward. Psalms 127:3 (AMP)

Progeny, that is, offspring, are a blessing and a reward from the Lord of the harvest:

Your wife shall be like a fruitful vine in the innermost parts of your house; your children shall be like olive plants round about your table. Psalms 128:3 (AMP)

The promise to Abraham, our father of faith, was that he would become the father of a multitude that would "possess the gate of his enemies":

In blessing I will bless you and in multiplying I will multiply your descendants like the stars of the heavens and like the sand on the seashore. And your Seed (Heir) will possess the gate of His enemies, Genesis 22:17 (AMP)

To "possess the gate" means to drive out the former inhabitants and to possess in their place. Here we see the promise of authority over the devil and all of his demons.

. . . I will build My church, and the gates of Hades (the powers of the infernal region) shall not overpower it [or be strong to its detriment or hold out against it].
Matthew 16:18 (AMP)

Every time you and I give birth to a new Christian through the gospel of Jesus Christ, we establish the authority of God at the gates of Hades. We cause the blessing promised to Abraham to be fulfilled and the desire of God to be realized.

The crown of the aged are their spiritual grandchildren.

April 22 - The Glory of Children is their Fathers

> . . . and the glory of children is their fathers.
> Proverbs 17:6 (AMP)

No one is more important to a child than their father.

To a young man, his father is his hero, his role model, his mentor and friend. Without being consciously aware of it, he will pattern his life after his father. The way his father treats his mother will be the pattern that molds his relationships with women and that will be used when once he marries. The father's morality, ethics and mannerisms will, to a great degree, establish the character of the son.

To a young lady, her father is her hero, her ideal man, her confidant, comforter and protector. When she comes of age, she will, subconsciously, look for a husband that is "just like dad." She will expect her husband to treat her just like her father treated her mother.

Children are greatly influenced by the presence, or absence of, their father. Our society has, for the most part, lost the knowledge of the importance of fathers in the family unit as it relates to the healthy development of children.

According to the above verse of scripture we find that fathers are the, *tiph'arah*, the glory, an ornament of beauty, the model and instiller of bravery, the one who gives honor and a majestic sense of being to a child.

Children should be able to expect an inheritance from their father. As it is written, "House and riches are the inheritance of fathers . . ." (Pro. 19:14 KJV).

They will be blessed by a godly father and their prophetic destiny sealed to them by the laying on of hands or they will suffer the curse of the ungodly.

May each young man strive to be the father that God has intended for him to be by making Jesus Christ his Lord and Almighty God his Father, Mentor and Friend.

April 23 - He Laid His Hands On Them

Now at the setting of the sun [indicating the end of the Sabbath], all those who had any [who were] sick with various diseases brought them to Him, and He laid His hands upon every one of them and cured them. And demons even came out of many people, screaming and crying out, You are the Son of God! But He rebuked them and would not permit them to speak, because they knew that He was the Christ (the Messiah). Luke 4:40-41 (AMP)

That there are many sick with various diseases and many tormented with demons it is evident to all with an eye toward the realities of the afflicted. People have the same needs today as they did in the days that Jesus walked on earth.

This is why His anointing is placed within and upon those who follow Him in this generation. The ministry of laying on of hands is still vitally needed in the land. Believers in Jesus the Christ, the Anointed One of God have received His anointing. It is written of them:

And these signs shall follow them that believe; In my name shall they cast out devils; they shall speak with new tongues; They shall take up serpents; and if they drink any deadly thing, it shall not hurt them; they shall lay hands on the sick, and they shall recover. Mark 16:17-18 (KJV)

Jesus said of them:

Verily, verily, I say unto you, He that believeth on me, the works that I do shall he do also; and greater works than these shall he do; because I go unto my Father. John 14:12 (KJV)

Are you a believer? If, in truth, you are, then you are called to meet the needs of humanity with the supernatural power of the Holy Ghost that dwells within you.

Ye are of God, little children, and have overcome them: because greater is he that is in you, than he that is in the world. 1 John 4:4 (KJV)

April 24 - He Is Risen!!!

You do not serve a dead God. Your God is Alive! As the angel said to the women gathered at Jesus' tomb:

He is not here: for He is risen, Matthew 28:6 (KJV)

We need to get this great truth settled deep down in our understanding. Jesus is not dead! He is Risen and very much alive! Hear His Words as recorded in Scripture:

I am he that liveth, and was dead; and, behold, I am alive for evermore, Amen; and have the keys of hell and of death. Revelation 1:18 (KJV)

- and again -

. . . These things saith the first and the last, which was dead, and is alive; Revelation 2:8 (KJV)

Beloved, you have a friend seated in the heavenly place of authority and power that is quite alive and able to help you in your time of trouble! [Joh. 15:14-15; Ephes. 1:20-23]

There is absolutely nothing that your God cannot do for you today!

And Jesus looking upon them saith, ... with God all things are possible. Mark 10:27 [Mat. 19:26; Luke 1:37]

Jesus Christ the same yesterday, and to day, and for ever. Hebrews 13:8 (KJV)

He desires to rescue, deliver, restore, heal, cure, protect, nurture, and provide for you. Today!

April 25 - They Forsook All

And after they had run their boats on shore, they left everything and joined Him as His disciples and sided with His party and accompanied Him. Luke 5:11 (AMP)

The verse tells us that "after they had run their boats on shore, they left everything and joined Him." Beloved, this is the secret to a Spirit-filled, Spirit-enabled life filled with revelation and power.

Each of us must come to an end of our works and "beach our boats" if we are to accompany Jesus. There is no looking back with a wistful eye if we are to realize the fulness of the call of Christ on our lives. Trying to carry the old life into the new will only cause our hearts to become more hardened than that of Lots wife when she was turned into a pillar of salt in the plain of Jordan (Genesis 19:26).

Jesus said to him, No one who puts his hand to the plow and looks back [to the things behind] is fit for the kingdom of God. Luke 9:62 (AMP)

The Christian life is not meant to be one of mixture but one of absolute dedication to the Kingdom of God and the King of the Kingdom. We are to leave "everything" and join Him as disciples. We are not to invite Him to come and walk with us. We are to yield to His call to come and walk with Him.

I have been crucified with Christ [in Him I have shared His crucifixion]; it is no longer I who live, but Christ (the Messiah) lives in me; and the life I now live in the body I live by faith in (by adherence to and reliance on and complete trust in) the Son of God, Who loved me and gave Himself up for me. Galatians 2:20 (AMP)

The call to follow Christ is one that necessitates our dying to self and living to Him. It is no longer we living a life of service to Him in absolute obedience but His life lived through us in every area. There is a huge difference. A difference that transforms through the power of resurrection life.

April 26 - We Ought Always to Pray

Also [Jesus] told them a parable to the effect that they ought always to pray and not to turn coward (faint, lose heart, and give up). Luke 18:1 (AMP)

Facing the world alone is a foolish and fearful thing to do. The Christian should never get tricked into thinking that he can go it alone. The devil would like nothing better.

The Bible, the Word of God, tells us that we are to "be subject to God. Resist the devil [stand firm against him]," and that "he will flee" (Jas. 4:7 AMP). We have authority against the devil and his demonic legions to the degree that we are walking with and submitted to God. This calls us to "be doers of the Word [obeying the message], and not merely listeners to it . . ." (Jas. 1:22 AMP)

It is from the Word of God that we receive our boldness of faith with which we withstand the fiery darts of the evil one (Rom. 10:17; Eph. 6:16). We are not quitters and we are not possessors of timid, cowardly, faint character: "For God did not give us a spirit of timidity (of cowardice, of craven and cringing and fawning fear), but [He has given us a spirit] of power and of love and of calm and well-balanced mind and discipline and self-control" (2 Tim. 1:7 AMP).

We also receive great encouragement and strength from our time in prayer. This is why the Lord taught His disciples to pray. He emphasized the importance of a consistent prayer life and would chastise those that were close to Him if they did not pray: "And He came to the disciples and found them sleeping, and He said to Peter, What! Are you so utterly unable to stay awake and keep watch with Me for one hour." (Matthew 26:40 AMP)?

Let me ask you a question today when our Nation and it's leaders need so much Divine intervention and guidance:

Can you keep watch with Me for one hour?

April 27 - I Will Send Forth Upon You

And behold, I will send forth upon you what My Father has promised; but remain in the city [Jerusalem] until you are clothed with power from on high. Luke 24:49 (AMP)

Jesus, Himself, said what we read above; "I will send . . . what My Father has promised. This "promise" was to cause the disciples to be "clothed with power." Not just natural power, but "power from on high."

This supernatural power is so important to every believer that they are to wait to move in ministry until they have received it. We read that John the Baptist said, ". . . He Who sent me to baptize in (with) water said to me, Upon Him Whom you shall see the Spirit descend and remain, that One is He Who baptizes with the Holy Spirit" (Joh. 1:33 AMP). From this we can see that the "promise of the Father" is the Person of the Holy Spirit and that the "power from on high" is resident in, and comes with, Him.

This power is so important to the believer that Jesus repeated His injunction in Acts 1:4 (AMP):

And while being in their company and eating with them, He commanded them not to leave Jerusalem but to wait for what the Father had promised, Of which [He said] you have heard Me speak. Acts 1:4 (AMP)

This, Beloved, is the precious Baptism in the Holy Spirit. This baptism can be both evidenced and heard.

Being therefore lifted high by and to the right hand of God, and having received from the Father the promised [blessing which is the] Holy Spirit, He has made this outpouring which you yourselves both see and hear.
Acts 2:33 (AMP)

Search the Scripture and you will see that it teaches clearly that every believer is to seek and receive the "promise of the Father," the baptism in the Holy Spirit with the evidence of speaking in other tongues.

April 28 - According to the benefit done

But Hezekiah did not make return [to the Lord] according to the benefit done to him, for his heart became proud [at such a spectacular response to his prayer]; therefore there was wrath upon him and upon Judah and Jerusalem. 2 Chronicles 32:25 (AMP)

How do we handle the many faceted blessings of God who loved us while we were lost and estranged from Him?

But God shows and clearly proves His [own] love for us by the fact that while we were still sinners, Christ (the Messiah, the Anointed One) died for us.
Romans 5:8 (AMP)

Do we "return {to the Lord] according to the benefit done to" us? In other words: Do we give Him our all or just a portion of our love, attention, energy and substance? Can we honestly say,

I have been crucified with Christ [in Him I have shared His crucifixion]; it is no longer I who live, but Christ (the Messiah) lives in me; and the life I now live in the body I live by faith in (by adherence to and reliance on and complete trust in) the Son of God, Who loved me and gave Himself up for me. Galatians 2:20 (AMP)

To consider ourselves more highly than we should, to get puffed up and prideful about our accomplishments and achievements, forgetting the working of God in our lives, is a sure road to destruction.

Pride goes before destruction, and a haughty spirit before a fall. Proverbs 16:18 (AMP)

Hezekiah showed himself to be a fool by not taking note of the Lord's spectacular response to his prayer and humbly proclaiming the greatness of God. Beloved, you and I must keep watch over, and guard, our hearts lest we find ourselves in the same situation as Hezekiah. God will not be mocked.

Let us always rejoice and be glad in our God who answers our prayers spectacularly.

April 29 - Spirit and Life

It is the Spirit Who gives life [He is the Life-giver]; the flesh conveys no benefit whatever [there is no profit in it]. The words (truths) that I have been speaking to you are spirit and life. John 6:63 (AMP)

Our very life comes from the Spirit of Life Himself:
[It is] the Spirit of God that made me [which has stirred me up], and the breath of the Almighty that gives me life [which inspires me]. Job 33:4 (AMP)

As the Amplified Bible suggests, this life is not merely natural life but is a life of excitement and inspiration. Jesus said, "... I came that they may have and enjoy life, and have it in abundance (to the full, till it overflows" (John 10:10 AMP).

There is no comparison between the life of the flesh and the life of the spirit. "The flesh conveys no benefit whatever." The Greek word, *sarx*, is used here to suggest that the carnal, fleshy, natural things offer no real lasting benefit or profit; while the spirit offers a life that is full, enjoyable, beneficial and profitable, both now and throughout eternity.

The life-giving Holy Spirit indwells us, if indeed, we are born-again. This ever present Spirit of resurrection life, leads, teaches, counsels, strengthens and comforts us every moment of every day as we learn to lean on, and listen to, His prompting.

As we open, read and ponder the Bible, the Word of God, He brings alive the words of the Lord and they become supernatural life to us.

For the Word that God speaks is alive and full of power [making it active, operative, energizing, and effective]; it is sharper than any two-edged sword, penetrating to the dividing line of the breath of life (soul) and [the immortal] spirit, and of joints and marrow [of the deepest parts of our nature], exposing and sifting and analyzing and judging the very thoughts and purposes of the heart. Hebrews 4:12 (AMP)

April 30 - What if Some did not Believe?

What if some did not believe and were without faith? Does their lack of faith and their faithlessness nullify and make ineffective and void the faithfulness of God and His fidelity [to His Word]?   Romans 3:3 (AMP)

One of the editors of our local newspaper was trying to convince me that homosexual marriages should be legal and that the homosexual life-style is acceptable. While expressing her arguments she wrote, "just because the majority of Americans believe something, it does not make it legal or moral." I, of course, could not agree more with that particular statement although it was nestled in a great bed of untruth. After all, Joshua and Caleb were surrounded by the majority when they gave a good report of the promised land (Numbers 13:30-33). The founding fathers of this great nation understood that simple truth and fashioned a Republic instead of a Democracy.

Just because the majority believe something, it does not make it true, but God is true. His Son is "truth" (John 14:6 KJV) and "faithful".

. . . These are the words of the Amen, the trusty and faithful and true Witness, the Origin and Beginning and Author of God's creation: Revelation 3:14 (AMP)

God is unwilling and, by His nature, unable to lie or deceive:

God is not a man, that He should tell or act a lie, . . . Numbers 23:19 (AMP)

If none believed, not even you and I, the Word of God and God Himself would remain to offer to rest to whosoever would reach out to Him in faith believing.

[Resting] in the hope of eternal life, [life] which the ever truthful God Who cannot deceive promised before the world or the ages of time began. Titus 1:2 (AMP)

MAY

May 01 - Faith Comes

So faith comes by hearing [what is told], and what is heard comes by the preaching [of the message that came from the lips] of Christ (the Messiah Himself).
Romans 10:17 (AMP)

Are you aware that a person can listen but not hear? Way too often, if we are not careful, we fail to really pay attention to what is being spoken or preached. Many times it is because we think we know what is being said or that we already know the concepts being discussed.

The Greek word, *akoe*, expresses the idea of comprehending and considering the thing heard. We give audience to that which we hear preached as though it were coming directly from the lips of Jesus. Because we are hearing the words that the Anointed One has given to the speaker (preacher), we apply what we hear so that it becomes a vital part of our lives.

In so doing, we keep ourselves from the snare of the fowler that many find themselves entangled in; that of being idle listeners to the Word rather than those who hear and obey.

But be doers of the Word [obey the message], and not merely listeners to it, betraying yourselves [into deception by reasoning contrary to the Truth]. For if anyone only listens to the Word without obeying it and being a doer of it, he is like a man who looks carefully at his [own] natural face in a mirror; For he thoughtfully observes himself, and then goes off and promptly forgets what he was like.
James 1:22-24 (AMP)

Today, let us determine to listen carefully to the Word preached even when we think we know all about what is being said. Let's listen for that one idea, concept, view, or insight that will open the door of revelation into what we thought we clearly understood, knowing that there are at least seven levels of understanding in the Word of the Living God (Psalm 12:6).

May 02 - Mark Them

I appeal to you, brethren, to be on your guard concerning those who create dissensions and difficulties and cause divisions, in opposition to the doctrine (the teaching) which you have been taught. [I warn you to turn aside from them, to] avoid them. Romans 16:17 (AMP)

Unfortunately, there are those who call themselves Christian and yet act anything but Christian. These poor souls can be those who said the words of a "sinner's prayer" but never repented and received a heart change, or they could simply be those who have come to Christ so broken and torn by the enemy that they will need much love, prayer and deliverance to begin to realize the blessedness of salvation.

Those who are the most glaringly in the process of sanctification are those we must not brush off because of the difficulty of ministering to them. They, like spoiled little babies, will throw fits, threaten, kick and scream, and, yes, even throw the "fiery darts" of the enemy. These are those that need loving discipline, reproof, and instruction from the fathers and mothers of the faith. What they need is that love that never fails (1 Corinthians 13:8).

Your calling, beloved, is to draw them ever closer into the center of the family of God by letting love cover a multitude of sins (1 Peter 4:8).

As for those who are unteachable, unwilling, unresponsive, divisive and unable to receive sound doctrine, after all attempts have failed, turn out of your fellowship lest they, like leaven, pollute you and the whole congregation.

That may sound harsh in today's permissive society, yet this is the way that the Spirit of the Lord teaches us through Scripture. We, who will one day judge angels, must learn to rule the house of God well. What we will not allow must be what is not allowed in heaven, and what we allow should only be what is allowed in Heaven (Matthew 16:19; 18:18).

May 03 - Grace

For it is by free grace (God's unmerited favor) that you are saved (delivered from judgment and made partakers of Christ's salvation) through [your] faith. And this [salvation] is not of yourselves [of your own doing, it came not through your own striving], but it is the gift of God; Not because of works [not the fulfillment of the Law's demands], lest any man should boast. [It is not the result of what anyone can possibly do, so no one can pride himself in it or take glory to himself.] Ephesians 2:8-9 (AMP)

"Grace has been sacrificed at the altar of self-aggrandizing human ego." - Dr. George M. Stover Jr.

Grace is simply grace. The Greek word, *charis*, simply means, Divine unmerited favour. It is the merciful kindness by which God extends His free gift of salvation through Christ to, lavishes His love upon, bestows His benefits in and through, offers His keeping power over and grants His Presence and glory within.

When an individual begins to add something, like good works, acts of service, change of behavior, or whatever to become a recipient of the free gift of salvation, grace is no more grace.

But if it is by grace (His unmerited favor and graciousness), it is no longer conditioned on works or anything men have done. Otherwise, grace would no longer be grace [it would be meaningless]. Romans 11:6 (AMP)

So, beloved, quit trying to earn your salvation. It is impossible to add one thing to the complete work of Christ on the Cross at Calvary.

With that truth in you heart, allow the Holy Spirit to lead you into that perfect liberty that results from being born-again. You will begin to serve God and His Christ with gladness.

May 04 - Give Diligent Search

You search and investigate and pour over the Scriptures diligently, because you suppose and trust that you have eternal life through them. And these [very Scriptures] testify about Me! John 5:39 (AMP)

Within the pages of the Bible lie the wisdom of God Himself. You will find revelation after revelation of the mysteries hidden in glory.

Every human condition is addressed as is every answer to living a fulfilling and victorious life. Cover to cover discloses the plan of God for humanity and His precious gift of Jesus, the Christ, to restore the intimate fellowship lost through man's rebellion and disobedience.

Each and every day should begin with a visit into the life-giving Word of the Living God, the Bible. There is no other book like it in the world. Not only is it the most historically accurate book ever placed in the hands of man, but it is the only absolutely accurate record of the dealings of God with man in the supernatural realm.

The Scripture is living and filled with power beyond the natural ability of man to comprehend:

But the natural man receiveth not the things of the Spirit of God: for they are foolishness unto him: neither can he know them, because they are spiritually discerned. 1 Corinthians 2:14 (KJV)

For the word of God is quick, and powerful, and sharper than any two edged sword, piercing even to the dividing asunder of soul and spirit, and of the joints and marrow, and is a discerner of the thoughts and intents of the heart. Hebrews 4:12 (KJV)

Email or come in and ask for a Bible Reading Guide that will guide you through the Word of God in one year. It will change your life for the good forever. Meet with Jesus today.

May 05 - Ye are Enriched by Him

[So] that in Him in every respect you were enriched, in full power and readiness of speech [to speak of your faith] and complete knowledge and illumination [to give you full insight into its meaning]. 1 Corinthians 1:5 (AMP)

The King James Version says "in everything" you are "enriched by him." In other words, you are now made wealthy, *ploutizo*, in all Divine utterance. You are enriched supernaturally in the wisdom and mysteries hidden in the Word of God, Jesus Christ, the personal wisdom and power in union with God, *logos*.

You may say, How can this be? Beloved, is it not written:

For who has known or understood the mind (the counsels and purposes) of the Lord so as to guide and instruct Him and give Him knowledge? But we have the mind of Christ (the Messiah) and do hold the thoughts (feelings and purposes) of His heart.
1 Corinthians 2:16 (AMP)

God, in Christ, has given you and I the ability to speak of our faith with "knowledge and illumination" and enabled us to have "full insight into its meaning." This is what is called "the anointing of The Anointed One." For too long the believer has been tricked by the devil into believing that they need to remember everything that they have read in the Bible before they can witness or proclaim the glorious Gospel when, in fact, the anointing is available to accomplish the task.

But the Comforter (Counselor, Helper, Intercessor, Advocate, Strengthener, Standby), the Holy Spirit, Whom the Father will send in My name [in My place, to represent Me and act on My behalf], He will teach you all things. And He will cause you to recall (will remind you of, bring to your remembrance) everything I have told you.
John 14:26 (AMP)

Spend time in the Word and in prayer and watch what will flow out of your mouth as you speak concerning the things of God.

May 06 - Last Day or First Day Mentality?

Now Jesus, having risen [from death] early on the first day of the week, appeared first to Mary Magdalene, from whom He had driven out seven demons. Mark 16:9 (AMP)

Many look to the day of Pentecost as the beginning of the Church. True, it was the day that the Church was commissioned with supernatural visitation that endued its members with the power of the Holy Ghost. The Church carries within each individual member, the resurrection power of God.

The beginning of the beginning of this powerful covenant community took place on "the first day of the week" when its Head, Jesus, rose from the dead. His appearance to one of those members, Mary Magdalene, holds great significance. We, too, can expect the Lord's visitation as we gather on "the first day."

Many of America's churches are seeing Sunday attendance wane as people testify to being "tired," "worn out," "too busy," or "having to get ready for "Monday." This, beloved, is a "Last Day" mentality.

I'm not talking about the kind of "Last Day" mentality that looks for Armageddon with the fear and trepidation that many have. This is quite different from what the early Apostle was talking about when he admonished us to gather together as often as possible as we see the Lords return draw near:

Not forsaking or neglecting to assemble together [as believers], as is the habit of some people, but admonishing (warning, urging, and encouraging) one another, and all the more faithfully as you see the [last] day approaching. Hebrews 10:25 (AMP)

This "last day" mentality sees Sunday as the last chance to get ready for the week ahead, when it should be "the first day" of the week, met with the most energy, enthusiasm, and excitement that is possible in light of resurrection.

It should be the day when we plan the rest of the week with the One who holds our "times" in His hands (Psa. 31:15).

May 07 - Jesus Will Meet With You

Then on that same first day of the week, when it was evening, though the disciples were behind closed doors for fear of the Jews, Jesus came and stood among them and said, Peace to you! John 20:19 (AMP)

My Bible tells me that in order to please God a person must have faith (Heb. 11:6). We know that faith draws its power to work through love (Gal. 5:6) and that love casts out fear (1 Joh. 4:18). God has not given us a spirit of fear (2 Tim. 1:7)! Yet, we see Jesus appearing to His disciples when they were hiding behind closed [locked] doors for fear of the Jews. This word fear, is the Greek word, *phobos*, which means terrified. It is the word from which we get phobia (extreme or irrational fear).

Jesus "came and stood among them" and reassured and comforted them with the words, "Peace to you!" The Greek word used here for peace is, *eirene*, which conveys the idea of security, safety and prosperity because of their unity with Christ and His anointing.

Beloved, Jesus will meet you in whatever condition you are in. He prefers that you meet Him in faith believing, but He will strengthen you until His life giving words give you the faith to stand in every situation.

It is the spirit that quickeneth; the flesh profiteth nothing: the words that I speak unto you, they are spirit, and they are life. John 6:63 (KJV)

Consider with me too, that Jesus appeared to His disciples on the "first day of the week." This is an important day for those who follow Jesus. We are prepared for the days ahead on "the first day of the week." As we gather together, Jesus comes and replaces our fear with faith, our unsettled condition with peace and our uncertainties with hope for the future.

This is accomplished through life-giving spirit words spoken in faith from a called, spirit filled, spirit led man or woman of God on Sunday, "the first day of the week."

May 08 - A Memorial

And you shall put the two stones upon the [two] shoulder straps of the ephod [of the high priest] as memorial stones for Israel; and Aaron shall bear their names upon his two shoulders as a memorial before the Lord.
Exodus 28:12 (AMP)

The Old Testament priest would wear the names of the tribes of Israel on his shoulders in order to remember to pray for the people of God, the nation of what we now know as Israel.

Today every believer should lift the people of this nation to God and especially remember to pray for those who sacrificed their personal comfort to fight for the liberties that we the people take for granted.

Some gave the ultimate sacrifice and lost their lives while others lost limbs, were paralyzed or emotionally damaged in some way and lost friends at arms. Each was a hero deserving our respect and appreciation.

Families also sacrifice to allow their loved ones to serve this great nation and the cause of freedom. In fact, the only thing more difficult that going to war is loving and losing someone who does.

Freedom is precious and must not be yielded to any dictatorial aspirations of a power hungry godless few. True personal freedom comes only to those who acknowledge the God of Abraham, Isaac and Jacob and His only begotten Son, Jesus, as Lord and Savior. Societal freedom can only be maintained by a people who honor God and His written Word.

The Word of God, the Bible, is the only infallible, eternal guide for life and godliness. Its precepts, alone, can guide a nation and its leaders. It is only when leaders are yielded to God and the Word of God can they govern a free society.

When the [uncompromisingly] righteous are in authority, the people rejoice; but when the wicked man rules, the people groan and sigh. Proverbs 29:2 (AMP)

May 09 - Breaking Bread

And on the first day of the week, when we were assembled together to break bread [the Lord's Supper], Paul discoursed with them, intending to leave the next morning; and he kept on with his message until midnight.
Acts 20:7 (AMP)

The communion of the Saints was held "on the first day of the week" when the early Saints assembled together. This breaking of bread was attended to by the preaching of the word. In fact, the preaching of the Word of God is a breaking of The Bread of Life.

Dear One, the Scripture is a revelation of Jesus the Christ, the Anointed One of God. It is a closed book to the unbeliever and the carnal minded.

But the natural, nonspiritual man does not accept or welcome or admit into his heart the gifts and teachings and revelations of the Spirit of God, for they are folly (meaningless nonsense) to him; and he is incapable of knowing them [of progressively recognizing, understanding, and becoming better acquainted with them] because they are spiritually discerned and estimated and appreciated.
1 Corinthians 2:14 (AMP)

[That is] because the mind of the flesh [with its carnal thoughts and purposes] is hostile to God, for it does not submit itself to God's Law; indeed it cannot.
Romans 8:7 (AMP)

But, to the spiritually minded believer, the Book of books reveals the character and nature of God the Father, God the Son, and God the Holy Ghost [Spirit]. All the secrets and mysteries hidden in Christ are revealed to those who desire to know. The preaching of God's word (the breaking of Bread) should stimulate a hunger for the Word and what it contains.

People in the Apostle Paul's day didn't care how long the sermon went on. They wanted to know God and His Christ by His Spirit. This, Beloved, is the communion of the first day that sets the atmosphere for six more days of communion with the Lord in the affairs of everyday life.

May 10 - Put Aside Something

On the first [day] of each week, let each one of you [personally] put aside something and save it up as he has prospered [in proportion to what he is given], so that no collections will need to be taken after I come.
1 Corinthians 16:2 (AMP)

There is much to be gleaned from the phrase, "On the first [day] of each week." It establishes the importance of Sunday as the beginning of the week and that proportionate giving is to be done "each week," not in a hap-hazard, whenever it's convenient manner. We can also glean that this is personal, involving each individual believer.

One might ask, What is the "proportion" that each believer is to give on the first day of the week?" The Greek word for proportion is the word, *euodoo*, which assumes that the one prospered knows what percentage of his increase he is to "lay up in store" in order to give. The word, *tithemi,* together with, *thesaurizo,* tells us to set aside riches [what God has prospered us with] so that it can be given on the "first day of each week."

The proportion, or the "something . . . as he has prospered," was readily recognizable by those of that day as the tithe. The word tithe, *aser*, a Hebrew word, means a tenth part of (10%). Therefore, ten percent of what the Lord has prospered each believer with should be saved up and brought to the assembly on the first day of the week [Sunday] to be freely given "that no collections . . . need to be taken."

The word collections (AMP) or gatherings (KJV), *logia* (from *logos*) carries the idea of having to talk one into giving when they already should be ready to give "with simplicity" (Rom. 12:8 KJV), "not grudgingly, or of necessity," because God wants each believer to be "a cheerful (joyous, prompt to do it) giver [whose heart is in his giving]" (2 Cor. 9:7 AMP). This is the giver God loves.

May 11 - Christ Always Leads us in Triumph

Now thanks be unto God, which always causeth us to triumph in Christ, and maketh manifest the savour of his knowledge by us in every place. 2 Corinthians 2:14 (KJV)

According to the Strong's Concordance, the use of the Greek word, *charis*, to mean, thanks, is interesting. ***Charis***, means grace. This is returning to God that which affords joy, pleasure, delight, sweetness, charm, loveliness, good will and loving-kindness. All this, in Christ, is our portion from Him. We are recipients of the merciful kindness by which God, exerting his holy influence upon [our] souls, turns [us] to Christ, keeps, strengthens, and increases [us] in Christian faith, knowledge, affection, and kindles [us] to the exercise of the Christian and virtues. This is thanks for benefits, services, favors, recompense and reward for which He, and He alone, is responsible.

In Christ, The Anointed One, we are caused to triumph, ***thriambeuo***, or, made to triumph over our enemies. As you can see, this has nothing to do with us and everything to do with Him. It is the Father's good pleasure to give us the kingdom (Luk. 12:32 KJV), and the kingdom is righteousness, peace and joy in the Holy Ghost (Rom. 14:17 KJV). We can settle down and abide in complete safety and peace in the midst of our enemies: "Thou preparest a table before me in the presence of mine enemies . . ." (Psa. 23:5 KJV).

There, in the presence of your enemies, God manifests, ***phaneroo***, makes visible or known what has been hidden or unknown about Christ so that He can be plainly recognized and thoroughly understood. He makes you like a fragrance which permeates the atmosphere with the, ***gnosis***, perfect and enlarged knowledge of God and His Christ.

By your Christ-like life in times of pressure, your enemies are left without excuse before the Living God.

May 12 - The Lord Is The Spirit

Now the Lord is the Spirit, and where the Spirit of the Lord is, there is liberty (emancipation from bondage, freedom). 2 Corinthians 3:17 (AMP)

The devil has a counterfeit for everything. The amazing thing is that he can make it look so good that people still buy the lie.

Take for instance the idea of "liberty (emancipation from bondage, freedom)." Barna research group and others have tracked the most interesting tendency among each of the current generations of people. It goes like this. What ever Mom and Dad's generation did, we won't do. Why? Because we are Americans and everyone knows that Americans are a free people. To make this concept real, it becomes necessary to throw off everything, both good and bad, to prove that one is really free.

This lie from the devil is working like a fishing fly tied by a master fly fisherman. Most young people have taken this idea "hook, line and sinker." As you may, or may not, know, the fisherman's fly has a hook in it that is designed to cause the early demise of the fish. The devil's "bait" is made for the same purpose. "The thief cometh not, but for to steal, and to kill, and to destroy . . ." (John 10:10 KJV). So, now, the "free" are free to not go to church, free to not read their Bible, free to not pray, free to do "that which is right in his own eyes" (Deu. 12:8; Judg. 17:6; 21:25").

Beloved, the only true "liberty (emancipation from bondage, freedom)" comes from being "where the Spirit of the Lord is." You say, "He is in me." Yes, precious one, but He manifests Himself in the assembly of the believers, the family of His choosing, the local church (Mat.18:20; Acts 2:46) where you are free to receive from the spiritual father that God has given as a gift to you (1 Cor. 4:15; Eph 4:8, 11).

May 13 - Glory to Glory

And all of us, as with unveiled face, [because we] continued to behold [in the Word of God] as in a mirror the glory of the Lord, are constantly being transfigured into His very own image in ever increasing splendor and from one degree of glory to another; [for this comes] from the Lord [Who is] the Spirit. 2 Corinthians 3:18 (AMP)

Did you realize that as you read the Word of God you are seeing and coming to recognize the glory of the Lord? The Bible is a most amazing book. Men wrote it by inspiration of the Holy Ghost. The words within in its pages are God breathed.

Knowing this first, that no prophecy of the scripture is of any private interpretation. For the prophecy came not in old time by the will of man: but holy men of God spake as they were moved by the Holy Ghost. 2 Peter 1:20-21 (KJV)

The Word of God is alive and powerful, able to transform, yes, even transfigure us into the image of God's own Son.

For the word of God is quick, and powerful, and sharper than any two edged sword, piercing even to the dividing asunder of soul and spirit, and of the joints and marrow, and is a discerner of the thoughts and intents of the heart. Hebrews 4:12 (KJV)

Just think about it; God, our Father, has promised to change us from one degree of glory to another, to another, and to another. This metamorphosis, *metamorphoo,* this transfiguration, takes us from the natural to the heavenly. We are going to be like Jesus:

Beloved, now are we the sons of God, and it doth not yet appear what we shall be: but we know that, when he shall appear, we shall be like him; for we shall see him as he is. 1 John 3:2 (KJV)

Can it really be? Oh, Beloved, God has said it. That settles the whole matter! We shall be like Him!

May 14 - Therefore Have I Spoken

Yet we have the same spirit of faith as he had who wrote, I have believed, and therefore have I spoken. We too believe, and therefore we speak, 2 Corinthians 4:13 (AMP)

What we say is much more important than most of us understand. To the Christian, speaking what God says in His word and by His Spirit is critical to a victorious Christian life.

God is a speaking Spirit and we were created in His image and likeness. We, too, are speaking spirits. His words created everything that we can see and touch. His words created the environment in which we live. Before the fall everything was perfect, pure, lovely, good and very good.

Adam was able to speak the nature of an animal into being by naming it. His words were also creative.

Even after the fall, mankind is able to create an atmosphere of failure, or success, by what he speaks; especially when he speaks the living words of God that are found in the Bible.

The words spoken must be filled with faith. In other words, the speaker must believe that what he says will come to pass because God, who cannot lie, says so. Real faith is followed up with action that is in harmony with what is spoken. We will do what we say if we believe what we say.

It doesn't matter how much time passes between what we have said and its coming to pass. Our time is in the Lord's hands and He is faithful to perform what He has said.

For the vision is yet for an appointed time and it hastens to the end [fulfillment]; it will not deceive or disappoint. Though it tarry, wait [earnestly] for it, because it will surely come; it will not be behindhand on its appointed day. Habakkuk 2:3 (AMP)

Beloved, guard your confession, the words you speak, with all diligence and wait expecting the completion of all you have said.

May 15 - A New Creature

Therefore if any person is [ingrafted] in Christ (the Messiah) he is a new creation (a new creature altogether); the old [previous moral and spiritual condition] has passed away. Behold, the fresh and new has come!
2 Corinthians 5:17 (AMP)

How do we understand the marvelous truth that a person who receives Jesus as their Lord and Savior "is a new creation (a new creature altogether)?" Let's see if the original language can give some insight.

The above verse starts out with, *hoste ei tis*, which can be translated: So then, whosoever, and is followed by, *en,* which means in a fixed position, and a relation of rest, in and through the Anointed, *Christos*.

We see here a permanent "fixed position" of one who has truly given Jesus, the Anointed One of God, complete, absolute, authority and power over his life. This one, we are told, has undergone a, *ktisis*, creative transformation that has left a brand new man of the spirit in place of the old. This new spirit man has a moral makeup and outlook that is totally fresh and new, and that, not of himself. The, *archaios,* the original man that has been since his beginning is gone forever.

By means of a miracle, all that the man was, *pas,* is gone and the new has come into existence, *ginomai*.

This, *kainos*, man is a recently made, fresh, unused, unworn man of a new unprecedented kind.

Beloved, you were born-again after the God kind! You are now an heir of the promise, of righteousness, of the kingdom, of the world, of God, and joint heirs with Christ (Gal. 3:29; Heb. 6:17; 11:7; Jas. 2:5 ; Rom. 4:13; 8:17).

You and I may never completely understand the miracle of salvation, but we can live an abundant, joy filled, spirit filled life in the knowledge that we have.

May 16 - Lay Hold of the Divine Favor

So we are Christ's ambassadors, God making His appeal as it were through us. We [as Christ's personal representatives] beg you for His sake to lay hold of the divine favor [now offered you] and be reconciled to God. 2 Corinthians 5:20 (AMP)

The Greek word, *oun*, translated, So we are, should be understood to carry the weight of, Then, these things being so.

I ask, "What things?," and go back to the preceding text in 2 Corinthians 5 to find:

1. We know we are not dependent upon our flesh and blood body but that we have an eternal in the heavens and are not afraid, are even eager, to move into that realm (v.1, 2).
2. We thrill at the thought of mortality being swallowed up of life (v. 4).
3. We are confident that when we are not in the body we shall be with the Lord (v. 5, 6).
4. We walk by faith, not by sight (v. 7)
5. We know that we are accountable for what we do in this body (v. 9, 10)
6. We are persuaders of men (v. 11).
7. The love of Christ constrains us (v. 14).
8. We know no man after the flesh (v. 16).
9. We are not who we were; we are a new creation in Christ (v.17).
10. We are reconciled to God in Christ and have the ministry of reconciliation (v. 18, 19).

"So (Then, these things being so)," we are, **presbeuo huper**, diplomats (ambassadors) of the very highest rank and authority sent by the kingdom of heaven to represent Almighty God and His Anointed One, Christ Jesus.

It is in this official position that we beg those in and out of communion with Jesus to, **katallasso**, to "lay hold of Divine favor" by changing their position and being made compatible with God.

May 17 - Our Warfare

For though we walk (live) in the flesh, we are not carrying on our warfare according to the flesh and using mere human weapons. 2 Corinthians 10:3 (AMP)

Don't doubt it; there is a war going on all around you at this very moment. One-third of the demons, led by Satan, are waging a war that is bent upon destroying every man, woman and child on earth. The Bible warns us in the first part of 1 Peter 5:8 (KJV) to "Be sober, be vigilant; because your adversary the devil, as a roaring lion, walketh about, seeking whom he may devour."

Demonic forces work according to the nature of their leader, of whom it is written, "The thief cometh not, but for to steal, and to kill, and to destroy" (Joh. 10:10a KJV).

They use every means possible to keep people from accepting Jesus as their Lord and Savior. When that fails, they attack the newly born-again Christian in order to draw him into cultic error or convince him that he is not going to be able to live the Christian life. The devil "is a liar, and the father of it" (Joh. 8:44 KJV).

You, dear one, are a child of the light and have revelation, insight into the mysteries of God in Christ, and know that you have been given the weapons of your Father to "fight the good fight of faith" (1 Tim. 6:12 KJV).

You understand that the only truth is in Christ who is the truth (Joh. 14:6 KJV), and He has told you that He has come so that you might have life, and that more abundantly" (Joh. 10:10 KJV).

The Word of God has also promised that "no weapon that is formed against you shall prosper" (Isa. 54:17 KJV) and that you can put on the armor of God which will enable you to stand in the most evil of days (Eph. 6:13 KJV).

Nothing can separate you from the unlimited power of the love of God (Rom. 8:39 KJV). That means that you will always come out the victor in every battle!

May 18 - Grace, Love, Presence and Fellowship

The grace (favor and spiritual blessing) of the Lord Jesus Christ and the love of God and the presence and fellowship (the communion and sharing together, and participation) in the Holy Spirit be with you all. Amen (so be it). 2 Corinthians 13:14 (AMP)

Today I cannot but think of how important you are to Sharon and Me. We thank God for surrounding us with the blessing of family, friends and partners like you.

I thank my God upon every remembrance of you. Philippians 1:3 (KJV)

As we bask in the love of God and consider the precious gift of people like you that He has brought into our lives, we pray that His "favor and spiritual blessing" be evidenced in your life. We pray that He keeps you in perfect peace as you set your mind upon Him and that you are ever conscious of His love, presence and fellowship.

There is a level of "communion and sharing together" with the Holy Ghost that surpasses anything that can be realized in the realm of the natural. There is a "participation" that we are drawn into as we spend time with Him in the Word and in prayer.

Have you drawn away from the demands of the day? They will wait, you know? Have you set aside some time to be with the sweet Spirit of God in the quiet place? Have you taken advantage of the secret place of the Most High?

He who dwells in the secret place of the Most High shall remain stable and fixed under the shadow of the Almighty [Whose power no foe can withstand]. Psalm 91:1 (AMP)

There, in that place of grace, presence and fellowship, you will find the answer to your questions for today; strength, comfort, peace and joy, for today. "For we which have believed do enter into rest" (Heb. 4:3 KJV).

May 19 - Victory Is Come!

Then I heard a strong (loud) voice in heaven, saying, Now it has come—the salvation and the power and the kingdom (the dominion, the reign) of our God, and the power (the sovereignty, the authority) of His Christ (the Messiah); for the accuser of our brethren, he who keeps bringing before our God charges against them day and night, has been cast out! Revelation 12:10 (AMP)

Glory! When the Holy Spirit, the Spirit of Life, the Spirit of Resurrection, raised Jesus from the dead, He took Jesus' blood with Him. There it was sprinkled on the Mercy Seat where it now speaks throughout eternity.

And to Jesus, the Mediator (Go-between, Agent) of a new covenant, and to the sprinkled blood which speaks [of mercy], a better and nobler and more gracious message than the blood of Abel [which cried out for vengeance]. Hebrews 12:24 (AMP)

When our Christ arose, and the blood was sprinkled, Satan was cast out of Heaven.

And he said unto them, I beheld Satan as lightning fall from heaven. Luke 10:18 (KJV)

The word, beheld, is the Greek word, *theoreo*, which means to discern, to perceive, or to be a spectator of (as in a prophetic vision). Jesus spoke of what He saw would happen when He entered the heavenly tabernacle after His ascension. Hallelujah!

The accuser no longer has access to the throne of God. He can only accuse you to your family, friends, fellow church members, and, yes, you to you. Don't you dare listen to him! He has no right to accuse you. The accusations, the arguments against you have been "cancelled and blotted out and wiped away . . . by nailing it to [His] cross" (Col. 2:14 AMP).

May 20 - Doctor, or No Doctor

If thou wilt diligently hearken to the voice of the Lord thy God, and wilt do that which is right in his sight, and wilt give ear to his commandments, and keep all his statutes, I will put none of these diseases upon thee, which I have brought upon the Egyptians: for I am the Lord that healeth thee. Exodus 15:26 (KJV)

Have you ever felt condemned because the devil has convinced you that it is a lack of faith to use doctors and medicine when you need healing? If so, perhaps the following will bring peace to your heart.

The first, and most important, thing for you and I to understand is that, it is the will of God to heal you. One time your faith can be strong and you can believe the Word without wavering no matter the circumstances or symptoms tell you. Faith will appropriate your healing; no problem.

Another time, you find that your faith is not developed to the degree that will bring you victory so, then, the doctor can be your best friend. Healing faith is something that comes line upon line through revelation in the word of God.

So then faith cometh by hearing, and hearing by the word of God. Romans10:17 (KJV)

If you're not certain whether you have faith that is strong enough or whether you need the help of a doctor, let the Holy Spirit lead you.

If fear tells you to forget the doctor and stand in faith, then go see your doctor in faith. If, on the other hand, you have strong confidence within you that healing is your portion by faith, let your faith work its work and receive your healing. Remember, the issue is not whether or not you go to the doctor, it is what you do with the faith you have.

May 21 - You Cannot Fail

Therefore we are buried with him by baptism into death: that like as Christ was raised up from the dead by the glory of the Father, even so we also should walk in newness of life. Romans 6:4 (KJV)

Do you realize that, as a believer, you have the Spirit of Resurrection residing in you? You have the same new life God gave Jesus when He raised Him from the dead. The old you no longer exists, you have become a new creation in Christ!

Old habits, ways of thinking, stubbornness and selfishness will stop the flow of resurrection life from reaching every area of your life. We must "work out our salvation" (Phil. 2:12). In other words, we must bring that which God has put within us out into every area of our soul and body.

Resisting God and embracing the old sin nature will separate us from the power of God that is available in Christ. Living a self-centered, disobedient and carnal life will stop up the flow of resurrection life and the power that resides within. You may say, "But I'm born-again." Beloved, even born-again people can encapsulate the resurrection power of God with their own spirits by soulish, carnal attitudes and sinful actions.

Allow the new life that God has put within you to overcome sin. There is no other way. You can't do it on your own, only spending quality time in the Word of God, prayer and walking what you learn by the power of the Holy Spirit will give you the victory.

Yes, we must allow the Holy Spirit to help us. God will never violate our will. He waits for us to want to subdue our old fleshly habits and to take the first step. Then, all of the strength of heaven becomes available to help. You are never alone. The Holy Spirit will teach you and enable you to live a new life in Christ. The name of Jesus has been give you and the unfailing love of the Father is working in you. You cannot fail!

May 22 - Temple of the Living God

What agreement [can there be between] a temple of God and idols? For we are the temple of the living God; even as God said, I will dwell in and with and among them and will walk in and with and among them, and I will be their God, and they shall be My people.
2 Corinthians 6:16 (AMP)

One of the great truths of Scripture is that a Christian is the temple of the Holy Ghost (1 Cor. 6:19). The word used in both of these verses is the Greek word, *naos*, This word is specifically used only of the sacred edifice (or sanctuary) itself, consisting of the Holy place and the Holy of Holies. This is where God dwells. "Know ye not that ye are the temple of God, and that the Spirit of God dwelleth in you?" (1 Cor. 3:16 KJV)

The Christian thinking process, spiritual pursuits and physical desires are diametrically opposed to anything dead and lifeless such as an idol, *eidolon*. An idol can be an image or likeness of a false heathen god , a dead person "saint," or the term can be used to mean the shades of the departed, apparitions, spectres or phantoms of the mind and demons.

When we recognize Christ Jesus as our Lord and Savior, we are filled with the, *zao theos*, the living (not lifeless, not dead) and acting, powerful, efficacious God Himself (Father, Son and Holy Ghost). He comes to permanently live within, making His residence within, us.

The fellowship (lost because of the fall of man) of the Garden of Eden, where "The Voice" came and walked with Adam in the cool of the day is restored (Gen. 3:8) and now God says, I will be your ever present living in the now God, and you and your fellow believers shall be the people of my choosing and calling, who are found faithful (Rev. 17:14). I will be with you and walk in and with you. I Am your God and you are My, *laos*, tribe, My nation, and those who are of the same mind, stock and language.

May 23 - Where Are You?

And they heard the voice of the LORD God walking in the garden in the cool of the day: and Adam and his wife hid themselves from the presence of the LORD God amongst the trees of the garden. 9 And the LORD God called unto Adam, and said unto him, Where art thou? Genesis 3:8-9 (KJV)

The idea of "The Voice" walking has always captivated me. The invisible God, the Word, walks with His people each and every day. He is walking toward you today. *Selah*!

After Adam and his wife rebelled they were devoid of the covering of glory that they had from their creation. They were so aware of the loss that they covered themselves and hid from God. Beloved, my heartache today is that many have lost the glory and, like Samson of old, have no clue that it's gone. They don't even notice that they are naked, destitute and alone.

Were you in church this past week end (actually, week beginning)? Were you there because you desired to meet with "The Voice" or were you there out of obligation or a sense of duty? It does matter. Did you gather together your tithe and offering before you came? Did you bring your gift as to God Himself? If you have made a pledge, did you bring it as promised?

These are serious questions. I'm not trying to condemn but am sounding the alarm as any good watchman should. To walk in covenant with God you must not exploit grace for the sake of your fleshly dictates. Obedience is better than sacrifice and a sacrificial gift of obedience is a sweet smell of incense in the courts of the King.

"The Voice" is walking toward you today and asking, "Where are you?" He is calling you to closer fellowship with Him.

May 24 - Forgive!

And when ye stand praying, forgive, if ye have ought against any: that your Father also which is in heaven may forgive you your trespasses. But if ye do not forgive, neither will your Father which is in heaven forgive your trespasses. Mark 11:25-26 (KJV)

Many times those in the Church ask why they are not getting an answer to their prayers. Too often it is because they have not dealt with their own flesh (carnal nature) and let go of the self-seeking, self-satisfying habit of holding grudges or, as the Bible calls it, they allow a root of bitterness to take hold in their life and become easily offended and refuse to forgive even the slightest offense (real or perceived). Beloved this will cut you off from the real relationships that would be your armor bearers in times of battle. Worse yet, your prayers are rendered powerless and unheard by the One who is your Defense.

"And when ye stand praying," *proseucomai*, is understood to mean: When you are persistently pressing in for an answer in prayer (standing in faith, believing) and not getting the answer for which you seek, "Forgive!"

"Forgive," is a command. The Greek word, **aphiemi**, is a strong word that leaves no doubt as to its meaning. It means to send away, yield up, let expire, to let go of, to never discuss, give up a debt owed, to forgive, to remit, to give up, to keep no longer, to not allow to hinder (relationship). This word tells us that we cannot go to a higher place in God until we abandon all claim to restitution or satisfaction.

Our unwillingness, or inability to forgive negates the forgiveness of the Father who originated the principle of forgiveness. He cannot break His own principles. We are expected to be obedient and not just hearing sons and daughters.

If you need to repent and forgive. Please do so now.

May 25 - Not Forgive?

And when ye stand praying, forgive, if ye have ought against any: that your Father also which is in heaven may forgive you your trespasses. But if ye do not forgive, neither will your Father which is in heaven forgive your trespasses. Mark 11:25-26 (KJV)

How could anyone who has been touched by the love of God not forgive? Perhaps it is because they do not understand how much they have offended God by their sins nor how much they have been forgiven. If they did they would be quick to forgive others in the same way God forgave them in Christ.

Wherefore I say unto thee, Her sins, which are many, are forgiven; for she loved much: but to whom little is forgiven, the same loveth little. Luke 7:47 (KJV)

Unforgiveness, bitterness, contaminates faith and defiles the one who refuses to forgive. Resentment, trouble and torment come as a result of holding what only God, the Righteous Judge, can deal with righteously. We are to warn one another and encourage each other so that this destructive sin has no place to gain a foothold in the believers life.

Exercise foresight and be on the watch to look [after one another], to see that no one falls back from and fails to secure God's grace (His unmerited favor and spiritual blessing), in order that no root of resentment (rancor, bitterness, or hatred) shoots forth and causes trouble and bitter torment, and the many become contaminated and defiled by it— Hebrews 12:15 (AMP)

You say, "I can't! You don't know what they have done to me." Beloved, you must, in Christ you can, let go of what the devil has meant to destroy you so that God can turn it for good.

No amount of self-satisfaction can replace the joy of being forgiven, cleansed and released from the bondage of a root of bitterness. Your release is one decision, one act of will, away.

May 26 - Submission?

> I beseech you, brethren, (ye know the house of Stephanas, that it is the firstfruits of Achaia, and that they have addicted themselves to the ministry of the saints,) That ye submit yourselves unto such, and to every one that helpeth with us, and laboureth.
> 1 Corinthians 16:15-16 (KJV)

What does it mean to submit? Who, exactly, should a Christian be submitted to? What exactly does this submission look like?

Let's look at the two verses given above and see if we can gain some insight into this interesting doctrine that helps to order the people of the house of God.

We'll start with the word submit. This Greek word "submit" is, *hupotasso*, means to arrange oneself under, or subordinate oneself to another for the sake of order. It carries the idea that the person submitted will yield obediently to one's admonition or advice. This is a Greek military term meaning "to arrange [troop divisions] in a military fashion under the command of a leader". In non-military use, it was "a voluntary attitude of giving in, cooperating, assuming responsibility, and carrying a burden."

Now, to whom should a Christian submit? The key to this understanding is in verse 16 where we learn that it is "unto such" that we "submit." "Unto Such, *toioutos*, is understood to mean, of this kind or sort. The "kind or sort" referred to is found in both verse 15, "they have addicted themselves to the ministry of the saints," and verse 16, "one that helpeth . . . and laboureth." The "addicted," *tasso*, also means, ordained, assigned and given authority, by mutual agreement, to arrange (the family of God).

One should also submit to those who partner with and assist them in their labor, *sunergeo*, until wearied from toil and effort, *kopiao*.

That, Beloved, is biblical submission.

May 27 - What Do You Think Would Happen?

And if the people of the land bring ware or any victuals on the sabbath day to sell, that we would not buy it of them on the sabbath, or on the holy day: . . .
Nehemiah 10:31 (KJV)

My wife, Sharon, and I were born in 1941, quite some time ago, and remember growing up in a community in Southern California where all the stores and businesses were closed on Sunday. We planned ahead and purchased what we might need the other six days of the week.

Although we neither of us was raised in a Christian home we never thought a thing about it. After all, we lived in a "Christian Nation" and that's just what we do.

When I served in the Armed Forces of these great United States I spent a couple of winters at a military base in Massachusetts. I remember that all the bars could not serve drinks after mid-night on Saturday through mid-night on Sunday. This, too, seemed natural.

As you well may have noticed; those days are gone. Now, practically every retail business is open on Sunday and, oh yes, all of the sports events for our kids and that adults watch are held and featured on Sunday.

The result is that there are very many who are not in church because "my kid is playing ... today," or "it's my only day off."

The Bible has much to say about this popular trend and mind set. Just about every Christian has heard, at one time or another, the admonition, "Not forsaking the assembling of ourselves together, as the manner of some is; but exhorting one another: and so much the more, as ye see the day approaching" (Heb. 10:25 KJV), but I wonder if we have noticed the verse above. It seems that they had the same problem way back in Nehemiah's day.

Did you notice how they dealt with the situation? They refused to purchase anything on the Lord's Day. That put and end to that. What do you suppose would happen if we did the same? Just a thought to consider for today.

May 28 - Yearning . . .

As the hart panteth after the water brooks, so panteth my soul after thee, O God. Psalms 42:1 (KJV)

AS THE hart pants and longs for the water brooks, so I pant and long for You, O God. Psalms 42:1 (AMP)

The deer, or stag, mentioned here is one found in the dry, arid desert seeking water to quench his thirst. There is an intense yearning to find water, without which, life will soon be over. He, *'arag,* longs for or pants after the **mayim *'aphiyq,*** that is, the channels or ravines that carry the watersprings or refreshing streams of the waters that bring and sustain life.

Beloved, our soul, like that of the Psalmist, should yearn after the Source of all life, Almighty God Himself. The word, soul, is the Hebrew word, **nephesh**, and it speaks of the very essence of a person, their desires, appetites, passion, thoughts and will.

There is something missing, and very wrong, when someone who is, supposedly, born-again can approach God haphazardly or casually. The life of the true believer becomes wrapped up in the Person of the Holy One and continually yearns for more of Him with each passing day.

Every facet of our being is focused on His refreshing Presence for we are bound in the bundle of the life of God Himself.

Though man is risen up to pursue you and to seek your life, yet the life of my lord shall be bound in the living bundle with the Lord your God. And the lives of your enemies, them shall He sling out as out of the center of a sling. 1 Samuel 25:29 (AMP)

I am crucified with Christ: nevertheless I live; yet not I, but Christ liveth in me: and the life which I now live in the flesh I live by the faith of the Son of God, who loved me, and gave himself for me. Galatians 2:20 (KJV)

May 29 - Passion . . .

The word, passion, carries, among others, two very interesting meanings. One is that of having an intense enthusiasm for something. That is, having an intense fervor that only comes from Divine inspiration. This is the compelling force that directs every thought, action and deed of a believers life.

Only a truly born-again believer can have this kind of enthusiasm for only such a believer is connected to the Source of divine inspiration and so filled with the understanding, life and vitality of God (Job 32:8).

The other meaning of the word, passion, that I would like you to consider with me is that of being willing to suffer extreme hardship for a worthy cause. Our example is that of Jesus "Passion" as He took our punishment and bore our sin.

Today's Western version of Christianity is a far cry from what the early Apostles considered a normal, healthy Christian life. In our present culture there seems to be an overwhelming self-centeredness that demands more and more comfort, convenience and caressing. There are not many of our number, "who through faith subdued kingdoms, wrought righteousness, obtained promises . . . out of weakness were made strong, waxed valiant in fight, turned to flight the armies of the aliens . . . were tortured, not accepting deliverance . . . had trial of cruel mockings and scourgings . . . bonds and imprisonment . . . were stoned . . . sawn asunder, were tempted, were slain with the sword . . . destitute, afflicted, tormented; (Of whom the world was not worthy:)" Hebrews 11:33-38 (KJV)

Perhaps this would be too "radical" in our society? Or would it?

This is the call of deep unto deep . . .
Selah.

May 30 - By Men of Strange Lips

It is written in the Law, By men of strange languages and by the lips of foreigners will I speak to this people, and not even then will they listen to Me, says the Lord.
1 Corinthians 14:21 (AMP)

Paul the Apostle teaches us through the Word of God that the supernatural gift of "stammering lips and another tongue" (KJV) in the public assembly is a sign to the unbeliever.

Thus [unknown] tongues are meant for a [supernatural] sign, not for believers but for unbelievers [on the point of believing], while prophecy (inspired preaching and teaching, interpreting the divine will and purpose) is not for unbelievers [on the point of believing] but for believers.
1 Corinthians 14:22 (AMP)

If this is so, why then are there so many "Pentecostal" and "Charismatic" churches that forbid speaking with other tongues in the assembly of the people?

Tongues is the initial evidence of being Baptized in the Holy Spirit (Acts 2:4 KJV) and is a grace given to declare "the wonderful works of God" (Acts 2:11 KJV).

Tongues is a powerful force within each believer that will cause supernatural strength to be released and the speaking believer to be built up in love (Jude 1:20, 21 KJV).

Tongues opens the windows and doors of the hidden mysteries and secrets of God (1 Cor. 14:2 KJV).

Tongues and interpretation of tongues constitutes prophecy and by it the church is built up (edified) (1 Cor. 14:5 KJV) and unbelievers and believers are struck with the presence of the Almighty (1 Cor. 14:22).

As I review these few examples of the wonder of God's gift of the Holy Spirit with the evidenced supernatural Spirit given utterance (Acts 2:4) I cannot but wonder what would happen if Pentecost returned to the assembly of the saints.

May 31 - Robbing Your Spiritual Father or Mother

Whoso robbeth his father or his mother, and saith, It is no transgression; the same is the companion of a destroyer. Proverbs 28:24 (KJV)

There are some verses of Scripture that just curl my hair and this is one of them. As a pastor, I have great love for the sheep and, yes, even the goats. Christ loved all, came for all, shed His blood for all, and died for all. Though I am well aware that I do not have the right to insist that anyone obey the Word of God, I do pray that they will see the wisdom in it and become doers of the Word.

The doctrine of Grace has been so abused by the willful that it has almost been destroyed for lack of knowledge. The casting away of "law" has become the mark of "freedom" to the extent that " many church goers who profess to be Christians find themselves of the same mind as that of those mentioned in the book of Judges: "In those days there was no king in Israel; every man did what was right in his own eyes" (Judg. 17:6 AMP).

Today it could be written, "There is no King (Father, Son and Holy Spirit); everyone is doing what is right in their own eyes" (Deut. 12:8; Judg. 21:25; Pro. 3:7; 12:15; 16:2).

We see from Proverbs 28:24 that one who robs father or mother is the companion of a destroyer, *chaber 'iysh shachath*. In other words, is knit together, a companion with, and an accomplice with a destroying demon.

How does one "rob" his spiritual father or mother? There are three main ways:

1) Withholding support.

2) Stealing their reputation by gossip.

3) Withdrawing your grace from the work that God called them to.

When we understand the principles in the Word of God we will find ourselves flowing in liberty and victory every day of our lives. Is it time to repent (1 Joh. 1:9 KJV)? ***Selah!***

JUNE

June 01 - Fathers

For though ye have ten thousand instructors in Christ, yet have ye not many fathers: for in Christ Jesus I have begotten you through the gospel.
1 Corinthians 4:15 (KJV)

Instructors are important for young Christians who have not yet developed enough spiritual maturity to have formed strong principles or to maintain integrity on their own These, *paidagogos*, schoolmasters or instructors were understood to be tutors i.e. "guardian and guide of boys. Among the Greeks and the Romans the name was applied to trustworthy slaves who were charged with the duty of supervising the life and morals of boys belonging to the better class. The boys were not allowed so much as to step out of the house without them before arriving at the age of manhood."

As important as these instructors were, they could not take the place of a father. Paul reminds his spiritual sons that he, alone, is their father on earth. He does not take the place of their Father in heaven but is His representative on earth for their well-being. He refers to himself as a generator or male ancestor, the founder of a family or tribe and the nearest ancestor. He uses the word, *pater*, to refer to his relationship with those he birthed in the spirit.

This conveys the idea of passing on the spiritual DNA or the same spirit as he himself possesses. He is saying that he stands in a father's place and looks after them in a paternal way that no "trustworthy slaves who were charged with the duty of supervising the life and morals" of their charges would do.

As their father it was his responsibility and joy to actuate and govern their mental pursuits according to the glorious gospel.

Fathers are connected in an intimate and lasting way that even the most dedicated hireling or servant would ever aspire to.

This coming Father's Day, remember and value both your natural and your spiritual father as you set aside time to honor your Father which is in heaven.

181

June 02 - That I may know Him

That I may know him, . . . ; Philippians 3:10 (KJV)

My goal, my passion, my utmost desire is to know Him and to know his ways. Moses knew His ways, whereas others knew His acts.

He made known his ways unto Moses, his acts unto the children of Israel. Psalm 103:7 (KJV)

Way too many people are familiar with the acts of the Holy Spirit but not His ways; the acts of Jesus but not His ways, the acts of the Father but not His ways. The ways of God was what was important about the ministry of Christ on earth and yet we focus on what He did. The miracles, healings, the feeding of thousands, the walking on water, all catch our attention and we forget to look underneath the acts done to the ways that brought them about.

You get to know some things about a person by what they do but you do not really know them until you know why they did what they did. To really know someone intimately, you must hear their heart, understand how they think and know their character and the motive for their actions in life.

It is just not enough to know what Jesus did, although His acts were spectacular and demonstrated the power of God and the power of the resurrection. For a Christian to be able to say, "I am crucified with Christ: nevertheless I live; yet not I, but Christ liveth in me: and the life which I now live in the flesh I live by the faith of the Son of God, who loved me, and gave himself for me" (Gal. 2:20 KJV), he must know His ways.

Even the most carnal Christian can do most of the acts of Jesus because of the resident authority in His name. That is why we read of Jesus saying,

Many will say to me in that day, Lord, Lord, have we not prophesied in thy name? and in thy name have cast out devils? and in thy name done many wonderful works? And then will I profess unto them, I never knew you: depart from me, ye that work iniquity. Matthew 7:22-23 (KJV)

May we know Him and His ways and then - His acts.

June 03 - That I may know Him - In The Power

That I may know him, and the power of his resurrection,
. . . ; Philippians 3:10 (KJV)

I love the way the Amplified Bible renders this verse:
[For my determined purpose is] that I may know Him [that I may progressively become more deeply and intimately acquainted with Him, perceiving and recognizing and understanding the wonders of His Person more strongly and more clearly], and that I may in that same way come to know the power outflowing from His resurrection [which it exerts over believers], and that I may so share His sufferings as to be continually transformed [in spirit into His likeness even] to His death, [in the hope]" Philippians 3:10 AMP

"My determined purpose is that I may know Him." The Greek word for "know" is, *ginosko*. This word not only means to perceive and understand, but carries a deeply intimate concept of "knowing" that can best be understood as how closely and intimately a husband and wife "know" each other during sexual intercourse. This is a "knowing" that is far beyond a casual acquaintance or having knowledge of.

As you can see, the Amplified Bible captures this idea with the phrase, "progressively become more deeply and intimately acquainted with."

Today, I want to focus on the "knowing" of His resurrection power. We will never be intimately acquainted with the power of resurrection until we submit ourselves to His crucifixion and death. The words, "I am crucified with Christ: nevertheless I live; yet not I, but Christ liveth in me: and the life which I now live in the flesh I live by the faith of the Son of God, who loved me, and gave himself for me" (Gal. 2:20 KJV), must be a result of having been to, and through, the Cross with Christ Jesus. Mortality must put on immortality in the spirit before it will ever become a reality in the realm of our character and our walk in this world. Life in the Spirit of resurrection power is Glorious! It is the right of every born-again son of God.

June 04 - That I may know Him - In The Fellowship

That I may know him, . . . , and the fellowship of his sufferings, . . . Philippians 3:10 (KJV)

Imagine, to share in fellowship with Christ is offered to every born-again, spirit-filled believer. But, you say, "I don't really like suffering." Beloved, you cannot escape its touch if you are committed to follow Jesus. You must embrace "the fellowship of his sufferings."

Firstly, we must understand just what this verse is asking of us. Secondly, we must make a decision to join Him in this fellowship.

The word used for "sufferings" is the Greek word, *pathema*, that deals with the afflictions which Christ underwent in behalf of the Father's cause.

The misunderstanding, rejection, maligning, hatred, mocking and, if necessary, the physical beating, torture and death, which Christ patiently endured. The emphasis is upon that which is of an inward state, an affliction, passion. It is the love of God unwanted, cast aside, ignored and otherwise trampled under foot that breaks the hearts of Christ and those who are in covenant with Him.

To share in the fellowship of His love for lost and dying humanity; to be moved with supernatural compassion for those suffering under the burden of sin and to be filled with a desire to seek and to save that which is lost is to enter into the fellowship of His sufferings.

To "have no fellowship with the unfruitful works of darkness . . ." (Eph. 5:11 KJV) and to have our "fellowship in the gospel" (Phil. 1:5 KJV) releases gifts in our lives so that as we "take upon us the fellowship of the ministering to the saints" (2 Cor. 8:4 KJV) we have all sufficiency in all things.

We enter into "the fellowship of the mystery, which from the beginning of the world hath been hid in God, who created all things by Jesus Christ" (Eph. 3:9 KJV) and we come to know Him.

June 05 - That I may know Him - Being Made Conformable

That I may know him, . . . , being made conformable unto his death; Philippians 3:10 (KJV)

It is written that a man must not cling to his life or he will lose it, and he must be willing to lose his life for Christ, and the cause of Christ, in order to find it. "For whosoever will save his life shall lose it; but whosoever shall lose his life for my sake and the gospel's, the same shall save it" (Mk 8:35 KJV).

To come to know Christ Jesus is to follow Him to, and through, the Cross. There must be a death, a burial, and a resurrection. There is a resurrection: "If by any means I might attain unto the resurrection of the dead" (Phi. 3:11 KJV).

There is a resurrected life to live here in this age. We are called to allow Christ to life in and through us, rather than we living our lives for Him. There is a very big difference between serving the Lord and living in Him.

Intimate knowing is possible, but only to degree that one wills to lay aside every personal agenda, future plan and preconceived notion of what life they might live.

It is not that the Lord will not give vision, a dream, or a plan to work toward. No, it is not that at all. It is the willingness to allow Him to bring us into His original plan, purpose and place of His calling for our lives. It is our allowing the Holy Spirit to take control and set the course for the good and the glory of God and mankind.

We are "dead" and, therefore, do not have our own aspirations of fame, greatness, or success. Our eyes are upon Him and our desire is to please Him in whatever way that we can. His passion is our passion, His purpose is our purpose, His will supersedes our will and even when we don't understand or are taken aback by what we see before us we can say, "Father, if thou be willing, remove this cup from me: nevertheless not my will, but thine, be done" (Luk. 22:42 KJV).

June 06 - What Is My Ministry?

Have you ever asked yourself this question? Have you ever asked God to show you what your ministry really is? What was His answer?

Beloved, here is your answer if you will receive it:

And as ye go, preach, saying, The kingdom of heaven is at hand. Heal the sick, cleanse the lepers, raise the dead, cast out devils: freely ye have received, freely give.
Matthew 10:7-8 (KJV)

As you go . . . Your "ministry" is one that will only unfold as you go. Too many Spirit-filled Christians are praying and seeking God to find out what their ministry "gift" is when the "it" they are asking for is already clearly presented in the Word. As you go . . . ; As you go to work. As you go to the store. As you go to Church. As you go about the affairs of the day. This is when you will have opportunity to be "faithful in little" so that your Father in heaven can "give you much."

Preach! Your first response may be, "I'm no preacher." Yes you are! Preaching is just proclaiming. Matthew 10:7 even tells you what to say. "The Kingdom of Heaven is at hand." This simply means that Kingdom rule, order and principle are in the now [God's ETERNAL NOW].

Jesus Christ the same yesterday, and to day, and for ever. Hebrews 13:8 (KJV)

June 07 - Freely Give!

Heal the sick! According to Psalm 107:20, God "sent His Word [Jesus], and healed them, and delivered them from their destructions." Christ is in you!

"... Christ in you, the hope of glory." (Col. 1:27 KJV)

Your "ministry" consists of what you allow Him to do through you!

Cleanse the lepers! Your "ministry" is to cleanse everything that eats away at humanity. Whether disease in the body or the ravages of sin in the spirit and soul. There is nothing outside the benefit of God's grace as manifest in the atoning work of Jesus at Calvary's Tree!

Raise the dead! This is a "ministry" that not many have reached for. Why not? Is one miraculous manifestation of the Almighty easier than another? I think not. God is calling us to be bold with concern to this "ministry."

Cast out devils! This "ministry" is one of the most misunderstood in the Christian family. Suffice it to quote the words found in the book of Colossians:

And having spoiled principalities and powers, he made a shew of them openly, triumphing over them in it. Colossians 2:15 (KJV)

Freely you have received, Freely Give! (Mat. 10:8 KJV)

You do have a "ministry!"

June 08 - What Do You Need?

What is the desire of your heart? What would you like your heavenly Father to do for you? Do you want Him to heal you or one of your loved ones? He will!

And whatsoever ye shall ask in my name, that will I do, that the Father may be glorified in the Son. ... ask any thing in my name, I will do it. John 14:13-14 (KJV)
[Isa 53:5; 1 Pe 2:24]

Just ask in faith believing! Jesus is waiting for a way to show you the great love of God that was displayed at Calvary's tree and in the Resurrection! He wants you to experience His life in the affairs of today. Perhaps you need a car, extra money, help with a decision, a new job or a promotion.

Ask, and it shall be given you; seek, and ye shall find; knock, and it shall be opened unto you: Matthew 7:7 (KJV)

You may be praying for a loved one to be saved. Be encouraged in the knowledge that God loves the lost and wants none to remain in that condition. He cares about the one you love. He has promised the lost to each believer as an inheritance.

Ask of me, and I shall give thee the heathen for thine inheritance, and the uttermost parts of the earth for thy possession. Psalm 2:8 (KJV)

Jesus is Risen! This revelation must be held close to your heart daily. He is Alive and waiting for you to call upon Him today.

You will always be welcomed when you come to Him. As recorded in the Living Bible:

... come to me ... and I will never, never reject [you]. John 6:37 (AMP)

Whatever your need, you can rest assured that He will meet it:

And this is the confidence that we have in him, that, if we ask any thing according to his will, he heareth us: And if we know that he hear us, whatsoever we ask, we know that we have the petitions that we desired of him. 1 John 5:14-15 (KJV)

June 09 - Show Me Your Ways

Show me Your ways, O Lord; teach me Your paths. Psalm 25:4 (AMP)

What more could we desire than to be shown the ways of God?

Our God and Father only shows those who are intimately acquainted with Him His ways. Scripture tells us that what God does could be seen by the children of Israel, but He reserved His purposes, intents, His very heart, to Moses. David wanted to go beyond seeing miracles to knowing God:

He made known his ways unto Moses, his acts unto the children of Israel. Psalm 103:7 (KJV)

The Hebrew word used in Psalm 25:4, Show, is, *yada*, which is, though it is a small word, a very powerful and intimate word. It carries the idea, or concept, of knowing which can be seen in the translation of Psalm 103:7. It means, to perceive and see, to find out and discern, to know by experience, and, therefore, to recognize, acknowledge and confess the Lord. The word goes beyond being acquainted with, to the intimacy of the marriage bed. It deals with receiving revelation of the One known.

So, David is asking the Lord God Almighty to make Himself known by revealing His nature and character. *Derek* is the word used for, Your ways. David wanted to know the paths of God, the manners and habits of God as well as His moral character and course of life. He wanted to be taught, *lamad*, trained and exercised in the ways and paths, *'orach*: God's way of living.

Imagine what our lives would be like if we were passionately seeking to know Him instead of wanting what He provides by way of provision, power, and peace.

Today, take a moment and ask God to show you His ways.

June 10 - Unprepared

Lest, if [any] Macedontians should come with me and find you unprepared [for this generosity], we, to say nothing of yourselves, be humiliated for our being so confident. 2 Corinthians 9:4 (AMP)

"Lest . . . we . . . be humiliated." Most born-again, church going, tithing individuals do not understand how their giving affects the community around them. In fact, most are learning nothing about giving because they close the ears of their hearts whenever they know that it is "offering time." It has become ritual and, therefore, something to be endured rather than celebrated.

Here in Las Vegas one can see multi-million dollar facilities everywhere. Everywhere that is, except, with rare exception, within the Christian community. The casinos, hotels, bars and restaurants flaunt their wares from expensive and lavishly appointed facilities while the church goes begging to raise enough money to build something, that is at best, presentable. People seem to think that fire works stands and bake sales are the answer when bringing "all the tithe into the storehouse" would meet every need both here and abroad

The national economy hinges on the willingness of the people of God to tithe and yet the Body of Christ still turns a deaf ear to the instructive Voice of God:

Ye are cursed with a curse: for ye have robbed me, even this whole nation. Malachi 3:9 (KJV)

The world mocks, sneers and laughs at the Church of the First-born without realizing that the Church moves ahead against, what appears to be, insurmountable obstacles within and without. The Spirit of the Living God uses the weak things to show His strength and the foolish things to manifest His wisdom:

. . . Not by might, nor by power, but by my spirit, saith the Lord of hosts. Zechariah 4:6 (KJV)

In spite of all, His Church will triumph gloriously! Of this we are unshakably confident.

June 11 - Are You Praying?

Christians have the privilege and the responsibility to pray. Many, however, do not avail themselves of the power of prayer and, so, live lives of aimless wandering rather than lives of focus and meaning.

Prayer brings focus to the plan and purpose of God for each supplicants life. Prayer is the time of dialogue between the Father's sons and daughters and Himself. In prayer there is communion, comfort for each trial, wisdom for each decision, knowledge for each task and timing for every purpose.

The Father's business is discussed and certain duties delegated to those who will spend the time to listen to the Voice of the Spirit and obey His promptings.

Herein are the strategies of the devil exposed and the plan of God drawn out and clarified in order to overcome every demonic strategy by the word of His children's testimony and blood of the Lamb,.

There is a warfare that is raging for the control of the nations, tribes and tongues of planet earth. For the faith filled praying Christian, this is a "good fight" that is already won at Calvary's tree.

Fight the good fight of the faith; lay hold of the eternal life to which you were summoned and [for which] you confessed the good confession [of faith] before many witnesses. 1 Timothy 6:12 (AMP)

[God] disarmed the principalities and powers that were ranged against us and made a bold display and public example of them, in triumphing over them in Him and in it [the cross]. Colossians 2:15 (AMP)

Believing Christians are to recognize that there is a war, seek the Lord for the heavenly strategies to bring the victory of the Cross to bear on the present skirmishes, and take the dominion authority that has been restored to them in the name of Jesus the Anointed One. The fight (battle) is not a natural one, but a supernatural one and must, therefore, be fought supernaturally:

"For the weapons of our warfare are not physical [weapons of flesh and blood] . . ." (2 Cor. 10:4 AMP).

June 12 - Robbing Your Spiritual Father or Mother

Whoso robbeth his father or his mother, and saith, It is no transgression; the same is the companion of a destroyer. Proverbs 28:24

There are some verses of Scripture that just curl my hair and this is one of them. As a pastor, I have great love for the sheep and, yes, even the goats. Christ loved all, came for all, shed His blood for all, and died for all. Though I am well aware that I do not have the right to insist that anyone obey the Word of God, I do pray that they will see the wisdom in it and become doers of the Word.

The doctrine of Grace has been so abused by the willful that it has almost been destroyed for lack of knowledge. The casting away of "law" has become the mark of "freedom" to the extent that " many church goers who profess to be Christians find themselves of the same mind as that of those mentioned in the book of Judges: "In those days there was no king in Israel; every man did what was right in his own eyes" (Judg. 17:6 AMP).

Today it could be written, "There is no King (Father, Son and Holy Spirit); everyone is doing what is right in their own eyes" (Deut. 12:8; Judg. 21:25; Pro. 3:7; 12:15; 16:2).

We see from Proverbs 28:24 that one who robs father or mother is the companion of a destroyer, *chaber 'iysh shachath*. In other words, is knit together, a companion with, and an accomplice with a destroying demon.

How does one "rob" his spiritual father or mother? There are three main ways:

1) Withholding support.

2) Stealing their reputation by gossip.

3) Withdrawing your grace from the work that God called them to.

When we understand the principles in the Word of God we will find ourselves flowing in liberty and victory every day of our lives. Is it time to repent (1 Joh. 1:9 KJV)?

- *Selah*

June 13 - This Is A Great Hour!

God is pouring out His love into the church like never before. This is an exciting time! Love Never Fails!

1 Corinthians 13:8 "Love never fails...."

As you read "listen" to what God is saying:

"And see, my child, how My love pours out to you. For truly I sent My own beloved, the only begotten, My Son, as a gift of love to you. That you might be able to receive all the fullness that I have to offer. For within My heart is the desire that you come into all that I Am and be behind in no good thing, lacking nothing.

Yes, I know what you have need of. For see, have I not fed the sparrow and clothed the lily and caused the cattle lowing on a thousand hills to be satisfied. Have I not provided all that is necessary for you and given you dominion and authority over it.

This is just a foretaste and a foreshadowing, for as you draw near to me I have promised to draw even nearer to you. This is so that within you and about you might be manifest My glory. So that you might come into realms and things that you've never dreamed of. Things that are beyond your wildest thoughts and imaginations.

Eye has not seen nor ear heard, what I have laid up in store for you. Not only in the ages to come but in this age. For I have not set you in a place where you have to wait longingly for all things. No, for I have poured out of Myself, by My Spirit, and My abundance shall flow to, through, and out of you."

June 14 - Don't You See?

The call of the Lord is for us to see . . . what His Spirit is saying:

"My abundance must flow and fill and immerse you. You shall be immersed in the heavenly waters of life in depths that will give you the ability to swim. Oh yes, and then where ever you go will spring forth streams of living waters. For out of your belly shall flow this stream and your words will bring life and encouragement for these are the leaves of healing that fall from the trees that line the river of God".

He who believes in Me - who cleaves to and trusts in and relies on Me - as the Scripture has said, Out from his innermost being springs and rivers of living water shall flow (continuously). John 7:38 (AMP)

"Every place that you go will, in it's barrenness, be turned into a fruitful field.

The trees will begin to bear fruit and all that grows up out of the ground shall blossom.

You shall see that I speak concerning the lives of mankind. They shall be changed, for I have come unto you and will move through you unto them. For I love you and I love them and My glory shall cover the face of the earth. Yes, and it shall be the glory of the only begotten, for you shall be like Him!"

Beloved, we are [even here and] now God's children; it is not yet disclosed (made clear) what we shall be [hereafter], but we know that when He comes and is manifested, we shall [as God's children] resemble and be like Him, for we shall see Him just as He [really] is. 1 John 3:2 (AMP)

June 15 - How Beautiful . . .

. . . upon the mountains are the feet of him that bringeth good tidings, that publisheth peace; that bringeth good tidings of good, that publisheth salvation; that saith unto Zion, Thy God reigneth! Isaiah 52:7 (KJV)

And how shall they preach, except they be sent? as it is written, How beautiful are the feet of them that preach the gospel of peace, and bring glad tidings of good things! Romans 10:15 (KJV)

Each and every Christian has a mandate from God to proclaim the Good News. Whether at home, at work or during set times of outreach or ministry we, as the people of God, are to be a light in the midst of darkness.

Ye are the Light of the world. A city that is set on an hill cannot be hid. Matthew 5:14 (KJV)

The people of the world will never know the Good News of the marvelous Gospel of Jesus Christ unless we allow the Holy Spirit to use us in His work of revealing Jesus.

We are admonished,

Let your light so shine before men, that they may see your good works, and glorify your Father which is in heaven. Matthew 5:16 (KJV)

You and I have the wonderful privilege of being in a position whereby we may glorify our Father!

Let us use whatever time we have in this earth to publish peace, bring glad tidings of good things, preach the gospel of peace and publish salvation!

For some, time is short; very short. You, or perhaps I, will be the last person they will ever speak to. Will we take the time to stop and share the good news. Will we recognize our window of opportunity?

Look carefully then how you walk! Live purposefully and worthily and accurately, not as the unwise and witless, but as wise (sensible, intelligent people), Making the very most of the time [buying up each opportunity], because the days are evil. Ephesians 5:15-16 (AMP)

June 16 - Submitted to What?!

To what are you submitted? To whom are you submitted?

Have you ever stopped to think about what, or to whom, you are really submitted? Have you questioned the motives behind what you do with your time each day?

Most Christians would say, "I'm submitted to God" or "I'm submitted to the will of God," or "I'm submitted to the Word of God."

If this is true then it is also true that you spend an hour or more a day in prayer, right? You read at least three or four chapters in the Bible each day and ponder what the Lord is teaching you by His living Word.

I ask again - To what are you submitted? To whom are you submitted?

Submitting to God is not the ministry to which we are called. Submitting to God is not our labor on the mission field. In other words, Submitting to God is not staying busy "in the work of the ministry."

Submitting to God is more relational than it is activity. He is calling us into relationship with Him. Our Lord wants us to hear His heart and He wants us to share our heart with Him. This brings submission into a whole different light.

Submitting to God, then, is prayer. It is the submission of quality time in our lives to Him. All of our actions of faith must come out of our relational time spent with Him. All that we are, and all that we do, should be the direct result of this time spent alone with Him.

For us to submit to His desire to spend time with us, we must recognize that time is owned, and controlled, by God Himself. The Psalmist passes on this revelation as, "My times are in thy hand . . ." (Psa. 31:15 KJV).

Therefore, our time is to be submitted to Him; not "His work."

Now, let me ask you once again - To what, or whom, are you submitted?

I pray that your answer now is a more considered one. I would that you and I reevaluate our position of submission and will set aside some meaningful time with Him each day.

June 17 - A Healing Jesus

When John the Baptist sent two of his disciples to ask Jesus, "Are You He Who is to come, or shall we look for another?" Jesus replied, "Go and tell John what you have seen and heard: "the lame are walking; the lepers are cleansed; the deaf are hearing; the dead are raised up; and the poor have the good news preached to them . . . And blessed is he who takes no offense in Me" (Mat. 11:3, 5, 6 KJV).

This the work reserved for the followers of Jesus Christ (believers).

> Heal the sick, cleanse the lepers, raise the dead, cast out devils: freely ye have received, freely give.

Matthew 10:8 (KJV)

> . . . they shall lay hands on the sick, and they shall recover. Mark 16:18 (KJV)

In fact, He has decreed that we are to do the "greater works."

> Verily, verily, I say unto you, He that believeth on me, the works that I do shall he do also; and greater works than these shall he do; because I go unto my Father.

John 14:12 (KJV)

The work, *ergon*, Jesus spoke of was referring to "the works of Him that sent" Him (Joh. 9:4 KJV). He was always about the Father's business (Luk. 2:49 KJV). The word work refers to an act, deed, thing done: the idea of working is emphasized in opposition to that which is less than work. Everything that Jesus did was a direct result of what He heard the Father say and what He saw the Father do (Joh. 15:19).

In this hour there is a great move of God to bring His body into something fresh and powerful; you are one of those chosen to be used of the Lord in this hour. Jesus said that you would do greater works than those that He did. The greater, *meizon*, here speaks of those signs, wonders, miracles (healing, raising the dead, etc.) being what He did and greater, and the fruitfulness of the harvest of souls being larger and accompanied by greater strength (stronger).

It is time now to step out and say, "Yes Lord, Yes to Your will and to Your way," and see what He will do with you!

June 18 - This Is A Great Hour!

God is pouring out His love into the church like never before. This is an exciting time! Love Never Fails!

"Love never fails...." 1 Corinthians 13:8 (KJV)
As you read "listen" to what God is saying:
"And see, my child, how My love pours out to you. For truly I sent My own beloved, the only begotten, My Son, as a gift of love to you. That you might be able to receive all the fullness that I have to offer. For within My heart is the desire that you come into all that I Am and be behind in no good thing, lacking nothing.

Yes, I know what you have need of. For see, have I not fed the sparrow and clothed the lily and caused the cattle lowing on a thousand hills to be satisfied. Have I not provided all that is necessary for you and given you dominion and authority over it.

This is just a foretaste and a foreshadowing, for as you draw near to me I have promised to draw even nearer to you. This is so that within you and about you might be manifest My glory. So that you might come into realms and things that you've never dreamed of. Things that are beyond your wildest thoughts and imaginations.

Eye has not seen nor ear heard, what I have laid up in store for you. Not only in the ages to come but in this age. For I have not set you in a place where you have to wait longingly for all things. No, for I have poured out of Myself, by My Spirit, and My abundance shall flow to, through, and out of you."

Don't You See? The call of the Lord is for us to see . . . what His Spirit is saying:
"My abundance must flow and fill and immerse you. You shall be immersed in the heavenly waters of life in depths that will give you the ability to swim. Oh yes, and then where ever you go will spring forth streams of living waters. For out of your belly shall flow this stream and your words will bring life and encouragement for these are the leaves of healing that fall from the trees that line the river of God".

June 19 - Nevertheless

And Simon (Peter) answered, Master, we toiled all night [exhaustingly] and caught nothing [in our nets]. But on the ground of Your word, I will lower the nets [again]. Luke 5:5 (AMP)

How many times have we done what we know how to do and, no matter how hard and long we labored, it just didn't work? All the planning, preparation and process was not producing what we had expected and wanted.

We were getting tired and frustrated.

Is it possible that we have put our trust in our knowledge, skill and ability while we ignored our need for the Lord? Could it be that we became so self sufficient that we needed a reminder that we were created to work together with the Lord and not develop our own plans and procedures?

After the fall in the Garden of Eden mankind was able to make critical moral and value decisions without the counsel of God Almighty.

But of the tree of the knowledge of good and evil and blessing and calamity you shall not eat, for in the day that you eat of it you shall surely die. Genesis 2:17 (AMP)

They would base their decisions on evil and calamity as well as on good and blessing rather than just the "good and perfect gift" of God. No decision ever need be fear based, but only love based as it flows from the heart of God.

Peter and his friends were working on what they knew in and through the natural realm. He was spiritually aware enough, however, to yield to the Word of the Lord and do what he could not see the value of. The result was a huge, supernatural, catch of fish.

You and I need rely upon the leading of the Lord rather than the understanding of our experience and knowledge. As we learn to follow the Spirit of God, not leaning on our own understanding (Proverbs 3:5), we will find great increase and fulfillment beyond any natural means.

June 20 - Things = Words = Things

> A good man out of the good treasure of the heart bringeth forth good things: and an evil man out of the evil treasure bringeth forth evil things. Matthew 12:35 (KJV)

This verse says that words are things. When we consider that God said, Let there be . . . , and there was (Gen. 1:3, 6, 14), we understand that good things came forth from His words (Gen. 1:12, 18, 21, 25). So, things are words, and words are things.

Our verse reads, "A good, *agathos*, man, *anthropos*, human being (male or female)." The, *agathos*, man is one who is of good constitution or nature. One who is pleasant, agreeable, joyful and happy. He is also one who possesses a good conscience and is distinguished, upright and honorable. This individual is one who is free from guile, and particularily, the desire to corrupt the people. He is pre-eminently of God, as consumately and essentially good. This person is one who has a kindness and attractiveness not necessarily possessed by one who merely measures up to a high standard of rectitude.

I submit to you that this is none other than the God Man, Jesus the Christ Himself who is being referred to.

> In the beginning was the Word, and the Word was with God, and the Word was God. The same was in the beginning with God. All things were made by him; and without him was not any thing made that was made. John1:1-3 (KJV)

The word, made, *ginomai*, carries the thought of having been brought forth into existence as recorded in the book of Genesis. Things were brought forth by the Word. The Word, Christ Jesus, is now in every believer and when we speak what we hear the Father speak we can be sure that the Word within will empower the word we speak, bringing forth good things.

June 21 - Summer Time

School is out and now, the family can go and play
If we miss church a bit, we're sure that will be OK
After all, God knows that, we need some time away
We'll stop in later to worship, join the Saints, and pray

The Lord is well aware, that we love Him in every way
Even when we're out and about on this His Sabbath day
When we return, and settle in, done with our summer play
Then we will think of church and tithing,
without any more delay.

Excited to get together with friends, both clergy and lay
We head for church on Sunday, and find to our dismay;
The church doors are closed,
and the pastor has passed away.
He died of a broken heart, you see,
and the bills he could not pay

by George M. Stover Jr.

June 22 - Where Thine Honor Dwelleth

LORD, I have loved the habitation of thy house, and the place where thine honour dwelleth. Psalm 26:8 (KJV)

This beautiful verse binds together the concept of the church as being both individual and corporate. Never fall into the error that God does not dwell within each of His children. Neither allow yourself to buy into the devilish lie that the local, visible, church is not important to God and His children.

YHWH, The Existing One, I have loved, *'ahab* or *'aheb*, have an appetite for, *ma'own* or *ma'iyn*, your dwellingplace and refuge in the temple, *bayith*, of our bodies and the gathering place of those who are your family (offspring), and the place, *maqowm* or *maqom*, within those who are Yours and the building set aside to honor Your Presence and filled with Your glory, *kabowd*, honor, abundance, riches, reverence, dignity, splendor, and reputation. This is the place, *mishkan*, where You receive the honor due.

Two verses come readily to mind as I consider, with you, the importance of the believer and the assembly, *ecclessia*.

The first is:

Know ye not that ye are the temple of God, and that the Spirit of God dwelleth in you? 1 Corinthians 3:16

and the second is:

Not forsaking the assembling of ourselves together, as the manner of some is; but exhorting one another: and so much the more, as ye see the day approaching. Hebrews 10:25 (KJV)

Both are equally important. Both are equally dependent upon the other.

If a Christian allows themselves to become disinterested in the church assembly they will eventually wander off, like lost sheep, into a multitude of errors. The sheep are safe in the fold when they recognize the church (ecclessia), assembly as a structural pillar in their lives.

But if I tarry long, that thou mayest know how thou oughtest to behave thyself in the house of God, which is the church of the living God, the pillar and ground of the truth. 1 Timothy 3:15 (KJV)

June 23 - Is There Not A Cause?

And David said, What have I now done? Is there not a cause? 1 Samuel 17:29 (KJV)

"Is there not a cause?" is a life changing question. Great things are only done when a person has a cause. For the Christian, the cause it that of God's cause. We must ask ourselves certain questions to determine if what we are thinking of doing is God honoring or self serving.

1 Samuel 17 holds the record of David's battle with Goliath. What made his cause worthwhile was that it was motivated by a desire to remove reproach from God and His people. David was concerned about removing the disgrace from his nation more than his own safety and comfort.

A great cause also holds a great reward. In David's case it was a promise of his family living tax free for life and his being given the hand of the kings daughter. So the cause of God will bring you prosperity and relationships of worth.

Like every worthwhile endeavor, a God honoring cause will bring persecution as it did from David's brothers. Yes, your family and close friends may be your worst enemies as you set out to fulfill your destiny in God.

Nothing of any value will be done for God without faith that speaks from the heart. David spoke to the Giant, told him how he would defeat him and reminded himself how God had given him previous victories when he defeated the lion and the bear.

Your God ordained cause will bring God all the glory and inspire others as it did the army of Israel.

Our nation is failing because it has turned its back upon God. "Is there not a cause?" I believe there is and I believe that you will allow the Spirit of God to send you into the heat of this spiritual battle between darkness and light.

And he said unto them, Go ye into all the world, and preach the gospel to every creature. Mark 16;16 (KJV)

June 24 - Dancing With God

Have you ever meditated on the word Guidance, You will notice the word "dance" at the end of the word.

I have read that doing God's will is a lot like dancing. When both dance partners try to lead, nothing works or feels right. Toes are stepped on and there is no graceful flow with the music. It just isn't a dance. The whole event becomes uncomfortable and jerky.

Traditionally, the man leads. When the woman realizes that she should let the man lead, both begin to flow in harmony with the music. The man gives gentle cues by gentle pressure to the back, hand or side. This light press or pull in one direction or another guides his partner. It's as if both partners have become one body, gracefully moving together in beautiful harmony of motion.

Dancing takes surrender, willingness, and attentiveness from the female and gentle guidance and skill from the male partner.

Let's look at the word Guidance again. It starts with a "G," as in "God." It is then followed by "u" and "I". "God," "(u) You" and "(I) I." God, you and I dance.

Do we, as the Bride of Christ, let Him lead?

After all, He is the Dancer. Are we willing to trust His guidance in our lives by His Word and Spirit. I am becoming more and more willing to let God lead. Dance with God to the symphony of life. Trust Him lead and to guide with gentle touches of His Spirit in your inner man.

Adapted from "Dancing with God" by an unknown author.- December 17, 2006 - gms

June 25 - On Moral Integrity

Why, exactly, do we need moral integrity? What, exactly, is moral integrity? Can there be individual integrity without a moral basis? This is something we all need to consider.

There is no possibility of the successful development of a society without a common value system to order the daily affairs of its members. It simply cannot withstand the pressures or heat that it must move through any more than the could the cruise ship Titanic or the space shuttle Columbia.

Even if there are only two individuals, there must be a set of ground rules by which one may relate to the other. In fact, an individual cannot function alone without a certain sense of purpose and worth. In other words, there must be a proper sense of being and adequate rules to live by. Recognizing this basic human need brings us face to face with the need to question who, or what, has the right to mandate or decree a set of moral values that could be the framework or basis of integrity?

Is mankind left to itself to develop and establish such a critical framework for interpersonal relationships, or is there someone who holds the right to hold the plumb line from which all society might gain direction?

We cannot speak of being moral without believing that there might be an absolute standard of behavior that would qualify a person as being moral or immoral. If integrity is partially defined as, the quality of having strong moral principles, then morality must be defined to the degree that all people within a given community could agree as to the absoluteness of its standard. And if we understand being moral to mean being concerned with the principles of right and wrong behavior, the goodness or badness of human character, and adhering to a code of behavior that is considered right or acceptable, or a standard of behavior, a principle of right and wrong, then we begin to see the need for an established and accepted norm of moral values.

Any nation, great or small, will eventually collapse and its world-wide influence fade as did the mighty Roman Empire if it does not have the absolute moral integrity that is found in the Word of God. People will either be ruled by their heart or by the sword. May it be that every Christian will endeavor to be heart led.

June 26 - Nothing New

As I read an old Special Issue 2006 copy of The Voice of The Martyrs I was captivated by a historical fact that I had never been aware of until now.

In my thinking, the United States was first attacked by Islamic hate mongers in February 1993 and again on the infamous 911 day of September 11, 2001 when, in fact, the first hostile act took place in 1785. The V.O.M. article, "Time to get on the train," is well worth reading and it included the following on page 3:

Americans were attacked by Muslims in 1785, before we even had a navy. Twenty-one American merchant soldiers had been kidnapped by Muslim pirates and held in Tripoli, Libya. One hundred fifteen were held in Algeria. The sailors who converted to Islam were given soft jobs. The ones who remained Christians had to crush rocks with hammers. Our new nation built its first navy so we could rescue these sailors in various battles lasting 12 years.

Did you notice, "The ones who remained Christians had to crush rocks with hammers."? When I read of Christians who will not yield their allegiance to Christ my eyes swell with tears because, unfortunately, there are way too few of them. To join such, one must come to know the tremendous price paid on Calvary's tree.

Iran's leader is spewing hatred and threats to annihilate Christian and Jew alike. If we think that this is just rhetoric we are sadly mistaken. As the Prime Minister of Israel, Benjamin Netanyahu, has said, reflecting upon the holocaust of Hitler's Nazi Germany, "When someone says that they are going to annihilate you - believe them."

What can the Christian do in times such as these? Join the Jihadists as hate mongers? Cower in fear? Avoid confrontation? Pretend that the problem will go away? No, We boldly proclaim the gospel in the power of the Spirit of grace. "We defeat the 'prophet of hate' when we share about the Prophet of Love."

Sharing the gospel with the lost, yes, even the Muslim lost, is what fulfills Luke 6:27-28 KJV: "But I say unto you which hear, Love your enemies, do good to them which hate you, Bless them that curse you, and pray for them which despitefully use you."

June 27 - Seeking Wealth - Speaking Peace

For Mordecai the Jew was next unto king Ahasuerus, and great among the Jews, and accepted of the multitude of his brethren, seeking the wealth of his people, and speaking peace to all his seed. Esther 10:3 (KJV)

Each and every Christian should realize that God wants to elevate them to places of governmental influence. Oh, I know, you don't "feel" called to politics. Well, be that as it may; you are still called to governmental influence.

John Maxwell has said, "Leadership is Influence, nothing more and nothing less." I couldn't agree more. Governmental influence is simply being willing to become a servant of people so that you can influence them.

This can take place in the home, the office, on the golf course, at the club, in church, through community volunteer service and/or in the political arena. What is important is that we be willing to let God place us where we can influence people for Christ. Christians are called to be salt and light in the midst of their respective societies.

This is so that the plan and purpose of God can be fulfilled and the harvest of souls can be brought in to the Father's embrace. This is what Jesus came, lived, shed His blood, was crucified, died, buried and raised from the dead for (Joh. 3:16).

Our goal should be that people have the leadership necessary to bring them righteousness, peace and joy in the Holy Ghost.

When the [uncompromisingly] righteous are in authority, the people rejoice; . . . Proverbs 29:2 (AMP)

Instead of seeking gain, authority or prestige for our own sake, we should be seeking to become all that our Lord Jesus died to provide in order to bring blessing to others.

We are to be a people who are "seeking the wealth of his people, and speaking peace to all his seed.." We have the words of life and understand the true prosperity that comes from the Prince of Peace Himself. We have the mind of Christ and the Word of life:

Let the word of Christ dwell in you richly in all wisdom; teaching and admonishing . . . Colossians 3:16 (KJV)

Let this year be a year of blessing others for His sake.

June 28 - All Fear Gone

I sought the Lord, and he heard me, and delivered me from all my fears. Psalm 34:4 (KJV)

Do you live a life without fear? If not, I want to give you the key to being fear free forever: Seek the Lord.

You must realize that ". . . God is love" (1 Joh. 4:8 KJV). *Theos*, God the Father, the first person in the trinity, Christ, The Son, the second person of the trinity, and the Holy Spirit, the third person in the trinity, esti, is and will always be love, *agape,* unconditional, unending love. This is expressed again in 1 John:

And we have known and believed the love that God hath to us. God is love; and he that dwelleth in love dwelleth in God, and God in him. 1 John 4:16 (KJV)

It's actually hidden away in one of the most well know verses in the Bible:

For God so loved the world, that he gave his only begotten Son, that whosoever believeth in him should not perish, but have everlasting life. John 3:16 (KJV)

God was, here, expressing His very nature toward mankind, specifically, you. After you accepted Him and His offer of Love, Jesus, He filled you with His Spirit of Love:

For God hath not given us the spirit of fear; but of power, and of love, and of a sound mind. 2 Timothy 1:7 (KJV)

The Lord wants you to know that fear is a spirit that has been replaced by His Spirit of power and love. His Spirit gives you a sound mind. F.E.A.R. is False Evidence Appearing Real and is played upon by demonic forces. Those forces were defeated at the Cross of Calvary and your victory over them was guaranteed there. Take a stand and know that you are in Christ, and Christ is in God Who is perfect love.

There is no fear in love; but perfect love casteth out fear . . . 1 John 4:18 (KJV)

King David understood the love of God and God as Love:

. . . whom shall I fear? the Lord is the strength of my life; of whom shall I be afraid? Psalm 27:1 (KJV)

When you receive the revelation of the love of God as David did, fear will be permanently put out of your life.

June 29 - One Thing Have I Desired

One thing have I desired of the Lord, that will I seek after; that I may dwell in the house of the Lord all the days of my life, to behold the beauty of the Lord, and to enquire in his temple. Psalm 27:4 (KJV)

There is only one thing that I desire, *lav sha'al* or *lav sha'el*, require, earnestly beg for and request of the Lord, *Yehovah*, "The Existing One," and that one thing I will seek after, *baqash*, as I seek His face.

My all consuming passion is to meet with Him and spend my life in, *yowm*, His house, His dwelling place, *bayith*, as one who is, *yashab*, married to Him and involved with His family and in His family affairs.

It is in this position of intimate fellowship that I can perceive with divine intelligence, *chazah*, and prophesy as one who sees in the ecstatic state of one who is in the spirit. Here, and only here, will I be able to provide an accurate prophetic glimpse into the things of God to those I minister to.

Here, in this place, I will behold, Men, *no'am*, the beauty, kindness, pleasantness, delightfulness, and favour of God and be able to, *baqar*, seek out, inquire of, and consider those things that are only found in the sanctuary of the heavenly temple, *heykal*, where He abides eternal.

He answered and said unto them, Because it is given unto you to know the mysteries of the kingdom of heaven, but to them it is not given. Matthew 13:11 (KJV)

And he said, Unto you it is given to know the mysteries of the kingdom of God: but to others in parables; that seeing they might not see, and hearing they might not understand. Luke 8:10 (KJV)

Beloved, the Father, Son and Holy Ghost, God Himself, is eagerly drawing you unto Himself in order to reveal to you the hidden mysteries of the kingdom found only in His abiding place.

June 30, 2013   Mysteries

For he that speaketh in an unknown tongue speaketh not unto men, but unto God: for no man understandeth him; howbeit in the spirit he speaketh mysteries.
1 Corinthians 14:2 (KJV)

The Greek word, **oudeis**, used here for, no man, simply means no man, woman nor anyone or anything; nothing. This is exciting in that this verse is telling us that no one and nothing but God, Himself, can understand what we are saying when we speak in the language of the Spirit.

God has provided a way for every believer to understand those things that are not understood by the natural mind. There are mysteries of the kingdom that only the spirit-filled believer will ever know. Even in the natural, Jesus spoke in parables to the unbelieving so that they would "hear yet not hear."

He answered and said unto them, Because it is given unto you to know the mysteries of the kingdom of heaven, but to them it is not given. Matthew 13:11 (KJV)

And he said, Unto you it is given to know the mysteries of the kingdom of God: but to others in parables; that seeing they might not see, and hearing they might not understand. Luke 8:10 (KJV)

The ministers of God are called, "stewards of the mysteries of God." How can they be stewards of that which they do not have? To ignore the command that Jesus gave in the book of Acts is a faithless position of rebellion (1 Cor. 4:1; Act 1:4).

Let the Holy Spirit reveal to you the mysteries of God as you cooperate with Him and allow Him to teach you to pray as you ought (Rom. 8:26).

JULY

July 01 - Commitment's Cost

For which of you, intending to build a tower, sitteth not down first, and counteth the cost, whether he have sufficient to finish it? Lest haply, after he hath laid the foundation, and is not able to finish it, all that behold it begin to mock him, Saying, This man began to build, and was not able to finish. Or what king, going to make war against another king, sitteth not down first, and consulteth whether he be able with ten thousand to meet him that cometh against him with twenty thousand? Or else, while the other is yet a great way off, he sendeth an ambassage, and desireth conditions of peace. So likewise, whosoever he be of you that forsaketh not all that he hath, he cannot be my disciple. Salt is good: but if the salt have lost his savour, wherewith shall it be seasoned? It is neither fit for the land, nor yet for the dunghill; but men cast it out. He that hath ears to hear, let him hear. Luke 14:28-35 (KJV)

Count the cost before you decide to make Jesus your Lord and Savior. He will not be your Savior if He cannot be your Lord.

If ye love me, keep my commandments. John 14:15

If ye keep my commandments, ye shall abide in my love; even as I have kept my Father's commandments, and abide in his love. John 15:10 (KJV)

Unfortunately, Christianity is marketed as a quick fix to a pressing problem when it is a needed fix for the sin sick human condition. To become a Christian is to be transformed by the blood of Jesus, the Lamb slain from the foundation of the world. The allowance for the old man is not tolerated because "all things become new" in Christ.

The grace of God is free, but not cheap by any stretch of the imagination and misappropriating its marvelous benefit leads to destruction.

Not every one that saith unto me, Lord, Lord, shall enter into the kingdom of heaven; but he that doeth the will of my Father which is in heaven. Many will say to me in that day, Lord, Lord, have we not prophesied in thy name? and in thy name have cast out devils? and in thy name done many wonderful works? And then will I profess unto them, I never knew you: depart from me, ye that work iniquity. Matthew 7:21-23 (KJV)

July 02- In Judah God Is Known

To the chief Musician on Neginoth, A Psalm or Song of Asaph. In Judah is God known: his name is great in Israel. Psalm 76:1 (KJV)

Jesus is the Lion of the tribe of Judah (Rev. 5:5). Judah, *Yehuwdah*, literally means "praised." This tribe descended from Judah the son of Jacob. The kingdom of Judah was comprised of the tribes of Judah and Benjamin which occupied the southern part of Canaan after the nation split upon the death of Solomon.

It would be reasonable and acceptable to say, "God, *'elohiym* (Father, Son and Holy Ghost), the true God is known. The Hebrew word, *yada`*, is a word that speaks of intimate knowledge. By it we understand that in praise, the One True God can be accurately perceived and seen, found out and discerned. The believing seeker who praises God can expect to know Him by experience and to be instructed by and acquainted with Him to the degree that God will make Himself known by revelatory declaration: ". . . the words that I speak unto you, they are spirit, and they are life" (Joh. 6:63 KJV).

In the following verse we come to understand that if we take praise to the next level of a, *tehillah*, praise song that expresses our praise, adoration, and thanksgiving (paid to God), His very Presence will come and settle down within us and He will be as One married to, and living with, us.

But thou art holy, O thou that inhabitest the praises of Israel. Psalm 22:3 (KJV)

This is one of the most wonderful, comforting and strengthening truths revealed to those who express their love for Him and to Him according to the teachings of the Word of God.

His desire is for you and I to love Him as completely as He loves us and to express that love through praise.

July 03 - Repair the Altar

Then Elijah said to all the people, Come near to me. And all the people came near him. And he repaired the [old] altar of the Lord that had been broken down [by Jezebel]. 1 Kings 18:30 (AMP)

Many people say, "Come near to me," but have nothing to give them once they do..

Whoso boasteth himself of a false gift is like clouds and wind without rain. Proverbs 25:14 (KJV)

A true man or woman of God will only gather people to build or restore the altar in their hearts.

The goal of church planters (Apostles) is to establish a "pillar and ground of truth" that will win the lost, connect them to Jesus and His Church, train (disciple) them so that they grow in grace and can be sent to do the same.

... the house of God, which is the church of the living God, the pillar and ground of the truth.
1 Timothy 3:15 (KJV)

When this happens the Word of God (Water) is preached, the gifts of the Spirit are present (Wind), and the fire of God falls (Glory /Anointing).

Water:

That he might sanctify and cleanse it with the washing of water by the word, Ephesians 5:26 (KJV)

Wind:

Quench not the Spirit. 1 Thessalonians 5:19 (KJV)

And these signs shall follow them that believe; In my name shall they cast out devils; they shall speak with new tongues; They shall take up serpents; and if they drink any deadly thing, it shall not hurt them; they shall lay hands on the sick, and they shall recover. Mark 16:17-18 (KJV)

Fire:

And it shall come to pass in that day, that his burden shall be taken away from off thy shoulder, and his yoke from off thy neck, and the yoke shall be destroyed because of the anointing. Isaiah 10:27 (KJV)

July 04 - When the Righteous Rule

When the [uncompromisingly] righteous are in authority, the people rejoice; but when the wicked man rules, the people groan and sigh. Proverbs 29:2 (AMP)

Our great nation was founded by "righteous" men who believed that they were "endowed by their Creator with inalienable rights."

The United States Declaration of Independence, which was primarily drafted by Thomas Jefferson, was adopted by the Second Continental Congress on July 4, 1776. The text of the second section of the Declaration of Independence reads,

"We hold these truths to be self-evident, that all men are created equal, that they are endowed by their Creator with certain inalienable Rights, that among these are Life, Liberty and the pursuit of Happiness."

When our founding fathers signed this great document they understood that they were created after the image and likeness of Almighty God Himself. This great truth was the foundation that would allow this nation to become great. God was honored and the principles of life being precious, each individual being created to live free and to have the right to pursue happiness was understood and revered.

Jesus, the Only Begotten Son of God, gave his life for humanity that they might have the opportunity to choose the "life and life more abundantly" that He promised to all who would come to Him.

His example caused many men and women to give their lives to provide and protect the right of Americans to have life, liberty and the pursuit of happiness written of in the Declaration of Independence.

The right to maintain life, liberty and to pursue happiness does not come without cost but is purchased at a great price. Men and women who hold the self evident truth of our nation being One Nation Under God have paid with the shedding of their blood, even unto death, to insure that the dream of America would remain for all who come after them.

Today, I pray for righteous leaders who will remember and honor them and bring us back to the God who alone will keep & guide us.

July 05 - A Kingdom Divided Will Not Stand

And Jesus knew their thoughts, and said unto them, Every kingdom divided against itself is brought to desolation; and every city or house divided against itself shall not stand: Matthew 12:25 (KJV)

Way too often, some give Jesus, the Christ of God, attributes that He most likely did not avail Himself of while He walked the earth. One idea that is held, especially among Pentecostal believers, is that Jesus could read the minds of those who were with Him. After all, it is said, "He is God."

While it is true that He was (is) fully God and fully Man, the Scripture tells us in Philippians 2:8 that He, *kenoo*, made His being God of none effect, and deprived of force His God nature to walk among men as man. This word translated "He made Himself of no reputation" carries the thought that He laid aside equality with, and the form of, God.

Where our text reads, "And Jesus knew their thoughts," many suppose that He read the minds of those He was with. The word, *eido*, however, leaves the impression that this knowing was more that of perceiving with the eyes, paying attention to or observing with the senses. If He did, indeed, know their thoughts, it was because the Father showed Him by His Spirit what they were thinking (Psa. 44:21; Psa. 94:11; Acts 15:8; 1 Cor. 2:11; 1 Cor. 3:20). Jesus communion with the Father was such that He only spoke and did what He heard and saw (John 8:28; 12:49; 14:10).

It is within the context of His human obedience to the Divine dictate that He teaches the danger of a kingdom, *basileia*, divided. This kingdom is not to be confused with an actual kingdom but rather the right or authority to rule over a kingdom. This is speaking of the royal power and dignity conferred on Christians in the Messiah's kingdom.

The believer must be in the total agreement and harmony with the word (will) of God that produces willing and immediate obedience. A double-minded Christian cannot stand.

July 06 - A House Of Prayer

And said unto them, It is written, My house shall be called the house of prayer; but ye have made it a den of thieves. Matthew 21:13 (KJV)

Jesus called the gathering place for the Church, "My House." During these times of emphasis on the "House Church" we must remember the "Temple."

And day after day they regularly assembled in the temple with united purpose, and in their homes they broke bread [including the Lord's Supper] . . . Acts 2:46 (AMP)

The regular gathering in the "temple" took place daily even as did the gatherings for fellowship and communion in individual homes.

I pray that we can learn from past mistakes and not "throw out the baby with the bath." The Holy Spirit is not leading people to homes in lieu of the church. It is not a matter of "either - or." The people of God are actually being called to more participation in church as well as more relationship and participation with each other.

Today, the Church is becoming complacent, self-seeking and self-serving. There is a "What's in it for me" attitude that must be done away with. The people of God are sleeping through the very things that are most important to their Lord.

And he cometh unto the disciples, and findeth them asleep, and saith unto Peter, What, could ye not watch with me one hour? Matthew 26:40 (KJV)

The Church should find its rooms filled with people of prayer who are seeking the face of God to learn the will and ways of God in this hour. There should be a renewal of holy fervor.

Even them will I bring to my holy mountain, and make them joyful in my house of prayer: their burnt offerings and their sacrifices shall be accepted upon mine altar; for mine house shall be called an house of prayer for all people. Isaiah 56:7 (KJV)

July 07 - He Cured Them

And the blind and the lame came to him in the temple;
and he healed them. Matthew 21:14 (KJV)

This verse follows the record of Jesus coming into the
temple in Jerusalem and declaring it to be the house of God. It
was His house and His house is meant to be the house of prayer.
The temple, the church building, the gathering of the *Ecclesia*, is
to be "the house of God," and "the house of prayer."
It was to that place where the, *tuphlos*, physically blind, or
mentally blind man and a man who was, *cholos*, lame due to
being maimed, deprived of a foot came to meet with Him.
Beloved, whether you are in need of a physical or mental
miracle from God, Jesus will meet you in the house of God that
is a house of prayer.
Just because there are buildings where people gather who
"hold a form of piety (true religion)," realize that there are those
who "deny and reject and are strangers to the power of it [their
conduct belies the genuineness of their profession]". Don't get
discouraged and give up. Simply avoid [all] such people" and
[turn away from them]" (2 Tim. 3:5 AMP).
Jesus said, "I will build My church, and the gates of Hades
(the powers of the infernal region) shall not overpower it [or
be strong to its detriment or hold out against it]" (Mat.16:18
AMP). There assemblies of faith-filled believers where Christ is
building His Church. Find one of those and go there.
He will meet each person who comes to Him in that kind
of place. "He healed them." Jesus, *therapeuo*, served them by
healing, curing, and restoring them to health. Both came, both
had different needs, and both were met with a miracle.

For God shows no partiality [undue favor or unfairness;
with Him one man is not different from another].
Romans 2:11 (AMP)

July 08 - Qualified And Fit

Giving thanks unto the Father, which hath made us meet to be partakers of the inheritance of the saints in light: Colossians 1:12 (KJV)

No one should be more thankful than a born-again, spirit-filled Christian! Life just doesn't get any better than that.

Unless, of course, that Christian is trying to live a "Christian" life in the flesh. That, my beloved friend, is torture, not the blessing of "righteousness, and peace, and joy in the Holy Ghost" (Rom. 14:17 KJV). This is because the life of the spirit is not meant to be lived by fleshly self-will. It can only be lived and enjoyed as it is lived out by the Spirit of God in the power of the resurrected Christ.

It was the sacrifice of God's only begotten Son, Jesus, that made atonement for our sin. It is the shed blood of the Lamb slain from the foundation of the world that cleanses us from all unrighteousness (Rev. 5:12; 13:8).

We can give thanks unto the Father because He has made us "meet," *hikanoo*, able, made sufficient, rendered fit, equipped us with adequate power to perform the duties of Himself. He did it, does it, and will continue to do it! Get over you. It's all about Him, His love and His power working within.

We are now fit to be the recipients, "partakers," *meris*, of an assigned part, a portion, and share of the "inheritance," *kleros*, of the portion of the ministry common to the apostles together with the part which one will have in eternal salvation which God has assigned to the saints "in light." This, *en phos,* is to be permanently shining or making manifest the heavenly light of God. This is the power to understand the Divine standard of moral and spiritual truth.

We can be thankful because it has been given to us to know the riches of His grace, the unsearchable riches of Christ, the riches of His glory, the mysteries of God which had been hidden from the foundation of the world, and to be partakers with Him of all that the Father has laid up in store for them that believe (Luk. 12:32 KJV).

July 09 - Study

Study to shew thyself approved unto God, a workman that needeth not to be ashamed, rightly dividing the word of truth. 2 Timothy 2:15 (KJV)

The word "Study" is the Greek word, *spoudazo,* which encourages us to exert ourselves, to endeavor, with do diligence, to learn the things of God in order to be "approved," *dokimos,* in the sense of being tried and found to be trusted with the truth of God's Word. The word was used in Jesus' time of money changers that were men of integrity, men that could be trusted to only deal in real, rather than counterfeit, money [Donald Barnhouse].

It is no wonder that this terminology is used when we compare it with that found in Philippians 1:10. The Amplified Bible version reads:

Approve and prize what is excellent and of real value [recognizing the highest and the best, and distinguishing the moral differences], and that you may be untainted and pure and unerring and blameless [so that with hearts sincere and certain and unsullied, you may approach] the day of Christ [not stumbling nor causing others to stumble].

This agrees with Proverbs 23:12:

Apply thine heart unto instruction, and thine ears to the words of knowledge. Proverbs 23:12 (KJV)

This diligent approach to the Word of God will enable us to "rightly divide" its message and intent.

For instance: To who is the text written? About who, or what people, is it written? The verse below is a good example for us to consider in light of world events today:

So that you may surely learn to sense what is vital, and Give none offence, neither to the Jews, nor to the Gentiles, nor to the church of God: 1 Corinthians 10:32 (KJV)

There are three people groups that God is dealing with in the earth. The Jews, the Gentiles and the Church. He has established an unbreakable covenant with the Jews and another with the Church. He has promised to deal with the Nations (Gentiles), or the people opposed to God and His Christ.

July 10 - Giving and Restitution

And Zacchaeus stood, and said unto the Lord; Behold, Lord, the half of my goods I give to the poor; and if I have taken any thing from any man by false accusation, I restore him fourfold. Luke 19:8 (KJV)

In verse six of the same chapter we read, "he . . . received him (Jesus) joyfully."

There is a total change of nature and character that takes place in a person who receives Jesus the Christ as Lord and Savior. The reception of such a lavish gift as the indwelling Person of the Holy Ghost (bringing Father, Son and Holy Ghost to abide within the believer) releases a spirit of giving and restitution.

This should not seem strange to us in that the love of God has been "shed abroad in our hearts" (Rom. 5:5 KJV). Recipients of God's love cannot but be dispensers of God's love.

Love, first of all, gives at its own expense for the benefit of another. We see Zacchaeus immediately knowing that it is his privilege to give for the benefit of others. Every born-again Christian should experience a release of the spirit of giving in their lives. Self-centeredness leaves and other-awareness enters the heart of those who are Christ's.

The desire to make restitution is the second awakening in the newly regenerated spirit man. Wanting to make right what has been damaged by the actions of our sin nature. This is not just feeling sorry for wrongs done to others, but a heart felt yearning to make it right. Zacchaeus second thought was to "restore him fourfold."

He did not consider how little he could get by with, but, for him, was expansive in his offer to make restitution that would settle any account against him. He realized, to some degree, the magnitude of the gift that Jesus had offered him.

This man of small physical stature had become of giant stature in the of the things of God.

The revelation of giving and restitution had permeated his being and attested to the fact that he was truly a new man.

July 11 - Seek and Save

For the Son of man is come to seek and to save that which was lost. Luke 19:10 (KJV)

Every person that says the "sinners prayer" should be taught the first things first. All too often the Church wants to immediately teach them all about the gifts of the Spirit (which can't be received by an unbeliever anyway), how to serve in the church meetings and that they should act a certain way (which tells them that they can live the Christian life carnally), when what they need is to learn what happened when they said "the prayer," what that means to them and how they can grow in the power and grace of the Spirit.

Vince Lombardi, famous Green Bay Packer football coach used to start every season by getting his team together, holding up a football, and saying, "This, is a football."

He had Super Bowl quality football teams because he never took for granted what anyone on the team knew or didn't know. Every season, he went back to the basics.

Never assume that because a person has been in church for a season that they are saved. Go back to the basics with them and confirm their salvation. If there is any hesitancy in their knowledge of what it means to be saved, or any question in their minds about who Jesus is, get back to the basics. Get in to the Word of God and show them what it says. This is biblical "confirmation."

Don't ever quit protecting, nurturing and caring for the new believer until he can stand on the Word and kneel in prayer on his own. You wouldn't leave a natural baby to fend for itself would you? Even then, be available to mentor and, most of all, live a life that will be an example so that you can say, "Be ye followers of me, even as I also am of Christ" (1 Cor. 11:1 KJV).

Once your new babe in Christ knows that he is saved, teach him what he is saved for: To win souls. Every true believer is brought into the kingdom to "seek and to save that which was lost." This will immediately give this new life purpose, without which, there will be no growth, no life, and no zeal whatsoever. It will take the new believer's mind off of himself and focus it where it belongs: Working the works of God (Joh. 14:12).

July 12 - Say So

Let the redeemed of the Lord say so, whom he hath redeemed from the hand of the enemy; Psalm 107:2 (KJV)

Nothing is more important than the testimony of the believer. Each follower of Christ must learn that they are called to proclaim the good news to a lost and dying world.

The most effective way that they can do this is to begin by telling the story of their born-again experience; how they came to know Christ and what that encounter has done in their lives.

The power of their witness cannot be over emphasized. The blood of Jesus is mingled with their words and the devil, and his devices, is overcome.

And they overcame him by the blood of the Lamb, and by the word of their testimony; and they loved not their lives unto the death. Revelation 12:11(KJV)

Do you protect yourself by shying away from witnessing to others what God in Christ has done for you? Beloved, you hold the salvation of a multitude in your mouth. Your words will determine the eternal destiny of those with whom you are in contact.

If you are one of the redeemed of the Lord, it is time that you began to move in the power of the Holy Spirit and say so. There is no more fulfilling act on earth than that of leading a lost soul to Christ Jesus. Your testimony will bring many to their moment of decision. Think about it: Would you be saved if no one had witnessed to you? Would you be living the life you live today if no one had cared enough to share the riches of Christ with you? Of course not. Someone cared enough to pray for you and witness to you.

The Lord even provide a special enduement of power to bring release to those who are held captive by sin.

But you shall receive power (ability, efficiency, and might) when the Holy Spirit has come upon you, and you shall be My witnesses in Jerusalem and all Judea and Samaria and to the ends (the very bounds) of the earth. Acts 1:8 (AMP)

July 13 - He Sent His Word

He sent his word, and healed them, and delivered them from their destructions. Psalm 107:20 (KJV)

The Everlasting Father, God, *shalach*, sent forth from Himself (or stretched Himself out and let go of) His, *dabar*, spoken commandment, or Word, in order to, *rapha'* (or *raphah*}, be their physician who heals their physical bodies and makes healthful their thoughts and emotions by healing their individual distresses.

He also heals the hurts and corrects the defects of nations and restores them to favor.

God also delivered, *malat*, them and causes them to slip away and escape speedily from, *shachiyth,* the destructions of the pit.

We can understand, *dabar*, the spoken Word of God to refer to Jesus the, *logos*, in this case, the Word, uttered by the Living Voice, as we see in John 1:1.

There, *logos*, denotes the essential Word of God, who is Jesus the Christ of God. He is the personal wisdom and power in union with God and the Minister of the Godhead in creation and government of the universe.

As the Strong's Concordance in the Online Bible states, He is "the cause of all the world's life both physical and ethical, which for the procurement of man's salvation put on human nature in the person of Jesus the Messiah, the second person in the Godhead, and shone forth conspicuously from His words and deeds."

"This term was familiar to the Jews and in their writings long before a Greek philosopher named Heraclitus used the term *Logos* around 600 B.C. to designate the divine reason or plan which coordinates a changing universe. This word was well suited to the writer's purpose in John 1.

Jesus, the Word, was sent to heal and deliver. He is the same yesterday, today and forever.

July 14 - Happy New Year !!!

"In July?", you say, "I always knew there was something strange about that guy in Las Vegas."

I can't help it. My spiritual clock seems to be set so that it winds down in mid-July. The Lord re-calibrates, oils, re-directs, and sets me in motion for the next twelve months by the first of August each year.

July is Jubilee time for me.

I realize that the Hebrew calendar is not the same as the one on my wall but perhaps Leviticus 25:9 can shed light on this phenomenon:

Then shalt thou cause the trumpet of the jubilee to sound on the tenth day of the seventh month, in the day of atonement shall ye make the trumpet sound throughout all your land. Leviticus 25:9 (KJV)

Jubilee is an acclamation of joy or a battle-cry. It is a time for the blowing of trumpets, rejoicing, and shouts of triumph and victory. It is also a time of breaking and breaking forth.

Every July Sharon and I draw aside with God. It is always a time of breaking old, outdated, patterns and habits and a breaking forth of fresh new revelation, bearing, and strength.

God is always so faithful to meet us and bring us into refreshing streams of rest that culminate in glorious times of triumphant celebration.

Our prayer is that you also will take extra time this month to seek the Fathers face. Together we will enter His rest as we listen, with our spiritual ear, for the sound of the shofar [trumpet] marking the beginning of jubilee.

Then, Beloved, we shall go forth to together "to proclaim liberty to the [physical and spiritual] captives and the opening of the prison and of the eyes to those who are bound . . .To proclaim the acceptable year of the Lord [the year of His favor], . . . that He may be glorified."[Isa 61:1-3]

July 15 - They Steadfastly Persevered

And they continued stedfastly in the apostles' doctrine and fellowship, and in breaking of bread, and in prayers. Acts 2:42 (KJV)

Continuing, persisting and being faithful to something over the long haul seems to be a lost art. The Christian is called to be faithful to, not only sound doctrine, but fellowship, communion and prayers.

In our verse for today we see the word "continued" used as the translators choice. This Greek word, *en*, can also be understood as were taught and were standing. So, they were taught the apostles doctrine and were standing steadfastly, *proskartereo*, in it. They were continuing steadfastly, attending continually to, and adhering to with great attention to every detail of what they were being taught. The word gives us the idea that they even showed great courage as they walked out what they were taught.

This kind of Christianity is foreign to most Westerners (North Americans). There is no room for the pick and choose variety of being a Christian that is seen in, and out, of most churches. If people do go to church it's on their own terms. Many opt out of "Church" because they don't think it has any relevance to their lives. This is simply selfishness; an unwillingness to give the Lord the time and attention He deserves.

This is certainly not biblical Christianity! Fellowship and communion, *koinonia*, are one and the same and are included in sound doctrine. This Greek word, *koinonia*, means fellowship, association, community, communion, joint participation, intercourse, the share which one has in anything, participation, intimacy, a gift jointly contributed, a collection, a contribution, as exhibiting an embodiment and proof of fellowship. Herein is the gathering of believers who steadfastly, as friends, eat together and offer prayers together.

July 16 - The Fire of The Lord

Hear me, O Lord, hear me, that this people may know that You, the Lord, are God, and have turned their hearts back [to You]. Then the fire of the Lord fell and consumed the burnt sacrifice and the wood and the stones and the dust, and also licked up the water that was in the trench. When all the people saw it, they fell on their faces and they said, The Lord, He is God! The Lord, He is God!
1 Kings 18:37-39 (AMP)

When there is a passion in one's heart that people might know the one true God, there will be a demonstration of His glory.

Beloved, when we build an altar in our hearts for the Lord, we are preparing ourselves for His fire to fall. When we offer ourselves as a living sacrifice to the Lord on that altar, we are preparing the way of the Lord for His fire to fall. When we soak our lives in the Water of the Word, we are setting the atmosphere for the Lord to rain holy fire upon our lives. God will send His holy flame and consume you with His love and power.

He will receive His Word as it is offered back to Him in faith and He will bring the fire of revival to the multitudes. When all the people around you see it, they will fall on their faces and say, "The Lord, He is God! The Lord, He is God!" as surely as they did when Elijah challenged the prophets of Baal.

As you consecrate yourself (set yourself apart for the Lord) you will usher in the greatest harvest of souls that the world has ever seen. Heaven's glory and power will be drawn to you and released through you during this great hour of the visitation of Almighty God Himself.

As it has been said, "God will not only show up, but He will show off" as He manifests His Presence in and through your life.

July 17 - My House

And said unto them, It is written, My house shall be called the house of prayer; but ye have made it a den of thieves. Matthew 21:13 (KJV)

Jesus called the gathering place for the Church, "My House." During these times of emphasis on the "House Church" we must remember the "Temple."

And day after day they regularly assembled in the temple with united purpose, and in their homes they broke bread [including the Lord's Supper]. . . Acts 2:46 (AMP)

The regular gathering in the "temple" took place daily even as did the gatherings for fellowship and communion in individual homes. My prayer is that we can learn from past mistakes and not "throw out the baby with the bath." The Holy Spirit is not leading people to homes in lieu of the church.

It is not a matter of "either or." The people of God are actually being called to more participation in church as well as more relationship and participation with each other.

Today, the Church has become complacent, self-seeking and self-serving. There is a "What's in it for me" attitude that must be done away with. The people of God are sleeping through the very things that are most important to their Lord.

And he cometh unto the disciples, and findeth them asleep, and saith unto Peter, What, could ye not watch with me one hour? Matthew 26:40 (KJV)

The Church should find its rooms filled with people of prayer who are seeking the face of God to learn the will and ways of God in this hour. There needs to be a renewal of holy fervor.

Even them will I bring to my holy mountain, and make them joyful in my house of prayer: their burnt offerings and their sacrifices shall be accepted upon mine altar; for mine house shall be called an house of prayer for all people. Isaiah 56:7 (KJV)

July 18 - Think On These Things

Finally, brethren, whatsoever things are true, whatsoever things are honest, whatsoever things are just, whatsoever things are pure, whatsoever things are lovely, whatsoever things are of good report; if there be any virtue, and if there be any praise, think on these things. Philippians 4:8 (KJV)

The Christian has been given the mind of Christ (1 Cor. 2:16) and a sound, well disciplined mind (2 Tim. 1:7), therefore, we are to make godly choices about what to think.

The right choices will cause our thoughts to seek out those things that are true. Actually, this word, *alethes*, calls us to be lovers of truth and those that speak the truth. We are to be lovers of those of honorable character, *semnos*, and who live lives in keeping with the commands of God, just, *dikaios*, and are, therefore in right standing with Him.

Pure things, *hagnos*, are those which excite reverence and are pure from carnality, chaste, clean, modest and without falsity. Those things that are, *prosphiles*, lovely, that is, acceptable and pleasing are also to be considered.

We are to set our minds on those things that are, *euphemos*, of good report. In other words, only listening to, or speaking, words that are favorable and bring about good success.

We are to seek out those things that, *arete*, bring about a virtuous course of thought, feeling and action or have to do with any particular moral excellence, such as modesty or purity. In every situation and as concerns everyone that we come in contact with, we should seek to find what is, *epainos*, praise worthy and commendable.

How different would be our lives and the lives of those with whom we spend our time each day if we would just "think on these things."

July 19 - My God Shall Supply

But my God shall supply all your need according to his riches in glory by Christ Jesus. Philippians 4:19 (KJV)

Paul is saying here that his God will supply the need of those who financially support his work in ministry. The Greek word, *pleroo*, used for "shall supply" means, to make full, to fill to the full, to cause to abound, to furnish or supply liberally. He is setting forth the biblical promise of partnership supply. In the previous few verses he has stated that he is more interested in the benefit that the giver receives than he is in receiving himself.

He knows that those who have supported him will be liberally supplied so that nothing shall be wanting to full measure. This is the word of God that cannot return to Him void and His plan to finance evangelistic discipleship (Mat. 28:18).

Every thing needful, *chreia*, or any necessity that you or I may have will be taken care of according to, *autos*, the Baffling Wind Himself and the, *ploutos*, fulness, abundance and plenitude of that with which He is enriched. *doxa*, in the sense of the absolute perfection of God as revealed in the personal excellency of Christ and the majesty to which He was raised after he had achieved his work on earth.

Now, that is a mouthful. Everything needful for you and Me is found in the glorious magnificence, excellence, preeminence, dignity, and grace of Christ Jesus. This is the full supply found in the glorious condition of blessedness to which true Christian partnership is privy. We receive now, in this life, and much more so after the Savior's return from heaven.

Nothing could more support this verse in Luke:

Give, and it shall be given unto you; good measure, pressed down, and shaken together, and running over, shall men give into your bosom. For with the same measure that ye mete withal it shall be measured to you again. Luke 6:38 (KJV).

July 20 - Entering the Kingdom

And when Jesus saw that he was very sorrowful, he said, How hardly shall they that have riches enter into the kingdom of God! Luke 18:24 (KJV)

One of the saddest things that exists today is the man or woman who has set their trust in the things they have. The majority of Christians in the Western World have their focus on the blessings of God more than the God of the blessings. In their rush to be rich in the richest country in the world, they have become poor.

Because thou sayest, I am rich, and increased with goods, and have need of nothing; and knowest not that thou art wretched, and miserable, and poor, and blind, and naked: I counsel thee to buy of me gold tried in the fire, that thou mayest be rich; and white raiment, that thou mayest be clothed, and that the shame of thy nakedness do not appear; and anoint thine eyes with eyesalve, that thou mayest see. Revelation 3:17-18 (KJV)

Nothing is more difficult to someone who trusts in their material wealth than to yield to the call of God to tithe (give ten-percent) on their increase, let alone, give over and above as an offering.

A person does not have to be rich to fall into the trap that the money they earn is theirs, and theirs alone, and that it is all they need to succeed. In fact even someone who is broke can have the same mentality. It is a blindness that must be healed in order to operate in, and receive, the blessing of God.

Are material things to be had and enjoyed? Of course they are. Our God has given us everything to enjoy.

Charge them that are rich in this world, that they be not highminded, nor trust in uncertain riches, but in the living God, who giveth us richly all things to enjoy; 1 Timothy 6:17 (KJV)

July 21 - Make the Master Rich

And he called his ten servants, and delivered them ten pounds, and said unto them, Occupy till I come.
Luke 19:13 (KJV)

It might be good to read Luke 19:12-27 and consider the call of Jesus to "Occupy till I come."

The Greek word, *pragmateuomai*, which is translated, "occupy," can be understood to mean, to be occupied in anything, to carry on a business, or to carry on the business of a banker or a trader. The concept that Jesus was teaching is that of bringing increase to the one who gave you your initial resource. This would include the resources of finance, gifts and talents, life and, certainly, the new life that comes with being born-again. Let me focus on the latter.

The initial promise to Abram (who became Abraham), the father of faith (Gal. 3:7 KJV), was that he would become the father of a multitude, innumerable as the stars of the sky. This promise has been fulfilled in his Seed Christ Jesus (Gal. 3:16). All he had to do was believe God and "Occupy till I come."

All the ten servants in Jesus' parable had to do was believe God and occupy until their Master came. Their occupation was to increase that which they had been given; no more and no less. Each was held accountable to their own ability and the resource given.

You see, Beloved, God does not ask more increase of you than He has given you resource and ability to work with. Don't measure your effectiveness by anyone else. Just be faithful with what you are given "til [He] come," *erchomai*. In our case this can be understood to mean until He be revealed at His returning. Jesus is coming back.

Will you have occupied and increased when He comes? Will you have sown His seed and be able to present Him with the precious sheaves of the earth? (Psa. 126:6)

July 22 - Kept

He will keep the feet of his saints, and the wicked shall be silent in darkness; for by strength shall no man prevail. 1 Samuel 2:9 (KJV)

Our Father watches over you and I, the objects of His affection, the apples of His eye, with care.

He found him in a desert land, and in the waste howling wilderness; he led him about, he instructed him, he kept him as the apple of his eye. Deuteronomy 32:10 (KJV)

His promise in 1 Samuel is to "keep," *shamar*, guard, keep watch and ward, protect and save the life of as a Watchman who observes and celebrates those cared for. He will "keep" the "feet," *regel*, the times and the complete journey of, according to the pace of perfection.

No weapon formed nor word spoken against you will prosper (Isa. 54:17) because the wicked, *rasha`*, the ungodly (who are hostile toward God or man) will be silenced, *damam*, struck dumb and destroyed.

We know that our strength and our weapons of warfare are supernatural. No one succeeds by human strength, *koach* (or *kowach*), wealth or demonic power. Those who belong to the Lord, however, have His strength, the help of the Holy Ghost and are strengthened by the ministry of angels.

Then he answered and spake unto me, saying, This is the word of the Lord unto Zerubbabel, saying, Not by might, nor by power, but by my spirit, saith the Lord of hosts. Zechariah 4:6 (KJV)

Be assured that the Lord is with you, leading and guiding by His Spirit and carefully watching over you. What ever you set you hand to will prosper

If it had not been the Lord who was on our side, when men rose up against us . . . - but - Our help is in the name of the Lord, who made heaven and earth. Psalm 124:2, 8 (KJV)

July 23 - Say What You Pray

And all things, whatsoever ye shall ask in prayer, believing, ye shall receive. Matthew 21:22 (KJV)

There is a great emphasis here on "all things," *pas*, being understood to be "whatsoever," *an hosos*, with the inclusion of "whosoever," as many as, whatsoever things, how great as, as far as, how much, how many, whoever.

The whole idea is that there is nothing left out, nothing excluded, nothing that will be unanswerable when you ask, *aiteo*, ask for what you desire, require and crave, even to the point of begging if need be.

Our asking takes on great power of influence when we ask, *en*, from (or "in") a (fixed) position (in place, time or state - as in a place or state of faith), and a relation of rest. The supplicate is resting in faith towards the One who has absolute authority and ability to bring into being, or bring to pass, what is asked for.

This prayer, *proseuche*, is a prayer addressed to God in a condition where the one praying cannot be distracted (as if in a place set apart for prayer). The "rest" comes as a result of faith, or as it reemphasizes, believing, *pisteuo*, a believing that commits the thing asked for to (one's) trust - here, the request is committed unto God Himself.

Having committed the request to God Himself, we place full confidence in receiving the answer. We think it to be true, and are persuaded of our answer to the degree that we credit it as done.

The believer, in this position of prayer, receives every time. "Ye shall receive." This is positive and powerful as can be seen in the use of the Greek word, *lambano*, which takes, as though with the hand, lays hold of, any person or thing in order to use it. In other words, one takes up a thing by faith and speaks of it as already being in their possession.

July 24 - Tradition

He replied to them, and why also do you transgress and violate the commandment of God for the sake of the rules handed down to you by your forefathers (the elders)? Matthew 15:3 (AMP)

The Church, so called, of America has drifted so far off from the core values of its inception and the original intention of God that it is no longer recognizable. The visible "Church" has devolved into nothing more than an irreligious community completely devoid of any understanding of God, His Word, or of the Son of God who said, "I will build My Church" (Mat. 16:18 KJV). Jesus has nothing to do with most of what is now called "Church."

Tradition has taken the place of Scripture. Please don't misunderstand me here; I believe in tradition where it has biblical foundation but when men set their hand to establishing tradition after their own unregenerate minds, there is a serious problem.

. . . ye made the commandment of God of none effect by your tradition. Matthew 15:6 (KJV)

Tradition has replaced heart felt worship with liturgical counterfeits. The gifts of the Spirit have been replaced with the imitations devised by man. We use sight and sound to generate an atmosphere that should be filled with dreams, visions, the songs of angels and, most of all, the Voice of the Almighty and the trumpet sound of His prophets.

Signs, wonders and miracles are things relegated to the past by unbelieving "shepherds" or have been replaced with the demonic manipulations of New Age practitioners.

What can be done? What if we soaked ourselves in the Word of God? What if we believed the biblical record? What if we lived by its precepts? What if we soaked ourselves in the presence of the Holy Ghost in seasons of prayer? What if we assembled together regularly and expected the Lord to meet with us? What if this was our cherished and lifestyle tradition?

July 25 - Who Do You Say That He Is?

He saith unto them, But whom say ye that I am?
Matthew 16:15 (KJV)

Who do you say that Jesus is? A great teacher? A powerful prophet? A charismatic personality?

He was and is all of these and more. He was and is and ever will be the Son of the Living God, the Messiah of Israel, the Savior of the world. He is the Seed of the Woman, Emmanuel, the One born of a Virgin, whose name is Wonderful, Counselor, The Mighty God, The Everlasting Father, The Prince of Peace (Isa. 9:6 KJV).

Let us not agree that He was a great teacher unless we can proclaim that He was, and is, The Way, The Truth and The Life without whom none can know God (Joh. 14:6 KJV). He is the Teacher who answered the high priest's question, "Art thou the Christ, the Son of the Blessed?," by saying, "I am: and ye shall see the Son of man sitting on the right hand of power, and coming in the clouds of heaven" (Mar. 14:61-62 KJV). He could not have been a "great teacher" unless He taught the truth. He was either a mad man or He was, indeed, the Son of God and Savior of the world.

We cannot agree that He was a powerful prophet unless we are willing to bow our knee to Him and confess that He is Lord, the Christ of God, for He spoke of fulfilling all that was written of Him and what He spoke concerning Himself as the Lamb slain from the foundation of the world came to pass exactly as He said.

We cannot agree that He was just a charismatic personality in that no natural man had ever done, nor would ever do, what He did but by His Spirit (Joh. 14:12). So great His impact on the whole earth that time itself is divided by His time here.

We must ask ourselves, "Who do we say that He is?" in the presence of all for the issues of eternal life rest upon our answer.

July 26 - Who Is This?

And when he was come into Jerusalem, all the city was moved, saying, Who is this? Matthew 21:10 (KJV)

What do people say about you when you show up on the scene? Is there a sense that someone of a different order has come to church? Does the atmosphere take on a certain air of expectancy when you arrive? Is the Holy Spirit evident in your life?

Whether Jesus came into a house or a city there was a ripple of wonder that ran through the people. "All the city was moved," tells us that no ordinary man had come. Did they question, "Who is this?" because of His deity or because He was a Man filled with the Holy Ghost and in relationship with the Father like none had ever been before Him?

I submit to you that He was walking as a man. Oh, Yes, I know that He was very man and very God, but the Scripture tells me that He became a man who depended upon the Spirit of God to empower and lead Him just like you and me. He said that the works He did were not of His own doing but of the Father which was in Him.

He told us that we would do what He did if we would but enter into a relationship with the Father through Him. We are to be like Him on the earth; filled with the Spirit, knowing God and doing exploits that will glorify Him.

Verily, verily, I say unto you, He that believeth on me, the works that I do shall he do also; and greater works than these shall he do; because I go unto my Father. John 14:12 (KJV)

When you or I walk into a room or a city we should cause a stir in the spiritual realm that will cause people, angels and demons to be moved and to say, "Who is this?" We should manifest the resurrected Christ Who is the greater One within us.

July 27 - Let My Prayer Be Set Forth

Let my prayer be set forth before thee as incense; and the lifting up of my hands as the evening sacrifice.
Psalm 141:2 (KJV)

Here, the Psalmist asks that his prayer be one that is set forth, *kuwn*. That is to say, one which has been prepared and arranged in a way that is pleasing to God; one that is morally steadfast (not given to satisfy personal selfish desire).

This prayer is to be like carefully prepared incense, *qatoreth*, which is perfumed smoke that gives the odor of burning sacrifice. It is prepared for the Lord, not for the supplicant. It is not for self, but for Him.

This special worshipful prayer is amplified by the physical expression of the lifting up, *mas'eth*, of hands, *kaph*, which when extended, is an utterance, or oracle, which rises to God as a signal that the prayers offered constitutes a gift; a willing offering, or tribute.

The hands lifted up are a type of palm branches (symbol of royalty and dominion power). We yield our delegated royal dominion and power to the One who gave it. They are also a type of clouds (in which God abides - Job 22:14; Psa. 18:11, and through which the Lord will return - Mat. 24:30; 26:64). We recognize that He is within reach, touchable, and near at all times.

This expression is as the evening, `*ereb*, sacrifice, *minchah*, the gift, tribute, present, or offering presented at sundown, not as an after thought, but as thanks for being guided, instructed and kept by the Good Shepherd during the day ahead (Gen. 1:5, 8, 13, etc.).

Let's take advantage of this great privilege of accessing God at any time and render the praise and worship that is pleasing to Him with all of our heart, mind and strength.

Evening, and morning, and at noon, will I pray, and cry aloud: and he shall hear my voice. Psalm 55:17 (KJV)

July 28 - Set A Watch

Set a watch, O Lord, before my mouth; keep the door of my lips. Psalm 141:3 (KJV)

Words are powerful. The Word of God spoken by a believing Christian is the most powerful thing loosed upon the earth since Jesus the Anointed One of God walked and talked here.

Words are creative. Once spoken their power remains until that which was spoken comes to pass. They can be words of health, wealth, vision and purpose or they can be words of sickness, poverty, hopelessness and purposelessness.

Words are like seed sown in the soil of the earth. The seed will bring forth a harvest after it's own kind. Words of lack will harvest lack, sickness of sickness, weakness of weakness, and so on. So, too, words of abundance will bring forth a harvest of abundance, health of healing and health, strength of vitality and strength.

Beloved, a church will not even win the lost until a desire to win the lost is spoken in the faith that brings about the action of witness. A church congregation will not give their tithe or offerings until words that teach the plan and purpose of God concerning the same are spoken. Lives are molded for evil or good by the words that flood into their ears and begin to create a mind set that brings wickedness or the blessing of righteousness.

Is it any wonder, then, that the Psalmist said, "Set a watch" over what comes out of my mouth. This word, *shiyth*, can be transliterated to mean, "Take a stand before me and put Your hand upon my mouth, Lord, and if any wrong word should slip out, lay it waste before it does any harm. The word, *shomrah*, simply reinforces the picture of this thought with that of a military guard or watchman.

A wise man will include such a request in his prayers from time to time. James 3:1-13 deals with this very consideration. It is the man who controls what comes out of his mouth that controls his very life.

July 29 - Treasure

But we have this treasure in earthen vessels, that the excellency of the power may be of God, and not of us.
2 Corinthians 4:7 (KJV)

You and I have the treasure, *thesauros*, the place in which good and precious things are collected and laid up; a receptacle in which valuables are kept; a treasury; storehouse, repository, magazine; the things laid up in a treasury, collected treasures. This Treasure is the Christ, the Anointed One and His Anointing, in whom are laid up all spiritual riches:
In Him all the treasures of [divine] wisdom (comprehensive insight into the ways and purposes of God) and [all the riches of spiritual] knowledge and enlightenment are stored up and lie hidden.
Colossians 2:3 (AMP)
This is "Christ in you, the hope of glory" (Col. 1:27). This mighty Spirit (2 Cor. 3:17) is within, *ostrakinos skeuos*, frail earthen vessels (men and women of quality, chosen instruments).
Though we are "chosen instruments of quality," yet we are frail, subject to the effects of this fallen world. Our minds needing daily washing with the water of the Word and our bodies resisting the grip of death through sickness, injury and aging by the quickening Spirit within.
All this so that the excellency, *huperbole*, the far more, exceeding more excellent, out of measure, beyond all measure, abundance, superiority, pre-eminence of His, *dunamis,* strength and ability, that inherent residing in Him by virtue of His nature. That which He exerts and puts forth as the power for performing miracles, moral power and excellence of soul, yes and even the power and influence which belong to riches and wealth. All this, and more, is contained within each believer.
Beloved, don't consider the vessel, consider the Treasure.

July 30 - Ministry

And all things are of God, who hath reconciled us to himself by Jesus Christ, and hath given to us the ministry of reconciliation; 2 Corinthians 5:18 (KJV)

God has reconciled, *katallasso*, returned us to favour with Himself by Jesus the Anointed One. He has received us into favor with Himself, His plan and His purpose.

This great privilege of position affords us the wonderful opportunity to work together with His Spirit in the reconciling of multitudes to Him.

For we are fellow workmen (joint promoters, laborers together) with and for God . . . 1 Corinthians 3:9 (AMP)

Sovereign though He is, He has chosen to work with and through men and women who have accepted the sacrifice of Himself in the Person of His Son and the leading of His Holy Spirit.

For all who are led by the Spirit of God are sons of God. Romans 8:14 (AMP)

There is no need for any born-again Christian to ask, "What is my ministry?" All true ministry begins with "the ministry of reconciliation," the service, *diakonia*, the ministering of those who execute the commands of God almighty. The ministry of those who by the command of God proclaim and promote the kingdom of God.

This ministry is not only prophetic, evangelistic and apostolic, it is practical in that it includes meeting the physical needs of people by service: the preparation and serving of food, clothing and/or shelter.

The "minister" is one who, "led by the Spirit of God," has made up their mind to care for the "sheep" of the Lord's pasture. He is the one who searches for the "lost sheep," tends the wounded sheep, and nurtures those in the fold. He is someone just like you.

July 31 - An Open Door

The season that lies before us is one of open doors of utterance. Revelation knowledge will freely flow to those who have spent time with Him in prayer. Ministry opportunities will avail themselves in increasingly supernatural ways. Many who have been "first" shall find themselves "last," and the last shall become first. Those heretofore unheard of and hidden will come to the forefront and move in the wonder working power of the Holy Ghost. Even those in prison will live and walk as freemen and find opportunity to speak as the oracles of God.

Withal praying also for us, that God would open unto us a door of utterance, to speak the mystery of Christ, for which I am also in bonds: Colossians 4:3 (KJV)

There is not one open door that man, nor the enemy, can shut. The Lord has set an open door before you, and who can shut that which He has opened?

This is a time of reward for those who have been faithful in the little. Now you will be given much; much more than you ever dreamed might be possible.

I know thy works: behold, I have set before thee an open door, and no man can shut it: for thou hast a little strength, and hast kept my word, and hast not denied my name. Revelation 3:8 (KJV)

What the Lord is doing is not dependent upon your strength, but He will reward the fact that you have kept and guarded His word in your heart.

Then he answered and spake unto me, saying, This is the word of the Lord unto Zerubbabel, saying, Not by might, nor by power, but by my spirit, saith the Lord of hosts. Zechariah 4:6 (KJV)

But without faith it is impossible to please him: for he that cometh to God must believe that he is, and that he is a rewarder of them that diligently seek him. Hebrews 11:6 (KJV)

Before you is the season of an open door into the fullness of the Christ of God because you have put your trust in Him. He will not fail you. Your season of harvest and increase is just ahead.

This is your season to excel in the things of God!

AUGUST

August 01 - Saith Not The Law

Say I these things as a man? or saith not the law the same also?
1 Corinthians 9:8 (KJV)

Many people today want to throw out the Old Testament as though it has nothing to do with the New Testament when, in actuality, the New unveils what is shadowed (hidden) in the Old. One without the other is partial truth at best.

Without the "Law of First Mention," in which God establishes precedent by speaking of a certain subject for the first time we would have no basis for much of our New Testament beliefs.

As Paul dealt with the question of support for those engaged in "full time" work for the Lord, he appealed to the authority of the scripture in the Old Testament, "saith not the law the same?" He based his concepts and dialogue on the Scripture of old as well as the words of Jesus.

It might be worth while here to mention that Jesus quoted various parts of 24 Old Testament books in much of His declaration and teaching. In fact, 34 books of the Old Testament were quoted in the New Testament. Ezra, Nehemiah, Esther, Ecclesiastes and Song of Solomon were the only 5 books that were not quoted in the New Testament.

Although men of old were moved upon by the Holy Spirit to speak and record the biblical record, the Old and New Covenant (Testament) writings are inextricably united as one book by One divine Author.

Paul recognized the "law" of God as unalterable and unquestionable. Prayerfully, you concede to this great truth and have not been drawn into the modern line of thought that uses grace to erase the spirit of the law of faith, ***nomos***.

We are to be "able ministers of the new testament; not of the letter, but of the spirit: for the letter killeth, but the spirit giveth life (2 Cor. 3:6 KJV).

August 02 - My Spirit, Who is Upon You

As for Me, this is My covenant or league with them, says the Lord: My Spirit, Who is upon you [and Who writes the law of God inwardly on the heart], and My words which I have put in your mouth shall not depart out of your mouth, or out of the mouths of your [true, spiritual] children, or out of the mouths of your children's children, says the Lord, from henceforth and forever.
Isaiah 59:21 (AMP)

New Testament believers have a covenant with the Lord. We are in league with God Almighty Himself. He has written an eternal constitution that establishes the relationship between Himself and those who are His.

Beloved, He has written its precepts and ordinances upon your heart and given you the authority to speak His words as though they are spoken directly by Him.

His words are "put in your mouth" as you yield to the prophetic unction of the Holy Spirit, Who is in you.

His Word is what you speak, not what you think, not what you feel, but what He says about every situation and circumstance.

Mark 11:23-24 (AMP) tells us that if we speak His word and believe that what He says, that there is nothing that will be impossible for us. Notice that our speaking is emphasized three times:

Truly I tell you, whoever says to this mountain, Be lifted up and thrown into the sea! and does not doubt at all in his heart but believes that what he says will take place, it will be done for him. For this reason I am telling you, whatever you ask for in prayer, believe (trust and be confident) that it is granted to you, and you will [get it].

. . . [Why,] all things can be (are possible) to him who believes! Mark 9:23 (AMP)

The wonderful thing is that, if we will speak the words of God and experience the power of them, our children and children's children will do the same thing and realize the benefit that the Lord has promised.

August 03 - What Can Man Do?

I called upon the Lord in distress: the Lord answered me, and set me in a large place. The Lord is on my side; I will not fear: what can man do unto me?
Psalm 118:5-6 (KJV)

No matter how distressing the situation is: when we call upon the Lord, He hears and answers us. Even if everyone we know turns against us, if God is with us, we need not fear.

The Hebrew word, *metsar*, the word used for distress, also means, pains or straits. This is dealing with emotions, physical and situational conditions. No matter how restrictive our condition, the Lord answers with an action that places us in "a large place," *merchab*, a broad or roomy place or wide, expanses. He will never let us remain shut in, boxed or walled in.

The Lord is on my side; I will not fear: what can man do unto me? Psalm 118:6 (KJV)

When life is met with difficulty and people become apparent enemies, we are to guard against fear; in fact, we are to rise in faith empowered by love. When we are "in Jesus Christ" we operate in "faith which worketh by love" (Gal. 5:6 KJV).

There is no fear in love; but perfect love casteth out fear: because fear hath torment. He that feareth is not made perfect in love. 1 John 4:18 (KJV)

God, Who is perfect love, "is on my side." When we accept this great truth and are perfected in love, we begin to speak what He says rather than what the situation, feelings or people may be saying.

What shall we then say to these things? If God be for us, who can be against us? Romans 8:31 (KJV)

Go ahead. Say it, "I will not fear" because "the Lord is on my side." Now say it again. How about once again? Now faith is coming because, ". . . faith cometh by hearing, and hearing by the word of God" (Rom. 10:17 KJV).

August 04 - You Set My Feet In A Broad Place

I will be glad and rejoice in Your mercy and steadfast love, because You have seen my affliction, You have taken note of my life's distresses, And You have not given me into the hand of the enemy; You have set my feet in a broad place. Psalm 31:7-8 (AMP)

One thing is sure, no matter what it looks or feels like, God knows what you are going through and He has not deserted you or left you without hope. Being a child of God assures each us of His constant overshadowing protection as we walk out our destiny in this fallen world.

His mercies are new every morning. Lamentations 3:22-23 (AMP) declares that -

It is because of the Lord's mercy and loving-kindness that we are not consumed, because His [tender] compassions fail not. They are new every morning; great and abundant is [the Lord's] stability and faithfulness.

With our heavenly Father near we can "be glad and rejoice" in whatever situation we find ourselves faced with.

Rejoice in the Lord always [delight, gladden yourselves in Him]; again I say, Rejoice! Philippians 4:4 (AMP)

You may feel shut in, bound, limited, restricted and without resource, but you can have a praise party because you know that the Lord has set your feet in a broad place.

This powerful truth has never been more evidenced than in our ministry. It looks as though we are small and insignificant but the ministry reaches around the globe through those we have encouraged and connected with.

The Devil is a liar and God is good, all the time!

August 05 - Afflicted

Before I was afflicted I went astray: but now have I kept thy word. Psalm 119:67 (KJV)

I don't know anyone who is real big on being "afflicted," do you? Yet, the Psalmist says that it can be beneficial if it serves to draw a person to the Lord. This Hebrew word, *'anah*, has various shades of meaning, including: afflict, humble, exercised, troubled and weakened. It can also mean, to be to be depressed or downcast, as well as, to be humbled or mishandled.

What King David is saying here is that the events that transpire in life have a way of showing a person, even a king, the value of knowing and keeping the Word of God. A few verses later he said,

It is good for me that I have been afflicted; that I might learn thy statutes. Psalm 119:71 (KJV)

Being humbled, exercised, troubled or weakened can, and should, as life experience can well do, tend to show us the frailty of our mortality and interest us in things concerning immortality. Even as great a warrior as was King David, he always recognized his dependence upon God.

By allowing life to happen, God gives us the chance to choose to live it with or without His guidance, help and strength. If we yield to His Word, which is His will, we are filled with the wisdom of God and are helped and strengthened.

There hath no temptation taken you but such as is common to man: but God is faithful, who will not suffer you to be tempted above that ye are able; but will with the temptation also make a way to escape, that ye may be able to bear it. 1 Corinthians 10:13 (KJV)

The Word of God will keep us in every situation - always.

. . . This is my comfort in my affliction: for thy word hath quickened me. Psalm 119:49-50 (KJV)

August 06 - Thy Word Is Settled

For ever, O Lord, thy word is settled in heaven.
Psalm 119:89 (KJV)

It is vitally important that we come to completely rely on the unfailing veracity of the Word of God. He says that what He has spoken is "settled." The Hebrew word used here is, **natsab**, which makes us to understand that the spoken words of God will be found to stand firm throughout eternity. His words are fixed in the fabric of the eternal now. They are timeless.

Have you ever heard someone say, "He is as good as his word"? We understand that a man is only as good as what he says. If he can't be trusted to do what he says, he is of no value whatsoever. God is not a man and He cannot, will not, lie.

God is not a man, that he should lie; neither the son of man, that he should repent: hath he said, and shall he not do it? or hath he spoken, and shall he not make it good? Numbers 23:19 (KJV)

And also the Strength of Israel will not lie nor repent: for he is not a man, that he should repent.
1 Samuel 15:29 (KJV)

The Lord has such regard for His Word that He set it's importance above His own name.

. . . thou hast magnified thy word above all thy name. Psalm 138:2 (KJV)

He has vowed that His words are established and to be trusted forever.

Heaven and earth shall pass away: but my words shall not pass away. Luke 21:33 (KJV)

This is so important that He personally watches over His word to make sure that it accomplishes what He means for it to.

Then said the Lord unto me, Thou hast well seen: for I will hasten my word to perform it. Jeremiah 1:12 (KJV)

For I am the Lord: I will speak, and the word that I shall speak shall come to pass; it shall be no more prolonged: for in your days, O rebellious house, will I say the word, and will perform it, saith the Lord God. Ezekiel 12:25 (KJV)

August 07 - Truth

Thy word have I hid in mine heart, that I might not sin against thee. Psalm 119:11 (KJV)

Your Torah, *'imrah*, (or *'emrah*), Your spoken Words, Your commandment uttered have I hid, **tsaphan,** treasured and stored up in the secret places of my heart, **leb**, my innermost being, my inner man of the heart, and made them my inclination, my resolution, and my determination of will, conscience as well as the seat of my emotions, passions, and the seat of my courage.

I have done this so that I might not sin, **chata',** that I might not commit any act, or hold any thought, that would be offensive to You, the only living God.

Your Word will keep me from missing the goal or path of right and duty so that I will not incur guilt nor incur penalty by forfeit because your Word is the only pure truth, **aletheia**, what is true in any matter under consideration and is of universal personal excellence. Truth that is that candour of mind which is free from affection, pretence, simulation, falsehood and deceit.

Sanctify them through thy truth: thy word is truth. John 17:17 (KJV)

Jesus is the Eternal Word (John 1:1) and, as such, is the only path of access to God. There is no other way.

Jesus saith unto him, I am the way, the truth, and the life: no man cometh unto the Father, but by me. John 14:6 (KJV)

As the believer hides the Word of God in their heart, he is developing a relationship of love with Jesus. He said,

If you [really] love Me, you will keep (obey) My commands. John 14:15 (AMP)

If you keep My commandments [if you continue to obey My instructions], you will abide in My love and live on in it, just as I have obeyed My Father's commandments and live on in His love. John 15:10 (AMP)

Life in Jesus is a life in love with the Word of Truth.

August 08 - Light For The Path

Thy word is a lamp unto my feet, and a light unto my path. Psalm 119:105 (KJV)

Your word, *dabar*, commandment, sayings, utterance is a lamp, *niyr*, or *nir*, a glistening glory light for my feet, *regel*, my journey according to the pace of God, and a light, *'owr*, a bright, clear, light like that of the morning sun, or a bright flash of lightning.

It is interesting that this word, also carries the meaning of the light of life, prosperity, instruction and, specifically, of having the Almighty Jehovah as our Light for every path, *nathiyb*, that we may travel on.

As we considered in yesterday's verse, the Word of God is absolutely sure and trustworthy. Every individual on planet earth can rest their eternal future upon the words that God has spoken. These words, as well as the historical dealings of God with man, and man with God, have been recorded in the Bible for our benefit.

In many separate revelations [each of which set forth a portion of the Truth] and in different ways God spoke of old to [our] forefathers in and by the prophets, Hebrews 1:1 (AMP)

All scripture is given by inspiration of God, and is profitable for doctrine, for reproof, for correction, for instruction in righteousness: 2 Timothy 3:16 (KJV)

Beloved, the Word of God is not a compilation of the teachings of man, but the very words of the Eternal, Almighty, Creator of heaven and earth, given to man to keep him in all his ways. This wonderful, supernatural, living Word is given as a gift so that those created after the image and likeness of God can live life, and life more abundantly (Joh. 10:10b).

There is no darkness that the light of God cannot dispel, no path or situation that the Word will not order aright, and no question that the Word will not answer. "Thy Word is Truth" (Joh. 13:13 KJV), absolute and complete.

August 09 - Let Us Go . . .

A Song of degrees of David. I was glad when they said unto me, Let us go into the house of the Lord.
Psalm 122:1 (KJV)

The songs of degrees were sung as the worshipers ascended to the Temple of God, many times out of Jericho in the valley below Jerusalem. In fact, the whole 119th Psalm was a "Song of Ascents" that was sung while moving up toward the Temple in the "Valley of the Shadow of Death," a common route from Jericho to Jerusalem and the Temple mount.

It was counted as a great privilege to, not only have a Temple, or House of Worship, but to be able to go there and gather with other believers to worship the Living God.

It is of great interest, distress, and anguish, to me that the North American people are in the process of casting off the great privilege of going to the "Church" to worship. True, there are many "churches," so called, that would not know a move of God, nor recognize the Word of God, let alone the God of the Word, if presented. Jesus addressed these kinds of gatherings in the book of Luke:

And he spake a parable unto them, Can the blind lead the blind? shall they not both fall into the ditch?
Luke 6:39 (KJV)

But, Beloved, don't throw away your money just because there are counterfeit dollar bills. Don't cast off the *ecclesia* just because there are counterfeit assemblies.

Not forsaking the assembling of ourselves together, as the manner of some is; but exhorting one another: and so much the more, as ye see the day approaching.
Hebrews 10:25 (KJV)

If you want to meet in a house, in a cell group, in a Bible study group, well and good, because you should. But, don't leave out the Temple [House of God] where the gifts of God may be of benefit to you (Acts 2:46; 5:2; 1 Tim. 5:13; Ephes. 4:8-16). Find one that is established by God, moving with God, and will teach you how to be a biblically active Christian.

August 10 - The Fear of the Lord

The fear of the Lord is the beginning of wisdom: a good understanding have all they that do his commandments: his praise endureth for ever. Psalm 111:10 (KJV)

I know, you thought "fear" was not of God.. You were right and you were wrong.

Let's look at the original language usage and perhaps we will see the difference between the fear that one man might have verses the fear of another. The Hebrew word, *yir'ah*, can mean fear, terror, an awesome or terrifying thing (object causing fear) or the fear (of God), respect, reverence and piety.

Much of our ability to understand languages other than our own is to know the context of the word we are considering. With this in mind we can look at the above verse and know that there are two possible meanings that present themselves to us.

God is Love, and as such, is not to be feared in the sense that we would be afraid of what He might do to us. It is true that we should "respect, "and hold in awesome "piety," this One who is God Almighty. Believers know Him as Father, Kind, Merciful and Longsuffering, therefore beneficent toward them.

An individual who does not know God personally would stand in utter terror before Him were He to show Himself to him. God is Holy and Just and the lost sinner knows he is guilty before Him and utterly without excuse in His presence.

Either "fear" should lead one to repentance and right standing with God through His Son, Jesus the Christ. This, Beloved, is the beginning, *re'shiyth*, the choicest, or chief, part of wisdom, *chokmah,* shrewdness, prudence, ethical and religious wisdom and skill in war. Those with "good understanding," *towb sekel*, that is, an ethical mind filled with insight, are obviously intimately acquainted with Him and act upon their knowledge of Him (They "know" Him).

His, *tahillah*, renown, fame and glory demanded by His qualities, deeds and attributes bring forth an eternal song or hymn of praise in them that know Him. Do you know Him?

August 11 - My Conscience

I say the truth in Christ, I lie not, my conscience also bearing me witness in the Holy Ghost, Romans 9:1 (KJV)

Jesus is the truth:
Jesus saith unto him, I am the way, the truth, and the life: no man cometh unto the Father, but by me. John 14:6 (KJV)
When we are in Christ, Who is "The Truth," we should speak the truth, live the truth, and never, never, never lie. Satan is the father of lies and has nothing to do with the truth.
Ye are of your father the devil, and the lusts of your father ye will do. He was a murderer from the beginning, and abode not in the truth, because there is no truth in him. When he speaketh a lie, he speaketh of his own: for he is a liar, and the father of it. John 8:44 (KJV)
The Christian must be a person whose word is trustworthy; a person of integrity. We are what we speak. Believers speak faith words, true words, honest, just, pure, lovely, virtuous words that bring a good report and are praiseworthy (Phil. 4:8 KJV)..
We having the same spirit of faith, according as it is written, I believed, and therefore have I spoken; we also believe, and therefore speak; 2 Corinthians 4:13 (KJV)
The Spirit-filled believer has a witness within that leads into all truth and warns against all lies.
Howbeit when he, the Spirit of truth, is come, he will guide you into all truth: . . . John 16:13 (KJV)
The Holy Spirit commingled together with your spirit speaks to you through your regenerate conscience. The conscience of the believer is a direct pipeline from the spirit of man to the conscious mind of man. Wherein it was unreliable in it's natural state, it is now a reliable source of prompting and information from God by the Holy Spirit to your spirit. Your spirit communicates to your conscious mind by means of your conscience and thereby guards and keeps your mind.

August 12 - Choose Life

I call heaven and earth to record this day against you, that I have set before you life and death, blessing and cursing: therefore choose life, that both thou and thy seed may live: Deuteronomy. 30:19 (KJV)

The will of God is that you would choose life and thereby receive blessing for you, your children and your children's children. The creation bears witness of His covenant desire.

The life, *chay,* that He wants us to choose is to live, *chayah,* to have a prosperous, sustainable, healthy life, that is free of sickness, discouragement, faintness and death. God wants you and I to be quickened, revived, refreshed and renewed by His Spirit.

Mankind is the recipient of the most precious gift that God could give besides His Only Begotten Son; that of having a free will. He has given man the ability to choose between "life and death, blessing and cursing, God and Satan, the truth and a lie."

He sets, as it were, a table before us and we are to take what ever we desire. Much like an earthly parent, He wills that we would choose a healthy diet that would strengthen and build. He warns us of the consequences of making the wrong choices, yet allows us to choose what we will.

As tempting as the desert dishes are, we know that to develop properly, we must balance our diet with the main course. So, too, as tempting as the things of the world are, we are called to choose the will and ways of God in order to develop suitably.

The Word of God is given as our main course. As we feast upon it we will find everything needful for life and godliness. We will be nourished properly and be full of the wisdom of God, realizing that making the right choice is vitally important.

All things are lawful unto me, but all things are not expedient: all things are lawful for me, but I will not be brought under the power of any. 1 Corinthians 6:12 (KJV)

August 13 - Another Man

And the Spirit of the Lord will come upon thee, and thou shalt prophesy with them, and shalt be turned into another man. 1 Samuel 10:6 (KJV)

In Old Testament times the Spirit of the Lord came upon men and women to wrought special works through them. It was a powerful anointing for a particular time and purpose. Whether it was upon the prophet to prophesy, or the soldier for supernatural strength and ability in battle, as in the case of David when he fought Goliath, it made them "another man."

Our verse for today is a record of what was spoken to Saul before he became king. This prophetic word came to pass and Saul prophesied with the prophets of that day.

And when they came thither to the hill, behold, a company of prophets met him; and the Spirit of God came upon him, and he prophesied among them. And it came to pass, when all that knew him beforetime saw that, behold, he prophesied among the prophets, then the people said one to another, What is this that is come unto the son of Kish? Is Saul also among the prophets?
1 Samuel 10:10-11 (KJV)

Today, in New Testament times, the Holy Spirit comes to indwell every believer rather than come upon and then withdraw as was the experience of the prophets and patriarchs of old.

What? know ye not that your body is the temple of the Holy Ghost which is in you, which ye have of God, and ye are not your own? 1 Corinthians 6:19 (KJV)

Now, every spirit-filled believer can prophesy and expect supernatural strength and ability to be manifest in their life on a regular basis. The Holy Spirit abides within.

There are, however, particular operations of the Holy Spirit that bring a greater anointing during special times or seasons to accomplish the will of God. Many testify of a "heavy anointing coming upon them" when they preach, teach or testify and those who know them attest to the fact that they have indeed become "another man."

August 14 - Believe That You Receive

Therefore I say unto you, What things soever ye desire, when ye pray, believe that ye receive them, and ye shall have them. Mark 11:24 (KJV)

There cannot be enough said about this powerful verse of scripture. Upon it rests the success or failure of the victorious Christian prayer life. How I have struggled with this great truth in times past.

The ability to believe that you receive before you see is foundational to the prayer of a mature Christian. This is prayer that pleases God and the subsequent answer is always the result.

Now faith is the substance of things hoped for, the evidence of things not seen. Hebrews 11:1 (KJV)

But without faith it is impossible to please him: for he that cometh to God must believe that he is, and that he is a rewarder of them that diligently seek him. Hebrews 11:6 (KJV)

I am well aware of the many sovereign works and acts of God where He has chosen to answer prayer that is, at best, hopeful but not of faith. This is not what I am considering today.

It is of great comfort to me to know that "faith comes by hearing, and hearing by the word of God" (Rom. 10:17). By this I know that whatever faith I need has been given, is given, and will be given, as I saturate myself in the living word of God. This places every desire of my heart (not my head) in the spiritual condition necessary to be fulfilled.

Delight thyself also in the Lord; and he shall give thee the desires of thine heart. Psalm 37:4 (KJV)

Believing prayer by those in covenant with God taps into the desire of the Father's heart to bless His children with every good and perfect gift. Hebrews 11:1 faith appropriates, possesses, and rejoices over what, though not yet seen by the natural eye, is seen with the eye of the spirit.

The possessor of this answer to prayer rests in the knowledge that the thing not seen will soon appear for all to see.

August 15 - Father of Many Nations

(As it is written, I have made thee a father of many nations,) before him whom he believed, even God, who quickeneth the dead, and calleth those things which be not as though they were. Romans 4:17 (KJV)

The above promise was made to Abraham and his Seed as well as to his seed. The promise was to all of those who would become heirs of the promise to Abraham.

Neither shall thy name any more be called Abram, but thy name shall be Abraham; for a father of many nations have I made thee. Genesis 17:5 (KJV)

His name was changed to prophetically seal him to the promise of God. One of his lineage, Jacob, also had his name changed to Israel.

The name change brought about a character change and pointed to the future plan and purpose of God concerning their lives. Abraham was to be the father of many nations and that has been fulfilled in Christ Jesus.

And if ye be Christ's, then are ye Abraham's seed, and heirs according to the promise. Galatians 3:29 (KJV)

Those who are "heirs according to the promise" literally come out of "every kindred, and tongue, and people, and nation."

. . . for Thou wast slain, and hast redeemed us to God by thy blood out of every kindred, and tongue, and people, and nation; Revelation 5:9 (KJV)

These heirs, two of which are you and me, are also becoming a multitude that cannot be counted (Heb. 11:12).

Beloved, you may not see yourself as the inheritor of a multitude, but you are! Consider the promise of God and begin to claim your inheritance and gather in the "nations." Begin, like God, to call "those things which be not as though they were."

Know that God is faithful and will give you what you ask:

Ask of me, and I shall give thee the heathen for thine inheritance, and the uttermost parts of the earth for thy possession. Psalm 2:8 (KJV)

August 16 - Know Them

And we beseech you, brethren, to know them which labour among you, and are over you in the Lord, and admonish you; 1 Thessalonians 5:12 (KJV)

We who are leaders of the Lord's flock are especially responsible to "know," *eido* or *oida*, them which "say" they labor among us. Not everyone that looks like a shepherd is a shepherd any more than everyone that looks like a sheep is a sheep.

We are strongly admonished to "know," *eido* or *oida*, those who declare themselves to be one of us. In the Greek we are being told to be close enough to someone to see them with our eyes and to have discovered them and discerned of what spirit they are. They are to be inspected, examined, interviewed, visited and proven.

We are to "know" those who labor for our benefit and serve as under-shepherds of the Great Shepherd because we are to honor, esteem and bless them in-as-much as they "watch over our souls" (Heb. 13:17).

Apostolic "fathers" are given to the under-shepherds (Pastors/Senior Elders) of every city to watch over, protect, advise, counsel, admonish, encourage and pray for them. They offer spiritual discerning, wisdom and understanding that can only come when it is combined with the experience of walking with God in their calling.

These are men of integrity, who know the ways of God as well as the acts of God. They are not more than any other but are given as gifts to those who are willing to be spiritual sons.

Sons may be fathers themselves but know that every great leader is also a great follower.

Do we not yet understand that we are to surround ourselves with wise counsel?

Where no counsel is, the people fall: but in the multitude of counsellors there is safety. Proverbs 11:14 (KJV)

Without counsel purposes are disappointed: but in the multitude of counsellors they are established. Proverbs 15:22 (KJV)

August 17 - Let Your "Yes" be "Yes"

But let your 'Yes' be 'Yes,' and your 'No,' 'No.' For whatever is more than these is from the evil one.
Matthew 5:37 (NKJV)

Why can't people say what they mean and mean what they say? Why would someone say that "The Lord told me . . ." and then later change their mind and say, "The Lord told me . . ." (Something entirely different)?

This, Beloved, is a breach of integrity. The Spirit of Truth is not working in some area of our life if we can not keep our word. If a Christian enters into a contract with a bank or another businessman and then finds that he made a mistake, he needs to admit he made a mistake, man up and keep his agreement (vow) and learn from the experience.

If a man makes a vow to the Lord, or swears an oath to bind himself by some agreement, he shall not break his word; he shall do according to all that proceeds out of his mouth. Numbers 30:2 (NKJV)

Keeping our word is not a matter of convenience but a mandate from the Lord Himself. He honors those that honor their word. How? By restoring whatever loss might result.

. . . But he [The Lord] honors those who fear the Lord; He who swears to his own hurt and does not change; Psalms 15:4b (NKJV)

Let's remember to think before we speak and to find out what God thinks before we think. Then, and only then, will our "Yes" be "Yes," and our "No," "No."

But above all, my brethren, do not swear, either by heaven or by earth or with any other oath. But let your "Yes," be "Yes," and your "No," "No," lest you fall into judgment. James 5:12 (NKJV)

The lesson begins at home and with an accountability between parent and child and child and parent. Parents need to keep their promises to their children and children need to keep their promises to their parents.

August 18 - Wise Counsel

For by wise counsel thou shalt make thy war: and in multitude of counsellors there is safety.
Proverbs 24:6 (KJV)

If we "know" them that labor among us we will not be drawn into the scam schemes and over-priced "deals" that regularly come along and seek to profit from the all-too-often naive under-shepherds of the flock of God.

Beware of false prophets, which come to you in sheep's clothing, but inwardly they are ravening wolves.
Matthew 7:15 (KJV)

Pastoral networks must be established in every city so that the "Gates" of the city are protected. There must be watchmen on the walls and "Elders" at the "Gate" who are filled with the Spirit and operating in the gift of Discerning of Spirits. These watchmen will "smell a rat (profiting prophet)" and move to either validate a worthy ministry or extricate any threat to the community of faith.

Pride is running rampant among those called of God. This separates the Body of Christ by breeding competitiveness. Every competitive spirit will soon give birth to "sheep stealing" which Paul addressed when he said, "Yea, so have I strived to preach the gospel, not where Christ was named, lest I should build upon another man's foundation" (Rom. 15:20 KJV). He addressed the same issue in 2 Corinthians 10:15-16 (KJV): "Not boasting of things without our measure, that is, of other men's labours; but having hope, when your faith is increased, that we shall be enlarged by you according to our rule abundantly, To preach the gospel in the regions beyond you, and not to boast in another man's line of things made ready to our hand."

This pride also removes the safety of a relational network that would expose unethical people whose only interest in the ministry is to gain access to its resources of people and finance.

The "Reverend" Sun Myung Moon took advantage of religious networks and built a public veil of credibility on the backs of undiscerning and naive ministers. Many are the financial "wolves" circling the flock with nothing but the profit of fleece in mind.

August 19 - Led Into The Wilderness

And Jesus being full of the Holy Ghost returned from Jordan, and was led by the Spirit into the wilderness, Luke 4:1 (KJV)

Even Jesus was led by the Holy Spirit to face the Devil and his lies in order to prove the power of the Word of God. Beloved, we must learn to prove the power of the Word of God and not be moved by deceptive spirits that spread fear and anxiety.

Many will promise wonderful and awesome things but the acceptance of doing things their way will only bring harm to the plan and purpose of God. Had Jesus "bought into" what the Devil was offering, He would have corrupted His life and destroyed His ministry. We would never have been rescued from sin by the Spotless Lamb.

There is no lack of "fathers" but most fathers are wondering where the "sons" are. Sons are willing to be led. They seek counsel before they make decisions (the decisions are still theirs to make) and they find that they excel in wisdom beyond those who rush ahead and reach their goals much easier and faster than those who are clearing their field alone.

For as many as are led by the Spirit of God, they are the sons of God. Romans 8:14 (KJV)

It has been an interesting thing to me as over the years young men have come to me and asked me to be their "father" only to distance themselves from me when I suggest an alternative to how they are doing things. This is not the spirit of a son. Mind you, I try to never give advice unless I am asked for an opinion and always allow that my advice can be ignored.

My spiritual fathers have a right to speak into my life whenever they deem it fit. I honor them with offerings each month and with other gifts as I am able. I know that the counsel of someone who loves and cares about me is priceless and cannot be bought. But, in my mind, a thank offering of appreciation is always appropriate. Relational accountability is the safety net of life.

August 20 - The Seed

For there shall the seed produce peace and prosperity; the vine shall yield her fruit and the ground shall give its increase and the heavens shall give their dew; and I will cause the remnant of this people to inherit and possess all these things. Zechariah 8:12 (AMP)

We, as Bible believing Christians, know that the Word of God is the Seed of God and that it will always produce good (peace and prosperity) in the soil of our lives. Why is it, then, that the promise is to "the remnant." Why is it that it is only the remnant that will "inherit and possess all these things"?

The "seed" of God is always good. The "seed" of God is the Word of God (Mar. 4:14; Luk 8:5).

Seed will lay dormant for a thousand years and still grow when it is put in the ground. It will produce after it's own kind.

The "seed" of man is always corrupt (Rom. 3:10, 23). When man fell in the Garden of Eden he began to make decisions about good and evil, right and wrong, outside of the counsel of God (Gen. 3:5, 22). Fallen man would now "know," *yada*`, in the sense of learning by experience and becoming acquainted with in his carnal nature, good and evil.

After being born-again many Christians still try to live the Christian life carnally. This is impossible (Rom. 8:6, 7; 1 Cor. 2:14). This is what the Parable of the Sower is speaking of in Mark 4:3-20. Everything in this parable deals with good seed being rejected by bad (corrupt) soil.

It is our responsibility to cultivate our ground so that it will receive the good seed. Good seed + Good ground = Good harvest. The "Vine" will yield her fruit based upon the seed; for good or evil. Beloved, you can have good seed and good ground but if you don't have the "dew of Heaven," the Holy Spirit moving in your life, quickening the seed in your ground, the Vine will not be able to produce to it's ultimate capacity.

August 21 - The Seed (Part Two)

There must be time spent in prayer, intimate relationship building prayer, worshipful times with God , where we flow in, and with, the Holy Spirit until He brings "heavens dew," the rain of the Spirit, the anointing, that brings fruitfulness.

The seed is good. The ground is giving it's increase (it is working to produce growth), the dew is falling from the clouds of glory, the Vine is responding to the light and winds of the Spirit, everything is wonderful; But: you are still not realizing the best that you know God has for you.

You are singing, "There must be more now Father. There must be more now Spirit. There must be more now Jesus. Rain down, Rain down."

The "I" (the I AM) must give the increase (2 Cor. 9:10). Increase only comes from Him (1 Cor. 3:7). You can be doing all the right things for the right reasons and He may still choose to set a season that is yet in the future so that you will not think that it is you who are producing what only He can produce.

When you receive the seed by providing good ground; When you nourish the Vine by giving it a place in the light; When you receive the dew of heaven by staying in the clouds of glory and yielding to the Holy Spirit; Surely the "I AM" will speak. What more can there be? Dear one, it is the acknowledgment of absolute dependence upon Him.

Ask. Ask with a pure heart to please Him with the answer to your request. He knows what you need, what you want and why you want it even before you ask; but, you must ask (Jam. 4:2-3). You must ask in faith believing (Mar. 11:23-24) knowing that everything depends totally upon His speaking the words of life (Joh. 6:63).

It is His declaration that produces the increase. (Genesis 1:3; Genesis 1:6; Genesis 1:11-12; Genesis 1:14; Genesis 1:20-22; Genesis 1:24-28; Psa. 29:3-9).

The "remnant" are those who ask in faith believing. It is they that shall "inherit and possess all these things."

August 22 - Lift Up Your Eyes

Say not ye, There are yet four months, and then cometh harvest? behold, I say unto you, Lift up your eyes, and look on the fields; for they are white already to harvest. John 4:35 (KJV)

It's harvest time! Look up! There has never been a time when so many people are seeking to find peace, purpose and purity in truth. There is no doubt about it. These are the days when the early and the latter rains will fall together on the precious fields of souls.

Be patient therefore, brethren, unto the coming of the Lord. Behold, the husbandman waiteth for the precious fruit of the earth, and hath long patience for it, until he receive the early and latter rain. James 5:7 (KJV)

The Lord said that there would be a day when the former and latter rains would fall and that the Spirit of Harvest would be poured out upon all flesh. He has been patiently waiting for this generation to arise and call in the clouds and beckon to the rain. He is waiting to answer our call and empower the Church once again for the work of the harvest.

And it shall come to pass afterward, that I will pour out my spirit upon all flesh; and your sons and your daughters shall prophesy, your old men shall dream dreams, your young men shall see visions: Joel 2:28 (KJV)

Joel's prophecy came to pass on the day of Pentecost and the rains began to fall.

And it shall come to pass in the last days, saith God, I will pour out of my Spirit upon all flesh: and your sons and your daughters shall prophesy, and your young men shall see visions, and your old men shall dream dreams:

Acts 2:17 (KJV)

Immediately following this recorded outpouring, 3000 souls were ushered into the kingdom with one sermon from the Apostle Peter's lips.

August 23 - Lift Up Your Eyes
(Part Two)

The uncertain, the coward, the weak of character, the one who denied the Lord before the cock crowed, became another man as the Spirit of God fell in the upper room.

These are days of signs, wonders and miracles that will arrest the attention of the lost. Agnostic, Atheist and followers of false religious systems will be met with the sudden visitation of God in the resurrection power of the Spirit in the name of Jesus the Christ.

These are the days when the uncertain, the coward, the weak of character, the intimidated will arise as another man with the anointing of God on his life and the prophetic word in his mouth. These are the days when, emboldened by the witness of the Spirit, common men and women will draw near to their God and do exploits.

It has begun. People, heeding the call to prayer, are catching the wind of the Spirit and hearing the words from the throne. They are beginning to speak to the clouds, until now the size of a man's hand, and they are declaring that rain come!

I hear the sound of abundant rain. I see the dark clouds of the spirit realm gathering over our City. I feel the excitement of the Lord of the Harvest and the Spirit of His Grace.

From the corners of the earth, I hear the cry of the martyrs, the call of the those who make brick without straw, as it were, those who labor in darkness at the driving of the cruel taskmaster.

I hear God say, "It is enough. Let My people go!" I hear the Lord say, "Who will go for Us?"

I hear the Bride say to the Bride Groom, "Here am I Lord, send me!" I see the Bride who is meet for her Bride Groom, who is perfectly adapted and suited for Him, stir herself and, like Ruth, move into the fields of Boaz to reap!

August 24 - Cooperation

But now bring me a minstrel. And it came to pass, when the minstrel played, that the hand of the Lord came upon him. And he said, Thus saith the Lord, Make this valley full of ditches. For thus saith the Lord, Ye shall not see wind, neither shall ye see rain; yet that valley shall be filled with water, that ye may drink, both ye, and your cattle, and your beasts. 2 Kings 3:15-17 (KJV)

There is nothing quite like the ministry of an anointed minstrel (an anointed worship musician) to bring the provisional prophetic anointing.

The Song of the Lord brings peace and clarity to every situation that can be clouded by situational circumstance. What we see with the natural eye often veils what we could see with our spiritual eyes. The prophet can "see" clearly in the realm of the spirit and speak what needs to be done in the natural realm to bring about supernatural intervention and supply.

After the prophet has spoken the hearers must obey in order to receive the benefit of the heaven sent life giving word. Obedience pleases God and He will respond to its action of faith.

Too many "ministers" think that physical work is beneath them or that it is not spiritual. This is simply the thinking of the spiritually immature and/or lazy. The Bible calls such, "sluggards." If you are not willing to put sweat and tears to the promise you will never realize the promise:

For as the human body apart from the spirit is lifeless, so faith apart from [its] works of obedience is also dead. James 2:26 (AMP)

The command was, "Make this valley full of ditches." This is work; hard work. This work had to come before anyone felt any breeze, saw any clouds or felt any rain fall. The word of the Lord had decreed that there would be provision for both man and beast when He said, "yet that valley shall be filled with water." Beloved, "Whatever He says to you, do it" (John 2:5 AMP).

August 25 - Can You Hear The Call?

He that hath an ear, let him hear what the Spirit saith unto the churches; To him that overcometh will I give to eat of the hidden manna, and will give him a white stone, and in the stone a new name written, which no man knoweth saving he that receiveth it. Revelation 2:17 (KJV)

God is speaking to those who have an ear to hear. The scripture records the words, "he that hath an ear, let him hear," seven times. One might think that, perhaps, it is important to hear what the Spirit is saying to the Church.

To the hearing is revealed the plan and purpose that God has for the overcomer. There is "hidden manna" to "eat," a "white stone" upon which is written "a new name" so personal, profound and private that "no man knoweth (it) saving he that receiveth it."

Beloved, if we are to be overcomers in this hour, we must begin to seek God while He may be found and learn to hear His Voice.

Seek ye the LORD while he may be found, call ye upon him while he is near: Isaiah 55:6 (KJV)

He will not be available to all forever.

And the LORD said, My spirit shall not always strive with man, for that he also is flesh . . . Genesis 6:3 (KJV)

Yet, to His own He is ever near.

Every true believer in God and His Christ, Jesus, the Only Begotten of God, thrills at the truth that God, in Christ, is within:

To whom God would make known what is the riches of the glory of this mystery among the Gentiles; which is Christ in you, the hope of glory: Colossians 1:27 (KJV)

He is now nearer than the sound of your voice. He is in you, with you; His Spirit commingled together with your spirit. You are one with God in Christ, eternally inseparable from Him. Wrapped in His love (Joh. 17:21,22).

. . . he hath a said, I will never leave thee, nor forsake thee. Hebrews 13:5 (KJV)

Listen. He is speaking. Can you hear?

August 26 - Eyes To See

And when the servant of the man of God was risen early, and gone forth, behold, an host compassed the city both with horses and chariots. And his servant said unto him, Alas, my master! how shall we do? And he answered, Fear not: for they that be with us are more than they that be with them. And Elisha prayed, and said, Lord, I pray thee, open his eyes, that he may see. And the Lord opened the eyes of the young man; and he saw: and, behold, the mountain was full of horses and chariots of fire round about Elisha. 2 Kings 6:15-17

Many wonderful servants of the Lord have yet to experience an open vision. They are, unfortunately, too busy or caught up in what they see in the natural to see into the supernatural.

Yes, there is a great deal of activity going on in the supernatural realm of the spirit that the physical man is not aware of. 2 Kings 6 gives us a perfect picture of a day in the lives of Elisha and his servant. An army hostile to the prophet and his servant surrounded the city in which they were. Fear struck the heart of Elisha's servant when he saw the number of soldiers, horses and chariots. The situation was quite hopeless. There was no way of escape; or so it seemed.

The prophet had a different view of the whole scene. Faith, not fear, was his portion and position. He was able to see with the eye of faith into the realm of the spirit where those who threatened God's two servants were surrounded by a heavenly host. Time, and time again, Sharon, I and our team of leaders here at Wellspring have been faced with seemingly insurmountable obstacles only to have our eyes opened to the innumerable company of the Lord's host that stand guard around and about us.

The angel of the Lord encampeth round about them that fear him, and delivereth them. Psalm 34:7 (KJV)

Remember, whether you can see them or not, "Fear not: for they that be with us are more than they that be with them."

My prayer is that, all God's servants have open eyes to see the resources available in the realm of the spirit.

August 27 - In Distress

To the chief Musician on Neginoth, A Psalm of David. Hear me when I call, O God of my righteousness: thou hast enlarged me when I was in distress; have mercy upon me, and hear my prayer. Psalm 4:1 (KJV)

As Christians we know that the Lord hears and answers our prayer. David also had the assurance that the God of his righteousness would, **shama**`, hear with attention or interest, understand the language of his heart and give heed to and consent to his request.

And this is the confidence that we have in him, that, if we ask any thing according to his will, he heareth us: 1 John 5:14 (KJV)

The Psalmists' experience during great distress, **tsar,** or **tsawr,** of narrow straits, attacks of adversaries, foes, enemies and oppressors that were as painful, worrisome and wearisome as a hard pebble in his shoe, had taught him that he would be developed in character.

This word, enlarged, **rachab**, teaches us that as we look to God in our distress we will develop a wider (broader) perspective that will cause us to come out of the restrictions and hindrances caused by our enemies and bring us into broad or roomy pastures (one translation calls them "a large room").

Now the Lord is the Spirit, and where the Spirit of the Lord is, there is liberty (emancipation from bondage, freedom). 2 Corinthians 3:17 (AMP)

As believers we have first hand knowledge of being emancipated from all bondage. Our liberty in Christ allows us to "walk through the valley of death" and fear no evil (Psa. 23:4). We are not moved by our situation or circumstance. We are not controlled by what we see. Our confidence is the God of our righteousness and that He will always hear and answer no matter how bleak and hopeless things appear to be.

August 28 - They That Know Thy Name

And they that know thy name will put their trust in thee: for thou, Lord, hast not forsaken them that seek thee. Psalm 9:10 (KJV)

Yada `, is the Hebrew word used in this verse to explain the intimacy that one should have with the, *shem*, the Name (His character, fame, report, reputation, glory). We are to know by the experience of Him having made Himself known to us by the revelation of His Spirit.

Intimate knowledge of the Lord includes being touched by His Spirit. *Yada* `, carries this implication: One who has been touched by the finger of God. This kind of knowing gives one a relationship of trust that will carry them through any situation or circumstance.

The Lord never, never, never forsakes those that seek Him:

Let your character or moral disposition be free from love of money [including greed, avarice, lust, and craving for earthly possessions] and be satisfied with your present [circumstances and with what you have]; for He [God] Himself has said, I will not in any way fail you nor give you up nor leave you without support. [I will] not, [I will] not, [I will] not in any degree leave you helpless nor forsake nor let [you] down (relax My hold on you)! [Assuredly not!] Hebrews 13:5 (AMP)

Teaching them to observe all things whatsoever I have commanded you: and, lo, I am with you alway, even unto the end of the world. Amen. Matthew 28:20 (KJV)

He has not, `*azab,* failed to fortify, help, restore and repair all who, *darash,* frequently search Him out in prayer and worship to enquire of Him as a necessity of life.

Beloved, when you seek Him you will find Him and all you have need of will be provided for you.

But seek ye first the kingdom of God, and his righteousness; and all these things shall be added unto you. Matthew 6:33 (KJV)

August 29 - The Rod of Iron

Whose feet they hurt with fetters: he was laid in iron: Until the time that his word came: the word of the Lord tried him. Psalm 105:18-19 (KJV)

The Amplified Bible renders verse 18 this way:
His feet they hurt with fetters; he was laid in chains of iron and his soul entered into the iron,
Psalm 105:18 (AMP)
Personal integrity is the "rod of iron" in our backs that is the result of experiencing and handling difficulty in the right way. Integrity is holiness and holiness is the heart of God. Holiness means being dedicated to, and set apart for, the pleasure and purpose of God in purity. Holiness is to be God-like; to be like Him in character. To walk and talk like Jesus the Christ.

But as he which hath called you is holy, so be ye holy in all manner of conversation; Because it is written, Be ye holy; for I am holy. 1 Peter 1:15-16 (KJV)
When you or I receive a promise from God, whether out of the written Word or a prophetic utterance, there is a time of waiting. During this time the word of the Lord will try us. In other words, patience will work its work and perfect that which pertains to each of us as individuals (Psa. 138:8).

But let patience have her perfect work, that ye may be perfect and entire, wanting nothing. James 1:4 (KJV)
How long will this work of perfecting last? Until our "soul [is] entered into the iron." Until we become mature enough to handle the "riches in glory by Christ Jesus" (Phil. 4:19) that the Lord has laid up in store as our inheritance.

Now I say, That the heir, as long as he is a child, differeth nothing from a servant, though he be lord of all; But is under tutors and governors until the time appointed of the father. Galatians 4:1-2 (KJV)
As we mature in our faith, our understanding of the ways of God, our selflessness, we will be given the position of full grown sons in the business of the kingdom and will save many alive.

August 30 - All Things

All things are delivered unto me of my Father: and no man knoweth the Son, but the Father; neither knoweth any man the Father, save the Son, and he to whomsoever the Son will reveal him. Matthew 11:27 (KJV)

There is nothing we possess, whether natural or spiritual, that does not come from our Father in heaven. The Amplified Bible says it this way:

Every good gift and every perfect (free, large, full) gift is from above; it comes down from the Father of all [that gives] light, in [the shining of] Whom there can be no variation [rising or setting] or shadow cast by His turning [as in an eclipse]. James 1:17 (AMP)

This supports our understanding that even the faith we have has been given as an extension of grace and the grace by which we are saved is a free gift of love given by God our Father.

So then faith cometh by hearing, and hearing by the word of God. Romans 10:17 (KJV)

For by grace are ye saved through faith; and that not of yourselves: it is the gift of God: Not of works, lest any man should boast. Ephesians 2:8-9 (KJV)

The Father is intimately acquainted with the Son beyond what you and I can understand short of divine revelation and that is only a glimpse beyond the veil into the hidden mysteries. The Holy Spirit sounds the depths of the mind of God and the heart of God and brings us His thoughts, purposes and desires.

The Son shares this unfathomable intimacy and therefore can reveal the one and only true God, the Almighty Creator of the Universe, the Ancient of Days, the Aleph and the Yod, the Alpha and the Omega, as none else can do. In seeing the Son with eyes anointed with heavenly eye salve, by receiving the ingrafted word and becoming born-again, we come to know Him who is unknowable to the unholy. In the Son He is revealed and we see Him high and lifted up and His train filling the temple (Isa. 6:1).

August 31 - The Men had Knowledge

And when they were gone over, they came into the land of Gennesaret. And when the men of that place had knowledge of him, they sent out into all that country round about, and brought unto him all that were diseased; And besought him that they might only touch the hem of his garment: and as many as touched were made perfectly whole. Matthew 14:34-36 (KJV)

A man who has first hand knowledge of the Lord cannot but noise abroad His arrival in his community. Witnesses to His willingness to minister, His compassionate nature, His supernatural power, and His marvelous works, have no second thoughts about telling everyone when Jesus shows up. They will go to great lengths to bring those who are afflicted by disease and every form of infirmity into His presence.

Beloved, we must be sure to provide a place for the men of our community to see, first hand, the power of God's Christ working. It is not enough to gather together a group of people and tell them about God. It is not enough to relate the stories of days gone by. It is simply not enough to give mankind a history lesson on what the Lord did while He walked on earth. Jesus has not changed one iota since He moved about the land of Galilee.

Jesus Christ (the Messiah) is [always] the same, yesterday, today, [yes] and forever (to the ages). Hebrews 13:8 (AMP)

What the world needs now is a fresh, new, dynamic demonstration of the resurrected Christ operating through believers today. There must be a place where seekers will not just be met with a sensitivity to where they are and a catering to what they think they want but will come face to face with a living, loving, confrontationally active and life changing Lord and Savior who saves, heals and delivers.

Seekers must meet the conquering Christ of the Cross of Calvary and participate in His death, burial and resurrection in order to find what they really need - to be made perfectly whole in the new birth that brings new life.

SEPTEMBER

September 01 - I Will Never Leave You

Let your conversation be without covetousness; and be content with such things as ye have: for he hath said, I will never leave thee, nor forsake thee. Hebrews 13:5 (KJV)

One of the first verses that I heard quoted after I received Jesus as Lord and Savior was Hebrews 13:5. To me this was the most important verse in the Bible after John 3:16.

I was the seventh son born of my natural mother. Each child had a different father. Right after birth my mother left me on the door steps of the Ventura Orphanage in Ventura, California. One thing is for sure, I am very glad that abortions were not in vogue at that time. It is obvious that God had a plan for my life that included becoming a Christian (which happened when I was 32 years old) and maturing for a while (I'm over 73 as I write this).

Adopted at 10 months old, I was given the Stover name and began to be a part of this Southern California family. My father, George M. Stover Sr. died when I was 12 and my mother disowned me when I was 17. It seemed that no one really wanted to keep me around; with one exception that is.

When I was 16 I met Sharon Heaton and we fell wildly in love. It was a love that lasted through my 2-1/2 year Army tour of duty over seas and brought us to the life long commitment of marriage when we were 20. Well, that was our intention in the beginning but after about 12 years things were pretty shaky. We were both alcoholics and not getting along like we had hoped.

That's when Jesus came into our lives and delivered us from alcohol, cigarettes and demons while restoring us to soundness of mind. The result has been a wonderful adventure that has allowed us to be celebrating our Anniversary next month. We're more in love today than we were when we got married and it has been over 53 years!

When Jesus came to us He made a commitment that was eternal. He said, "I will] not, [I will] not, [I will] not in any degree leave you helpless nor forsake nor let [you] down (relax My hold on you)! [Assuredly not!]" (Heb. 13:5 AMP). Now, that is a powerful commitment that gives complete assurance of love, acceptance and belonging. It is His eternal promise to you too.

September 02 - An Approved Workman

Study to shew thyself approved unto God, a workman that needeth not to be ashamed, rightly dividing the word of truth. 2 Timothy 2:15 (KJV)

This much quoted verse caught my attention the other day and I thought I would share it with you.

We start with the strong admonition to "study." This Greek word is, *spoudazo*, and means to "exert one's self, to be diligent in labor while studying. This is followed by the reason for the admonition to study which is that we "show ourselves approved of God." The word used for "to shew" is, *paristemi*, which could be understood as, "to offer such an argument, or so much proof, that your presentation would bring another into your fellowship of understanding and intimacy" with the Word of God and the God of the Word.

Our argument is easily embraced by others because we are called to be "approved" of God. This is the word in this verse that I found so interesting. The word "approved" is, *dokimos*. According to Donald Barnhouse we understand that, "In the ancient world there was no banking system as we know it today, and no paper money. All money was made from metal, heated until liquid, poured into moulds and allowed to cool. When the coins were cooled, it was necessary to smooth off the uneven edges. The coins, were comparatively soft and of course many people shaved them closely. In one century, more than eighty laws were passed in Athens, to stop the practice of shaving down the coins then in circulation. But some money changers were men of integrity, who would accept no counterfeit money. They were men of honour who put only genuine full weighted money into circulation. Such men were called, *dokimos,* or "approved".

Oh, that we Christians would be, *dokimos,* and learn to handle the Word of God without "shaving down" its full counsel.

My constant prayer is that we would each be willing to exert ourselves and be diligent in our study of the Word. Oh, that we would learn to present our testimony of its life giving power in a way that would draw the lost into fellowship with Christ, the *Logos* of God, and give them a hunger to seek intimacy with our God.

September 03 - Integrity

Then said his wife unto him, Dost thou still retain thine integrity? curse God, and die. Job 2:9 (KJV)

During Job's affliction by the devil, his wife mocked him and told him to curse God and die. Such will do those who do not have a relying trust in the Lord when things are not going the way they want them to.

In the book of Acts as we read the story of Stephen the evangelist it Chapter 7, we see those who are opposed to the Gospel message becoming enraged to the point that, in order to silence him, they stoned him to death.

And cast him out of the city, and stoned him: and the witnesses laid down their clothes at a young man's feet, whose name was Saul. Acts 7:58 (KJV)

These are but two instances of men in the Bible who refused to lose their integrity neither for the sake of loved ones nor for the crowd. These are followed by many others who at one time or another have had to make a decision as to whether to yield to the animosity of a family member or the popular opinion or political correctness of society even at the cost of their own life.

Little did Job's wife know that, in actuality, to "curse God" was to "die." Stephen's antagonists, one of which was a young Saul of Tarsus who would follow him in martyrdom after his conversion, did not understand that they could kill Stephen's body but not his inner man.

Today there is a bold line drawn in the sand between those who "curse God and die," though they think that they live, and those of you who will suffer anything and "still retain thine integrity."

The New Birth transforms the inner man of the spirit, the soulish man of the will, intellect and emotions and the physical man of flesh. Integrity demands that there be no schism between spirit, soul and body. The Christian with integrity will openly maintain their confident confession of Jesus as Christ in every situation no matter the pressure to yield.

September 04 - Comfort Them

Who comforteth us in all our tribulation, that we may be able to comfort them which are in any trouble, by the comfort wherewith we ourselves are comforted of God.
2 Corinthians 1:4 (KJV)

Our God is "the God of all Comfort." In answer to the prayer of Jesus, He has sent us the "Comforter," the Holy Spirit.
And I will pray the Father, and he shall give you another Comforter, that he may abide with you for ever; John 14:16 (KJV)
Whatever we face, whatever we go through, and we do "go through," whatever our human experience, we are comforted by the Holy Ghost. Because of the work of the ever present "Comforter," we can bring comfort to others in their troubles.
We also have been taught of Him in those times of testing so that we can "wage a good warfare" and "having done all, stand" (1 Tim. 1;18; Eph. 6:13). Whatever Word we need will be brought to our remembrance so that we can abide in the power of the living Word.
But the Comforter, which is the Holy Ghost, whom the Father will send in my name, he shall teach you all things, and bring all things to your remembrance, whatsoever I have said unto you. John 14:26 (KJV)
There is also the wonderful promise that when the "Comforter" comes, He will tell us all that He has experienced with Jesus the Christ. He testifies of Jesus the Christ to those who want to know of Him. He is the Spirit of truth and will lead us into all truth.
But when the Comforter is come, whom I will send unto you from the Father, even the Spirit of truth, which proceedeth from the Father, he shall testify of me: John 15:26 (KJV)
Jesus is the truth and the Holy Spirit reveals Him as the Word of truth, the *Logos*, the living, working, reasoning (the mind) of God incarnate ("the mind of Christ" 1 Cor. 2:16).
Jesus saith unto him, I am the way, the truth, and the life: no man cometh unto the Father, but by me.
John 14:6 (KJV)

September 05 - Identification Determines Destiny

I am crucified with Christ: nevertheless I live; yet not I, but Christ liveth in me: and the life which I now live in the flesh I live by the faith of the Son of God, who loved me, and gave himself for me. Galatians 2:20 (KJV)

Paul's consciousness lies here. He had nothing to lose. He was crucified with Christ. You must understand who you are because identity determines destiny. Remember this: Identity Determines Destiny.

According to secular thought, we are shaped by (a Genetic determinism, (b Psychological determinism, and/or (c Environmental determinism. In other words; where we came from genetically, what our psychological propensities are, or the environment we were born and raised in determines our destiny.

But, when you are born-again, Jesus gives a whole different identification and redetermines your destiny. We now live according to the Epistles. It has been said, "You are what you eat." This is a great spiritual truth. You need to feed in, and be nourished by, the Epistles.

Romans, Chapter 5, tells us that: Adam made the mess (Genetic determinism) and then Christ fixed the mess (Creative determinism). Our destiny, as believers, is now determined by creative determinism.

When you were born-again, much like a CD, cassette tape or video tape, what was written on you was erased and a new Master was used to imprint information on (in) you. The life, nature and mind of Christ was superimposed upon you. Now, it is not you, but Christ that lives!

You are in Christ. You fight the good fight of faith and never enter the ring as contender. Now, you enter as the champion (Heb. 11:1). Victory is the substance and evidence of faith.

Now, you are the son of God! God loves you exactly the same as He loves Jesus. You are the righteousness of God in Christ (2 Cor. 5:21). The Old man was crucified (executed) (Rom. 6:6).

Agree with God and you will fulfil your destiny. It is the work of faith. "The life I now live, I live by faith."

September 06 - Integrity of the Upright

The integrity of the upright shall guide them: but the perverseness of transgressors shall destroy them.
Proverbs 11:3 (KJV)

The integrity, *tummah*, quality of being honest and morally upright and the state of being whole or unified, of the upright, *yashar*, straight, upright, straightforward, just, fitting, proper and righteous, shall guide them.

Integrity, for the Christian, is living in a state of agreement with God concerning His will for that which is spirit, soul and body. In other words, for a Christian to be a person of "integrity" they would need to be "doers of the word, and not hearers only" (Jam. 1:22 KJV), applying the Word of God to every area of life. All of the Christian's dealings with others would be honest and straight forward. These principles of character are fitting, proper and righteous.

To be otherwise would leave such a one in a state of deceiving themselves and not knowing what manner of person he actually is (Jam. 1:22, 24 KJV). Sadly, many of the beloved of God are wilfully self-deceived in the quest for immediate personal gratification and, so, drift into thinking and the resultant behaviors that secular society has imprinted upon their lives.

Our verse goes on to say, the perverseness, *celeph*, crookedness and crooked dealing of transgressors, *bagad*, the unfaithful man who acts or deals treacherously, faithlessly and deceitfully, shall destroy, *shadad*, utterly ruin, them.

Wouldn't it be prudent to read, study, meditate on, and commit to memory, the Word of God and yield to its wisdom, insight and instruction? Being the Word is profitable (2 Tim. 3:16), would it not make sense to embrace its dictates and reap the benefit of Gods will for our lives?

Is anything more important than finding and fulfilling the plan and purpose of God for every area of one's life? I think not.

May this day find each of us prospering and in good health, even as our soul is prospering (3 John 1:2).

September 07 - Friend of God

> And the scripture was fulfilled which saith, Abraham believed God, and it was imputed unto him for righteousness: and he was called the Friend of God.
> James 2:23 (KJV)

Have you heard the song, "I am a friend of God"? What a marvelous thought put to music so beautifully. When I first heard it I couldn't stop singing the chorus, "I am a friend of God, I am a friend of God. He calls me friend." I believe that to be called the friend of God burns in the heart of every true believer.

After I got over the thrill of the moment, I began to consider what it takes to be "a friend of God." It wasn't quite such an ecstatic flight in the realm of reality.

To be "the friend of God" requires that a person be a believer. The words, "Abraham believed God," carry the powerful truth that to be "the friend of God" demands a faith that results in absolute obedience. After all, "faith without works is dead" (Jam. 2:20, 26).

Abraham was justified by the work of faith when he offered Isaac on the altar (Jam. 2:21) and that action of faith is what made his faith perfect (Jam. 2:22) and endeared him to the heart of God as "friend."

Believing in God is really of no value to those who do not mix action with their faith. Scripture declares that, "the devils also believe, and tremble," but of what value is that to them or to God. No devil has ever been called the friend of God though they believe that He is.

The true believer must not only believe that God is, but that He is a rewarder of them that diligently seek Him (Heb. 11:6). That is to say that, the believer is in a covenant relationship with Him that brings the rewards of relationship. This kind of believing is the same as that which is required of those who "receive" Christ as Lord and Savior. It is that belief of heart, accompanied by confession of mouth, that confirms the covenant relationship between man and God, God and man, which results in a changed life that receives imputed righteousness, activated and worked out by and through faith.

September 08 - Son of God

According as he hath chosen us in him before the foundation of the world, that we should be holy and without blame before him in love: Ephesians 1:4 (KJV)

The only thing better than being a friend of God is being a child of God. This, Beloved, is exactly what God the Father has done in and through Christ Jesus. Now I enthusiastically sing, "I am a son of God, I am a son of God, I am a son of God, He calls me son." Glory!

The love of God manifest in and through Jesus was not an afterthought to God. He chose, *eklegomai*, chose out for Himself out of many those to be peculiarly His own. Now, you are a part of a chosen generation. You are "called, and chosen, and faithful."

But ye are a chosen generation, a royal priesthood, an holy nation, a peculiar people; that ye should shew forth the praises of him who hath called you out of darkness into his marvellous light: 1 Peter 2:9 (KJV)

These shall make war with the Lamb, and the Lamb shall overcome them: for he is Lord of lords, and King of kings: and they that are with him are called, and chosen, and faithful. Revelation 17:14 (KJV)

As God's own children, by His choice, we "should be holy and without blame before him in love." We should, by our life-style and our words, reveal to the world what it means to be a child of God and joint-heirs with Christ.

And if children, then heirs; heirs of God, and joint-heirs with Christ; if so be that we suffer with him, that we may be also glorified together. Romans 8:17 (KJV)

And because ye are sons, God hath sent forth the Spirit of his Son into your hearts, crying, Abba, Father. Wherefore thou art no more a servant, but a son; and if a son, then an heir of God through Christ.
Galatians 4:6-7 (KJV)

Selah

September 09 - Except it Die

Thou fool, that which thou sowest is not quickened, except it die: 1 Corinthians 15:36 (KJV)

You and I have been delivered from a spirit of fear.

For God hath not given us the spirit of fear; but of power, and of love, and of a sound mind. 2 Timothy 1:7 (KJV)

Even death fails to hold us in the grip of fear once we are born-again.

And deliver them who through fear of death were all their lifetime subject to bondage. Hebrews 2:15 (KJV)

Fear is simply negative faith. It believes the lie of the deceptive forces of Satan in the world. Fear will believe that you are going to die and not live. It believes that you are going to go broke, lose your house, live on the street and perhaps even starve to death. It believes that your ministry will never come into the fullness you had planned.

The devil loves to convince people, those who call themselves Christians, especially those called into the ministry offices of the Church, that they are fools to follow Christ, give money to the Church and spend their time pursuing the things of God.

God, on the other hand, in Christ, has delivered such from all that is attached to fear. We have been translated into His marvelous light and walk in the love filled realm of faith. God, who is Love, has bestowed upon those He loves, You and I, exceeding precious promises. All of this is available the moment we are willing to die to self and accept life in Christ.

Faith comes alive when love comes. Perfect love comes when flesh yields to death. When flesh dies, the life of the spirit rises in resurrection power. The sons of God are manifest in resurrection glory. They know their God and do exploits enabled by the love, life, and power of the Almighty. The name of Jesus provides all sufficiency in all things. Giving becomes a joyful river of provision. There is no lack to them that live in Christ.

September 10 - My Covenant

My covenant will I not break, nor alter the thing that is gone out of my lips. Psalm 89:34 (KJV)

"My covenant, **beriyth**, will I not break," establishes the position of God in relation to those who put their trust in Him. He has made an alliance of friendship that is irrevocable. He has pledged to be in league with us, world without end.

God has said, ". . . I will never leave thee, nor forsake thee" (Heb. 13:5 KJV). The Amplified Bible renders the verse in this way: "I will not in any way fail you nor give you up nor leave you without support. [I will] not, [I will] not, [I will] not in any degree leave you helpless nor forsake nor let [you] down (relax My hold on you)! [Assuredly not!]."

This is reminiscent of the Lord's words to Joshua:

There shall not any man be able to stand before thee all the days of thy life: as I was with Moses, so I will be with thee: I will not fail thee, nor forsake thee. Joshua 1:5 (KJV)

God, who cannot lie, has cut covenant with those whom He has chosen and called. The blood of Jesus was shed, the spotless Lamb of God sacrificed, to ratify the covenant of God to those who would receive the Token of this great and precious promise (Titus 1:2; Heb. 10:29; Rev. 17:14).

The Almighty God has given to us Him whose "name shall be called Wonderful, Counselor, The mighty God, The everlasting Father, The Prince of Peace" (Isa. 9:6 KJV). Jesus, the Christ, leaves nothing lacking in our covenant relationship with our Creator, God and Father. He who was dead is mediating this eternal covenant to see that it is never altered. Even death and hell are subject to Him

I am he that liveth, and was dead; and, behold, I am alive for evermore, Amen; and have the keys of hell and of death. Revelation 1:18 (KJV)

What, then, could trouble us? Who can be against us being that our God is in covenant with us and will not change His mind? (Rom. 8:31)

September 11 - Fear Not!

> Fear not, O land; be glad and rejoice: for the Lord will do great things. Joel 2:21 (KJV)

Fear is crippling. It is the great enemy of faith. In fact, it is negative faith that empowers the enemy of our soul, life and ministry. The simple truth is that F.E.A.R. is False Evidence Appearing Real. The majority of what we fear never happens. The rest is overcome by faith in the promises of God.

I just love it when the Lord shows up or sends His angels to help us. The greeting is always the same, no matter the situation and circumstance. The Lord comes on the scene and says, "Fear Not!" Our verse today tells us that the Lord has promised to do great things, *gadal*. His means that He will magnify Himself in and through you by making you great and powerful in the strength of His might. We see this in the New Testament where we are told that there are no limits to what we can do in Christ:

> I can do all things through Christ which strengtheneth me. Philippians 4:13 (KJV)

I don't know about you, but that gives me great deal of confidence and hope for the future. This lays the foundation for faith to arise and to see the enemies of God scatter.

Our verse for today records the Lord speaking to the land, *'adamah*. This is speaking of land in the sense of your piece of ground, territory or country. We are told to be glad and rejoice because of what the Lord is wanting to do in, and through, you. He is going to do great things, *gadal*. That is, He is going to magnify Himself in and through you by making you great and powerful in the strength of His might.

You see, the Lord is in and for you. There is nothing and no one that can stand in the way of His mighty working in your life except you yourself.

Open your heart and let God arise. Let the Word of God speak to you and let faith arise. As you do, you will see your enemies scatter and victory be your portion.

September 12 - Be Not Afraid!

Be not afraid, . . . : for the pastures of the wilderness do spring, for the tree beareth her fruit, the fig tree and the vine do yield their strength. Joel 2:22 (KJV)

"Be not afraid," is the same Hebrew word, *yare',* that is used in the previous verse translated, "Fear Not." The word is spoken to all of creation to bring comfort and hope:
Because the creature itself also shall be delivered from the bondage of corruption into the glorious liberty of the children of God. For we know that the whole creation groaneth and travaileth in pain together until now. Romans 8:21-22 (KJV)
The "tree" spoken of here is the Cross, the tree of life. We are told that "the tree" will bear her fruit. This is speaking of Christ and the Christian who were crucified on it.
The fig tree is nothing other than Israel and the vine is, without doubt, Christ and His Church, the covenant Bride.
The promise, then, to all of creation, Israel and the Church is that they will yield, *nathan.* We understand this to mean that they will commit, entrust, give over, deliver up, produce, yield, or bestow their strength.
Strength, *chayil,* host, forces, valiant men of valour, riches, wealth, power, substance and might is the yield of the covenant people of God.
We can see that the working of God on earth will be manifest through both covenant groups of; Israel and the Church. Yes, both have a covenant with God. The covenants differ in their administration but they are just as binding in both instances. There is a third group of people and they are without covenant though God will deal with them. They are the gentiles; the unbelieving ones. This is what is being taught in 1 Corinthians 10:32 (KJV): "Give none offence, neither to the Jews, nor to the Gentiles, nor to the church of God." These are the only people groups recognized by the Almighty.
These days in which we live will show forth the dealings of God with each of these people groups to fulfill His plan and purpose. The three-fold chord of God, His chosen people, the Jews, and His children, the Church will be displayed in strength.

September 13 - How Are You Known?

Even a child is known by his doings, whether his work be pure, and whether it be right. Proverbs 20:11 (KJV)

My Mother used to say, "Do as I say, not as I do!" Unfortunately, this never works. We learn more by what we see than what we hear. Of course, what we speak is vitally important but if it is not backed by corresponding action it is nothing. The Bible says it this way:

But wilt thou know, O vain man, that faith without works is dead? James 2:20 (KJV)

For as the body without the spirit is dead, so faith without works is dead also. James 2:26 (KJV)

Another translation says: "Faith without its corresponding actions is dead.

Many so called Christians prefer to live like they want with no regard for the wants of the Father or honor of the Lord. They are self-seeking and self-gratifying in action while spouting the promises of God as though they had claim to them.

The simple truth is, however, that those who truly love the Lord will put action to their professed faith. They're not afraid of what God will do to them if they live an unholy life but are concerned what they will do to God. Jesus said:

If ye love me, keep my commandments. John 14:15 (KJV)

If ye keep my commandments, ye shall abide in my love; even as I have kept my Father's commandments, and abide in his love. John 15:10 (KJV)

Our love for God demands that we are concerned with how He looks at our behavior. Love calls us to desire to please Him and not ourselves. Beloved, let us, then, heed the call:

I beseech you therefore, brethren, by the mercies of God, that ye present your bodies a living sacrifice, holy, acceptable unto God, which is your reasonable service. Romans 12:1 (KJV)

As 1 Corinthians 6:20 (KJV) says, "For ye are bought with a price: therefore glorify God in your body, and in your spirit, which are God's." *Selah*

September 14 - He Grew

And Samuel grew, and the Lord was with him, and did let none of his words fall to the ground.
1 Samuel 3:19 (KJV)

A parent would think it a disturbing thing if their new-born child did not begin to grow. Growth is a natural process subsequent to birth. This is true in the natural and it is true in the spirit.

When a baby is fed and cared for properly it will take on strength and stature day by day. This is growth. The little human being begins learning even in the womb. This learning process accelerates during and after birth. There is a physical yearning for food and a mental yearning for knowledge just as certainly as there is a desire to be loved and wanted.

As the individual develops there is noticeable change in physical appearance, mental acumen, emotional maturation and self-control. At least, this is what is expected.

Christian parents also develop their children spiritually, feeding them with the Word of God and modeling the Christ life rather than the self life. This is without argument the most important responsibility of Christian parents. They are called to produce righteous seed after the God kind; their kind.

Samuel had been wholly dedicated to the Lord by his parents. In fact they had given him into the care of Eli the priest so that he could grow into the fullness of that to which he was called.

Our verse for today declares, "Samuel grew." This word "grew" is the Hebrew word, *gadal*, which means, not only to grow, but to become great or important, to be promoted or to be made more powerful in order to do great things.

As you and I feed on God's Word and are nourished, cared for, protected by, taught and guided by the Holy Spirit we cooperate with the process whereby we are becoming great or important (as did Joseph in Egypt) and are being promoted and made to be more powerful in order to do great things for our Father and our God in Christ (Dan. 11:32b).

September 15 - The Lord Was With Him

And Samuel grew, and the Lord was with him, and did let none of his words fall to the ground.
1 Samuel 3:19 (KJV)

Not only did Samuel grow, but "the Lord was with him." When you and I are willing to feed ourselves on the Word of God, willing to spend time with, and yield to, the Holy Spirit, we will grow spiritually until we reach the measure of the stature of the fullness of the Christ and the completeness found in Him.

[That it might develop] until we all attain oneness in the faith and in the comprehension of the [full and accurate] knowledge of the Son of God, that [we might arrive] at really mature manhood (the completeness of personality which is nothing less than the standard height of Christ's own perfection), the measure of the stature of the fullness of the Christ and the completeness found in Him. Ephesians 4:13 (AMP)

This developmental process that we experience as we cooperate with His work within (Phil. 2:12b) will bring us to "oneness in the faith and in the comprehension of the [full and accurate] knowledge of the Son of God." This is how the believer reaches spiritual maturity ("really mature manhood").

It is in this marvelous condition that we, as mature believers, come to realize the great truth that the Lord is with us, in us, and, in fact, manifest in and through us (Joh. 4:21; Rom. 8:19; Heb 13:5; Col. 1:27; 1 Joh. 4:4;).

As you and I grow, the Lord is with us to bring us into His determined destiny for our lives. Beloved, you and I will complete the plan and purpose of God for our lives. We won't do it by our own strength, but He will do it with, in, and through us.

. . . Not by might, nor by power, but by my spirit, saith the Lord of hosts. Zechariah 4:6 (KJV)

It shall be said and known that, "the Lord was, and is, with you!"

September 16 - The Lord Appeared Again

And the Lord appeared again in Shiloh: for the Lord revealed himself to Samuel in Shiloh by the word of the Lord. 1 Samuel 3:21 (KJV)

Beloved, don't lose heart. If you haven't had one of those high times, if you haven't heard the Voice as you once did, if it has been some time since you had a dream or a vision: Don't lose heart.

Stay in the Word, stay in the Word, stay in the Word. Be washed by the washing of regeneration that can only come by the Word of the Living God. Your working for the Lord will never accomplish what waiting on Him after having been washed by waters from the well of salvation will.

Not by works of righteousness which we have done, but according to his mercy he saved us, by the washing of regeneration, and renewing of the Holy Ghost; Titus 3:5 (KJV)

That he might sanctify and cleanse it with the washing of water by the word, Ephesians 5:26 (KJV)

As we are immersed in the flowing water of His Word we will be moved into a position where the Lord will appear again. Rest assured, He will appear again!

I will never forget a time in my life when it seemed as if the heavens had become brass and the Lord had closed up shop for a vacation. I immersed myself in the Word and prayed fervently. I confessed everything I had ever done, thought of doing or even thought I might ever think of doing. It was a miserable time, yet a grand time. I fell in love with the word. It carried me as nothing else ever had. Then, after a year and a half, as though He had only taken a breath between words, "the Lord appeared again" and spoke.

I asked Him, "What happened, Lord? I thought I had somehow offended you." Gently, but oh so powerfully, He said, "You were leaning too much on experience and feeling so I left you to get anchored in My Word. Now you can walk by faith into the victory that has been provided you in Christ."

September 17 - By The Word of The Lord

And the Lord appeared again in Shiloh: for the Lord revealed himself to Samuel in Shiloh by the word of the Lord. 1 Samuel 3:21 (KJV)

I have always been a bit of a mystic. By that I mean that I love the things of the Spirit of God and all that accompanies them. I love to see visions, have dreams and hear the Lord speak by His Spirit. I lay great stock in the prophetic and the ministry of the Prophet in this hour.

Every encounter I have had with the supernatural has only served to make me more hungry to know the Lord and His ways. I do realize that all of the manifestations of the Spirit of the Lord are the revealing of His acts and not necessarily a revelation of His ways.

To know the ways of God requires that we be serious students of, and adherents to, His Word. His acts are seen in the miraculous intervention of the natural order, in whatever way He chooses, to bring benefit to His creation. His ways, on the other hand, are only found by revelation in His Word.

And if thou wilt walk in my ways, to keep my statutes and my commandments, as thy father David did walk, then I will lengthen thy days. 1 Kings 3:14 (KJV)

In the Book of books are the words of life. It is the Word of Life, the *Logos*, the Living Light of the World, Who, incarnate, walked the earth in human flesh.

That which was from the beginning, which we have heard, which we have seen with our eyes, which we have looked upon, and our hands have handled, of the Word of life; 1 John 1:1 (KJV)

To know His ways is to know His Son. To know His Son is to know His Word. To know His Word requires that it be honored and kept. Then, it will come to pass that "the Lord revealed himself . . . by the word of the Lord." Our love for Him will cause us to revere and obey. Thus shall we know His ways.

September 18 - Prisoners of Hope

Turn you to the strong hold, ye prisoners of hope: even to day do I declare that I will render double unto thee; Zechariah 9:12 (KJV)

A stronghold is not just a word used for a fortress. It is also a word used for a treasury, a store house, or a vault where valuable items are kept safe and secure.

Once born-again, once we have embraced the Christ of God as our personal Lord and Savior, entering in to a covenant relationship with Him, we are possessors of God's riches in glory by Christ Jesus:

But my God shall supply all your need according to his riches in glory by Christ Jesus. Philippians 4:19 (KJV)

We are "prisoners of hope;" that is, we are bound, *'aciyr*, to hope, *tiqvah*, filled with expectation for the thing longed for and the outcome committed to by salvation's covenant promise.

When we have moved away from our promised possession through the ignorance of a lack of teaching or neglect, we are beckoned to "Return," *shuwb*, or to be restored in order to recover that which was lost.

Many times we do not appropriate what Christ died to provide because of the deceits of the Devil. He is the thief and always comes to steal:

The thief cometh not, but for to steal, and to kill, and to destroy: I am come that they might have life, and that they might have it more abundantly. John 10:10 (KJV)

Jesus, however, came to give life, and life more abundant. By His Spirit He calls to us in love:

Return to the stronghold [of security and prosperity], you prisoners of hope; even today do I declare that I will restore double your former prosperity to you. Zechariah 9:12 (AMP)

As we respond to Him, He restores a second order, *mishneh*, or double of what was lost. It is never too late.

September 19 - Completion

Use the rest of this year to compete those things that have been started. It is a season of drawing upon the Resource of heaven and embracing the promise of your God given dream and vision.

The battles you have fought in the realm of the spirit have been won and it is time to reap the Victor's spoil.

For the weapons of our warfare are not carnal, but mighty through God to the pulling down of strong holds; 2 Corinthians 10:4 (KJV)

The word "strong holds," is, *ochuroma*, and does not just speak of a fortification, but of a treasury vault that holds its contents safely.

Our weapons of warfare, Beloved, are supernaturally endued with power by Almighty God Himself to "pull down," *kathairesis*, from the word, *kathaireo*, which also means to take down from the Cross of crucifixion, without violence, the One crucified.

In other words, we can draw out of His riches in glory by Christ Jesus those things that Christ purchased on Calvary's Tree. The exceedingly precious promises that are ours in Christ are ready for delivery to those who are ready to receive by faith.

Your "good fight of faith" has been completed and your faith has pleased God. This has released the reward of heaven into your account for disbursement.

But without faith it is impossible to please him: for he that cometh to God must believe that he is, and that he is a rewarder of them that diligently seek him. Hebrews 11:6 (KJV)

You might as well shout for joy now because you are about to walk into the manifestation of your long awaited promised possession.

Now faith is the substance of things hoped for, the evidence of things not seen. Hebrews 11:1 (KJV)

September 20 - None of His Words Fell to the Ground

And Samuel grew, and the Lord was with him, and did let none of his words fall to the ground.
1 Samuel 3:19 (KJV)

When you are willing to grow in the Lord, yielding to the prompting of His Spirit, being taught of Him and led by Him, being nourished by His Word, you will experience His mighty presence moment by moment each and every day.

This is how you can come to the place where it can be said of you, "[He] did let none of his words fall to the ground." This simply means that what you say will be accomplished. Your words will be honored by God and will establish your future.

For verily I say unto you, That whosoever shall say unto this mountain, Be thou removed, and be thou cast into the sea; and shall not doubt in his heart, but shall believe that those things which he saith shall come to pass; he shall have whatsoever he saith. Therefore I say unto you, What things soever ye desire, when ye pray, believe that ye receive them, and ye shall have them. Mark 11:23-24 (KJV)

The above verse is not a promise loosely given to just anyone who says that they are a Christian. The power of words is not limited to the redeemed child of God but supernatural power is superimposed upon the words of those in covenant with Him.

Those at the tower of Babel were using the natural power of common words and common purpose but those of the Upper Room were using the supernatural power of divine words and divine purpose.

When the Lord is with us and we are with Him, we speak "as the oracles of God" and we minister "of the ability which God giveth: that God in all things may be glorified through Jesus Christ, to whom be praise and dominion for ever and ever. Amen" (1 Pet. 4:11 KJV).

He will not allow what we speak to "fall to the ground" without accomplishing what has been said.

Receive. Rehearse. Require. Rejoice and Realize.

September 21 - He was established

> And all Israel from Dan even to Beer-sheba knew that Samuel was established to be a prophet of the Lord.
> 1 Samuel 3:20 (KJV)

As we learn to receive the engrafted Word and rehearse what God speaks to our hearts, to ourselves and those around us, we will find faith becoming a stronger and more powerful guiding force in our lives.

What we speak with our mouth is directly connected to what we believe in our hearts. "Out of the abundance of the heart the mouth speaks" (Mat. 12:34; Luk. 6:45). We must learn to speak what is in our heart rather than what is in our head and is observed by our senses. The soul must, often times, be convinced of the spiritual truths received and held in the heart. This is done by rehearsing that which God has spoken to us.

> So then faith cometh by hearing, and hearing by the word of God. Romans 10:17 (KJV)

What is spoken in our spirit by the Spirit is what we receive by faith until it becomes apparent in the natural. We not only receive the promises of God in word, dream or vision, but require it of God who cannot lie.

The time between word, dream or vision and the realization of that which has been seeded in our hearts must be passed with rejoicing. We will only rejoice in the midst of trial, testing and time passing when we have received that for which we believe by faith.

This is the walk of the prophetic. It is specifically and habitually the walk of those called to be a Prophet. Every Christian is called to be a prophetic voice in their generation. Whether walking in the prophetic life as salt and light or walking the land in the ministry office of a Prophet, you and I are "established to be a prophet of the Lord" to the multitudes who are withering away in the "valley of decision" like dry parched bones without any hope of life. We have come for such a time.

September 22 - Shout the Shout of Victory!

Yes, shout for joy oh prisoners of hope and lay hold of what you have seen by the Spirit.

Let them shout for joy, and be glad, that favour my righteous cause: yea, let them say continually, Let the Lord be magnified, which hath pleasure in the prosperity of his servant. Psalm 35:27 (KJV)
Your Father's good pleasure is to give you the Kingdom. This has been His plan all along. Now is the time, the fulness of time, for that which concerns you to come to fruition.
Do not be seized with alarm and struck with fear, little flock, for it is your Father's good pleasure to give you the kingdom! Luke 12:32 (AMP)
Will He withhold any good thing from you?
. . . the Lord will give grace and glory: no good thing will he withhold from them that walk uprightly. Psalm 84:11 (KJV)
Our Lord works in the proper seasons of our lives. There are appointed places, times, seasons and meetings, as is expressed in the Hebrew word, *mow'ed*. This word is akin to the Greek word, *prothesmios*, which means, a time appointed, set beforehand, appointed or determined beforehand or prearranged.
Hear the Lord as He would say to you:
"My dear one, you may not like what you have been going through, but trust in Me. It was not meant, nor allowed to be, for your destruction nor was it allowed to harm you.
Like My son Joseph, it was to place a rod of iron in your back and to prepare you for this day and the new thing which I will bring forth in this coming year. Just as Samuel grew, *gadal*, so grew Joseph and so have you that you might be promoted or made to be more powerful in order to do great things in the days ahead.
In this prearranged and appointed time I have determined to release you as a 'beloved son, in whom I am well pleased.'"

September 23 - Open My Eyes

Open thou mine eyes, that I may behold wondrous things out of thy law. Psalms 119:18 (KJV)

Open thou mine eyes, *'ayin,* mental and spiritual faculties, the fountain of my spirit, that I may, *nabat,* be able to pay attention to and consider the wondrous things, *pala',* those things that separate God from man because of their extraordinary and difficult to understand nature known only to God.

The Psalmist is asking that Almighty God reveal Himself through His Word.

You may have come to realize that the Word of God holds things hidden beneath the surface of the words read. Surely, you have read a verse for the fourth, fifth or umpteenth time and, all of a sudden, it leaps off the page with a whole new depth like never before.

This has happened to me so many times. One verse can hold truths that are not seen by the casual reader. In fact it can hold multiple truths (none taking away from the original meaning) that are life changing.

I believe that there are at least seven levels of truth found in the words and promises of God that are only revealed by the Holy Spirit in times determined by God for each believer and for each season of time :

The words and promises of the Lord are pure words, like silver refined in an earthen furnace, purified seven times over. Psalm 12:6 (AMP)

No wonder that the Word of God is never boring, always fresh and pertinent to our daily lives and society's condition. The Eternal is eternal and knows the beginning from the ending and His Word is a living rule and guide for all generations.

I encourage you to become, not just a reader, but a student of the Word of God. If you will spend the time to become intimate with the Word of God you will become intimate with the God of the Word.

The Holy Spirit will help you too; if you ask.

September 24 - My Chosen One

I have made a covenant with my chosen, I have sworn unto David my servant, Psalm 89:3 (KJV)

Today's verse literally says, "I have cut a covenant, *karath beriyth*, of alliance and friendship. This covenant is one of divine ordinance accompanied with signs and pledges and ratified by My oath, *shaba*`. It is a covenant between Me and My chosen, called and anointed servant, `*ebed*.

This word, servant, `*ebed*, is not the servant slave that we might think. This is the worshiper of God, the prophet, priest servant. This is the word used as a form of address between equals. This is what Jesus was speaking of when He said,

Greater love hath no man than this, that a man lay down his life for his friends. Ye are my friends, if ye do whatsoever I command you. Henceforth I call you not servants; for the servant knoweth not what his lord doeth: but I have called you friends; for all things that I have heard of my Father I have made known unto you. John 15:13-15 (KJV)

Jesus is the "David," *daw-veed*`, the "Beloved" of God Who is the Chosen, Called and Anointed Servant, Prophet and Priest. The wonderful thing is that you and I are also the "beloved" of God in Christ. We are the object of His affection and the purchased of His life through the blood of the Lamb.

In Christ we are now the chosen, called and anointed servant king priests that walk the earth and carry the anointing to set the captives free as we rule and reign.

But ye are a chosen generation, a royal priesthood, an holy nation, a peculiar people; that ye should shew forth the praises of him who hath called you out of darkness into his marvellous light: 1 Peter 2:9 (KJV)

The Kingdom of God is in, and manifest through, the Beloved and His beloved. Now are the praises of God shown forth to all who are groping in darkness until this day. We "servants" bring the marvelous light of God to bear where ever we go.

September 25 - Go For Yourself

NOW [in Haran] the Lord said to Abram, Go for yourself [for your own advantage] away from your country, from your relatives and your father's house, to the land that I will show you. Genesis 12:1 (AMP)

If we are not careful, we can pickup a spirit of unworthiness and begin to allow religion to crush our ego. Self-esteem, or our sense of worth as an individual, is not to be done away with but is to be sanctified. In other words, You are important and valuable in the eyes of God and, therefore, should be valuable and important in your eyes and in the eyes of others.

You and I recognize that our righteousness falls far short of the righteousness of God and that there is nothing wholesome or righteous about us. We were born to a fallen world.

For we have all become like one who is unclean [ceremonially, like a leper], and all our righteousness (our best deeds of rightness and justice) is like filthy rags or a polluted garment; we all fade like a leaf, and our iniquities, like the wind, take us away [far from God's favor, hurrying us toward destruction]. Isaiah 64:6 (AMP)

But, once born-again, once cleansed by the covenant blood of Jesus the Christ, we become the very righteousness of God by imputation.

For our sake He made Christ [virtually] to be sin Who knew no sin, so that in and through Him we might become [endued with, viewed as being in, and examples of] the righteousness of God [what we ought to be, approved and acceptable and in right relationship with Him, by His goodness]. 2 Corinthians 5:21 (AMP)

Now, you and I can accept and obey the call and desire of God to bless us. The only way that this can happen is to leave everything behind and "Go for yourself [for your own advantage] away . . ." The Lord came to redeem and restore that which was lost. It is time to leave and receive.

September 26 - Die To Your Seed

I assure you, most solemnly I tell you, Unless a grain of wheat falls into the earth and dies, it remains [just one grain; it never becomes more but lives] by itself alone. But if it dies, it produces many others and yields a rich harvest. John 12:24 (AMP)

There is nothing more frustrating that sowing your seed and having crop failure.

One day I was sitting in front of my upstairs window looking out over our church property watching my wife, Sharon, drive round in our modified golf cart. When the Lord blessed us with the ability to purchase this beautiful four acre ranch I also purchased this cart from the former owner. It was quickly modified into our personal "tractor" and "tote-mobile."

Sharon was riding around spraying super strength Roundup © on the weeds and the area where weeds normally spring up each year. This treatment keeps the seed from moving through the growth cycle that results in cockle burrs and tumble weeds galore.

Too many of us give money, time and talent to the kingdom and then spray it with spiritual Roundup © by not dying to the "seed sown."

We give money but demand where it be spent. We give time and talent only to demand when and where it be used and many times insist that it be showcased.

Thou fool, that which thou sowest is not quickened, except it die: 1 Corinthians 15:36 (KJV)

God is not pleased with such acts of flesh. God will only accept that which has been offered as a sacrifice for destruction, *qorban*. There are many Hebrew words used for offering but this one is of particular importance due to the total release of ownership spoken of. The thing offered is seen as belonging to God and not to the giver. The Lord can do with it as He pleases.

Spiritual crop failure comes when the seed sown is kept in the hand of our heart and not released into the good soil of the heart and hand of God.

September 27 - God Never Forgets

For God is not unrighteous to forget your work and labour of love, which ye have shewed toward his name, in that ye have ministered to the saints, and do minister. Hebrews 6:10 (KJV)

God, *theos*, The Father, The Son, and The Holy Spirit, The Godhead, or Trinity, will never, ever forget nor stop caring about, *epilanthanomai*, your work, *ergon*, what you undertake to do or the, *kopos*, trouble and toil you have endured. You have honored His name, *onoma*, everything which His name covers, everything the thought or feeling of which is aroused in the mind by mentioning, hearing or remembering His name, because you work through trouble and toil in, *agape*, God's kind of limitless Love.

The Lord says, "You have ministered and do minister to My born-again, sons and daughters with the same kind of, *agape*, Love I have loved them with and I will never forget."

The Church has missed the tremendous regard that God, Who is Love, has for those who move in the realm of that Love. The Western world, especially the English speaking world has never been able to gain a revelation of the Love of God.

It is only when the Church begins to move in the Love of God that she will begin to do the greater works that Jesus assured her she would to.

I assure you, most solemnly I tell you, if anyone steadfastly believes in Me, he will himself be able to do the things that I do; and he will do even greater things than these, because I go to the Father. John 14:12 (AMP)

The level of faith necessary to do the "greater things" is only released to the degree that, *agape*, Love is received and released by the one who ministers.

For [if we are] in Christ Jesus, neither circumcision nor uncircumcision counts for anything, but only faith activated and energized and expressed and working through love. Galations 5:6 (AMP)

September 28 - The Drip Line

And I will give you [spiritual] shepherds after My own heart [in the final time], who will feed you with knowledge and understanding and judgment. Jeremiah 3:15 (AMP)

Recently, a 30 foot pine tree in our back yard just dried up and died. We fertilized it and did everything we knew to do. Little did we know that the original owners had an irrigation system put in that only watered next to the trunk of the tree.

A tree expert friend of ours came and looked at it and told us that most likely it was root bound and was unsalvageable. Sure enough, he was right. All the water was going straight down and did not challenge the roots to spread as they should. The tree could not get adequate nourishment to survive. The water should be at the drip line (that's where the branches reach to).

Many Christians run around getting "water" that is close to their "trunk." They don't want what will cause them to stretch and grow properly. They want what is easy and light. The result is that they are becoming "root bound" and soon will wither and die. Their roots don't go deep and wide into the river of God and so they cannot stand during a real storm life.

Pastors are a gift to the believer from Jesus, the Great Shepherd of the sheep. They know how to water the "trees" of the Lord properly.

And His gifts were [varied; He Himself appointed and gave men to us] . . . some pastors (shepherds of His flock) and teachers. Ephesians 4:11 (AMP).

They are responsible to water them at the "drip line." Rather than always bringing a light, easy, uplifting message, they bring "water" that will cause the "roots" to go wide and deep. They feed them nutrients that will allow them to grow to maturity in grace and a systemic word that will protect them from the attacks of blight and pestilence.

Don't be running around to get what is easy and light. Settle in to a local church and ". . . be like a tree firmly planted [and tended] by the streams of water, ready to bring forth its fruit in its season; its leaf also shall not fade or wither; and everything he does shall prosper." Psalm 1:3 (AMP)

September 29 - Through Faith . . .
We Understand - Part I

> Through faith we understand that the worlds were framed by the word of God, so that things which are seen were not made of things which do appear.
> Hebrews 11:3 (KJV)

As I considered this familiar verse of scripture I decided to take a look at the original language and see what I might find hidden in it.

Much to my surprise I found another reason to believe those brave scientists that are championing the "young earth" model of creation. The tragedy is that so many scientists and theologians have been corrupted by Darwinian theory and are still trying to come up with a multi-millions of years creation theory; the scientists refusing to recognize the possibility of a Creator and the theologians by yielding the biblical record to the whims of godless thinkers.

Let's start here: By means of faith, *pistis*, that is, our conviction of the truth based upon the character of the One who can be relied on, we understand, *noeo*, or we perceive with our mind, that the worlds, *aion*, translated as, the worlds, but also meaning, the universe and all that is in them, were framed, *katartizo*, that is, rendered, sound and complete.

Can you see that? The creation was put in order, arranged and adjusted to fit in completed form. God spoke the Word, *rhema,* that is, the spoken living word from His mouth and what He spoke was what appeared. It was, as it were, translated from what was not to what could be seen. This agrees with Hebrews 4;12a (AMP) that reads, "For the Word that God speaks is alive and full of power [making it active, operative, energizing, and effective];"

We also are assured that what God created was created to last through the fall and every subsequent convulsion. Don't let earthquakes or man made pollution frighten you. The earth was rendered sound and fixed. It will last until God removes it and replaces it with a "new heaven and a new earth" (Rev. 21:1).

September 30 - Through Faith . . . We Understand - Part II

Through faith we understand that the worlds were framed by the word of God, so that things which are seen were not made of things which do appear.
Hebrews 11:3 (KJV)

Yesterday we learned that the creation was spoken into existence as a complete and secured work. Now we will finish our study of the verse.

The Word of God was that which is or has been uttered by the Living Voice, of God, *theos*. This word, *theos*, speaks of the Godhead, Father, Son and Holy Spirit.

Now consider these little words that follow. so that things, *eis ho*, can be translated, toward the end that, things, The Son and the things He created, which are seen, *blepo*, or, perceived by the use of the eyes and therefore understood, were, *ginomai*, made to appear in history or brought to pass as a finished miracle, and not, *me ginomai*, or rather, not translated and made, brought into existence, *ek*, out of, things which do appear, *phaino*, are brought forth into the light and have become evident, appear so as to be seen.

What I'm seeing here is that this verse teaches us once again that Christ was at the center of creation and took full part in it -

All things were made by him; and without him was not any thing made that was made. John 1:3 (KJV)

- and that everything we can see, hear, touch, smell and taste was spoken into existence in completed form.

For the invisible things of him from the creation of the world are clearly seen, being understood by the things that are made, even his eternal power and Godhead; so that they are without excuse: Romans 1:20 (KJV)

307

OCTOBER

October 01 - Behold What Manner Of Love

Behold, what manner of love the Father hath bestowed upon us, that we should be called the sons of God: therefore the world knoweth us not, because it knew him not.
1 John 3:1 (KJV)

Behold, *eido*, turn your eyes, your mind, and your attention to the quality, *potapos*, of Love, *agape*. This love is the character and essence of God Himself (God is Love).

This word, Love, could be translated, Covenant Relationship. God has bestowed, *didomi*, given of His own accord into our care, His pledge of Himself and all that He is and has. He has committed into our care His cause and that which is given forth from Him.

This covenant relationship eternally establishes us in the family of God. He has adopted us with a promise to never break covenant. We can boldly call Him "*Abba*," Father and declare that we are a child (son or daughter) of His.

Once we receive a revelation of this quality of Love, the power of this covenant commitment, we will no longer be known, *ginosko*, by the world, *kosmos*. That is to say that the unsaved, the society of the world, will no longer have intimate knowledge of who we are. They will neither understand nor comprehend our relationship with God nor our way of thinking and living.

Just as those of Jesus' time did not recognize the time of their visitation, neither will the lost of this age recognize the presence of the manifest sons of God. We will not be "known" because He was not "known." We will not be understood because He was not understood.

Without a revelation of the Love of God there is no way to understand, regard nor value the people who are the loved of God. Consider this when you feel that people don't understand you now that you are saved. Consider the love bestowed.

October 02 - It Doeth Not Yet Appear

Beloved, now are we the sons of God, and it doth not yet appear what we shall be: but we know that, when he shall appear, we shall be like him; for we shall see him as he is. 1 John 3:2 (KJV)

I simply love this word, Beloved. This is the Greek word, *agapetos*, a word which is derived from, *agape*, the God kind of Love. This wonderful favorite of mine means, dearly beloved, well beloved, esteemed, favorite, and worthy of love.

Did you catch that? "Worthy of Love." How did such a thing happen? What makes us worthy of the God kind of love that issues from the Father to us ward?

God chose you and Me. He called you and I into covenant relationship with Him because He wanted to. He imputed righteousness to us because of the atonement wrought in Christ Jesus.

For he hath made him to be sin for us, who knew no sin; that we might be made the righteousness of God in him. 2 Corinthians 5:21 (KJV)

He adopted us into His family. "Now are we the sons of God."

This is exceedingly, abundant and above anything that I can wrap my mind around, let alone express, yet, He tells us that this glory we experience is nothing compared to what is to come. "It doth not yet appear what we shall be," holds a promise that is beyond imagination and causes one to thrill at the thought of what this might mean.

Then, we are told, when He comes, we shall be like Him. The Father's promise will be fulfilled just as assuredly as every word spoken by Him comes to pass. He cannot lie.

For those whom He foreknew [of whom He was aware and loved beforehand], He also destined from the beginning [foreordaining them] to be molded into the image of His Son [and share inwardly His likeness], that He might become the firstborn among many brethren. Romans 8:29 (AMP)

October 03 - Tongues of Men and of Angels

Though I speak with the tongues of men and of angels, and have not charity, I am become as sounding brass, or a tinkling cymbal. 1 Corinthians 13:1 (KJV)

"Though I speak" makes a clear and simple statement that the Apostle Paul speaks in "tongues" and is addressing those who also practice this empowering gift of glossolalia.

His point, however, is that no matter how much one speaks in tongues and no matter how many tongues are spoken, even angelic ones, it is a useless pursuit if not an out flow of Love (charity = *agape*): God's uniquely distinctive kind of covenant Love).

We can preach our hearts out, we can speak "as the oracles of God," we can be the greatest orator of all time, we can see and speak into the spirit realm, but if we have not love, it is grating and irritating, entirely useless "hot air."

The key to receiving the power, the revelation, the benefit of praying in tongues is that of allowing yourself to walk in covenant love with your brethren and to extend the offer of it to the lost.

Beloved, let us love one another: for love is of God; and every one that loveth is born of God, and knoweth God. 1 John 4:7 (KJV)

God is Love (1 Joh. 4:8, 16). His very character is Love. To receive anything from Him is to receive an outflow of His Love. What I'm say is, that when we speak in tongues, it must be an outflow of the love that God shed abroad in our hearts in order for us to realize the benefit of speaking mysteries (Rom. 5:5).

The Word of God teaches us that a heavenly language is given so that, in the spirit, the believer can speak mysteries and be able to build himself up on his most holy faith as well as praise and magnify the Lord (1 Cor. 14:2, 4, Jude 1:20).

Love is the key that unlocks the heart of God and allows the believer to experience covenant blessing through tongues.

October 04 - I Am Nothing

And though I have the gift of prophecy, and understand all mysteries, and all knowledge; and though I have all faith, so that I could remove mountains, and have not charity, I am nothing. 1 Corinthians 13:2 (KJV)

The word translated "charity" is the word for God's special kind of love, *agape*. This God kind of love is only experienced by the born-again believer who develops a covenant relationship with the King of Glory. This is the love by which faith works (Gal. 5:6). The very nature and character of God is this kind of love. It is not natural, human, nor humane, love but is supernatural in its origin.

Too many Christians, unwittingly, claim that they are something they are not. They have received a gift and have operated in it with great success for some time. They have prophesied, received revelation regarding some of the mysteries of the kingdom and have come to know a certain amount of spiritual truth. They have come to a knowledge of how faith works and had a great deal of visible success because of it. They may have a large following of supporters and believe that they have arrived in the blessing of the Almighty.

Unfortunately, if the God kind of love is not present in their life, God considers them to be nothing. Yes, that's right, God considers them nothing. If this were not true, Paul never would have said that without love "I am nothing."

Jesus came to seek and to save that which was lost. He came to seek out and restore individuals into the covenant love relationship that Adam had before the fall. He came to bring to full measure the covenant that God made with Abraham. Jesus was the love of God expressed in human form.

For God so loved, *agapao*, the world, that he gave his only begotten Son, that whosoever believeth in him should not perish, but have everlasting life. John 3:16 (KJV)

Gifts only work properly when activated and empowered by this kind of love.

Beloved, let's live in this God kind of love.

October 05 - No Profit

And though I bestow all my goods to feed the poor, and though I give my body to be burned, and have not charity, it profiteth me nothing. 1 Corinthians 13:3 (KJV)

Way too many folks are lulled into a sense of well being by how benevolent they are. They feed the hungry, clothe the needy, provide housing for the homeless during the icy winter months or give toys to the kids at Christmas. That these are noble and right things to do, there is no doubt. But, how does God look at such things?

Others are filled with a kind of spiritual pride at how sacrificially they serve their God, their Church, their Organization, Community or a favorite cause. Unfortunately, the only benefit they will ever realize is how good it makes them feel at the moment.

You see, everything that is done with a selfish motive is useless and sinful in the sight of the Lord. Self gratification is the furthest thing from the heart of God that there can be. Motive is everything. Even feeding starving children can be a sinful act motivated by self-centered pride, a gnawing guilt, or fear.

Don't misunderstand me here. I'm not saying that doing any of these acts of kindness are sinful in and of themselves. In fact, quite the opposite. I thank God for any need that is met by one who cares for others, no matter what the motivation.

What I want to point out is the simple but profound truth that is found in our verse for today. In the economy of God, there is no profit to the benefactor who does such acts without them being an overflow of the love, *agape*, of God.

This simply means that our show of benevolent intent should have its beginning in the heart of God and that it should be an expression of His love through us. It is the same for sacrificial service of any kind. Even "missions" can be a sinful act if it puffs up and makes the flesh proud. The love of God in Christ for the souls of every kindred, tongue, people and nation is the only acceptable and profitable cause for the missionary. Gods love felt and expressed is the only right motive of the Christian.

October 06 - Supposing Him To Be

But they, supposing him to have been in the company, went a day's journey; and they sought him among their kinsfolk and acquaintance. Luke 2:44 (KJV)

This verse speaking of a young Jesus slipping away to be with the religious leaders of the day caught my eye in a different way. I thought, "Many church goers are in this condition. They suppose Jesus to be in their company and look to those around them to validate His presence." Beloved, just because there is a crowd does not mean that the Lord is in their midst. The music and message may be uplifting, but is He there?

The tragedy is that many "Christian" churches are filled with people who do not realize what His parents realized on their journey home. He was not with them.

What do you do when you realize that Jesus is not in your "caravan"? Change direction. It is time to turn back to the last place where you were with Him and seek Him.

And when they found him not, they turned back again to Jerusalem, seeking him. Luke 2:45 (KJV)

It may take some time to reestablish your connection but when you do you will reconnect with His plan and purpose.

And it came to pass, that after three days they found him . . . Luke 2:46 (KJV)

When they did they heard Him say,

" . . . wist ye not that I must be about my Father's business? Luke 2:49 (KJV)

We must be aware that when we leave off being interested in the Father's business, we will find ourselves separated from the Son. The "caravan" may be moving along but it may be missing the One who should be at the center of everything.

October 07 - Flesh & Spirit

Now there was long war between the house of Saul and the house of David: but David waxed stronger and stronger, and the house of Saul waxed weaker and weaker. 2 Samuel 3:1 (KJV)

The war between the house of Saul and the house of David was a war between the man of the flesh and the man of the spirit. You will note that it was a "long war."

Too many Christians believe that there should be no "war" after someone is born-again. This, dear one, is just not so. The flesh dies hard.

The good news is that the man of the spirit will wax "stronger and stronger" and the flesh will wax "weaker and weaker."

This is accomplished through reading and meditating on the life giving, living, Word of God so that we are renewed daily and transformed into the image of Christ rather than being conformed to the world of the flesh.

And be not conformed to this world: but be ye transformed by the renewing of your mind, that ye may prove what is that good, and acceptable, and perfect, will of God. Romans 12:2 (KJV)

Don't despair. The war we wage is that of a "good warfare" according to the prophetic promises of God:

This charge I commit unto thee, son Timothy, according to the prophecies which went before on thee, that thou by them mightest war a good warfare; 1 Timothy 1:18 (KJV)

Our fight is a good fight that has already been won at the Cross and is affirmed by our profession of victory:

Fight the good fight of faith, lay hold on eternal life, whereunto thou art also called, and hast professed a good profession before many witnesses. 1 Timothy 6:12 (KJV)

October 08 - Love Suffers Long

Charity suffereth long, and is kind; charity envieth not; charity vaunteth not itself, is not puffed up,
1 Corinthians 13:4 (KJV)

Love, *agape*, God's kind of love, suffers long, *makrothumeo*. This is the kind of love that is laden with patience, long patience. It never loses heart as it perseveres patiently and bravely in enduring misfortunes and trouble.

The love of our Lord is patient in bearing the offenses and injuries of others, is mild and slow in avenging, slow to anger and slow to punish.

Our society is filled with time saving devices. Microwave ovens, washing machines and dryers, computers, automobiles, ships and airplanes. We can have a meal ready in a minute and a half, go do other chores or run to the store while the clothes are being washed or dried, type letters without white-out (you may be too young to remember typewriters) and communicate via fax, text messages or email. Moving along at 60 plus miles an hour we can go from one city to another in a very short amount of time. Our ships carry us over the water quite speedily and we can go half way around the world in less than a day on our favorite air carrier. All of which makes us less and less able to be patient about anything.

If we are not careful we may allow the ability to get things done in a hurry to begin to place expectations on our children to grow up faster, do more or be more before they are mentally or emotionally mature enough. We may place unreasonable demands upon them and everyone else we know to meet our expectations. This same tendency can come into the church and our spiritual relationships as well. I have found myself falling into this kind of mentality without even noticing the change. This is unjust and unloving to say the least. I must, and do, repent.

After all, if it has taken the Lord this long to get me where I am, and I'm not completely whole yet, how can I expect anyone else to be changed any faster?

How about you?

October 09 - Love Is Kind

Charity suffereth long, and is kind; charity envieth not; charity vaunteth not itself, is not puffed up,
1 Corinthians 13:4 (KJV)

Just as love suffers long, so love, *agape*, God's kind of love, is kind, *chresteuomai*. This word, kind, carries the idea of someone who shows themselves mild and one who uses kindness.

The word, kind, is also used to express the sameness of likeness of something or someone to another. For example, Christians are of the same kind. We were created after the God kind, if you will, after His image and likeness:

God said, Let Us [Father, Son, and Holy Spirit] make mankind in Our image, after Our likeness, and let them have complete authority over the fish of the sea, the birds of the air, the [tame] beasts, and over all of the earth, and over everything that creeps upon the earth. So God created man in His own image, in the image and likeness of God He created him; male and female He created them. Genesis 1:26-27 (AMP)

So, the love of God that works in and through us is of the same kind. Our regard for one another is that of being equals, co-laborers, and joint heirs in Christ. We are "in the same boat," so to speak. This kind of love dictates that we treat one another as mutual recipients of the manifold grace of God.

And be ye kind one to another, tenderhearted, forgiving one another, even as God for Christ's sake hath forgiven you. Ephesians 4:32 (KJV)

Kindness flows from the love of God that sent Christ to bleed and die for us in order to forgive us, for none has been so kind to us as our God and Father.

I am endeavoring to be more kind to those I live with, those I work with and those I meet with on a regular basis. The love of God is shed abroad in our hearts so that we can be loving and kind to all who are in the process of sanctification and who are yet to be redeemed.

October 10 - Love Does Not Envy

Charity suffereth long, and is kind; charity envieth not; charity vaunteth not itself, is not puffed up,
1 Corinthians 13:4 (KJV)

The love, *agape*, of God does not, *ou*, absolutely does not ever, envy, *zeloo*. Envy is desire gone beyond its bounds. It covets earnestly and boils over with hatred and anger. Many times this envy leads to character assassination and, in its extreme, murder.

A perfect example of this kind of envy is found in Jezebel's husband, King Ahab. We can see the record of Ahab envying Naboth his neighbor and coveting his vineyard.

The first thing that envy did was cause the king to pout and have a pity party: "he laid him down upon his bed, and turned away his face, and would eat no bread" (1 Ki. 21:4). Then, he whined to his wife when she inquired about his obvious depression and told her, "Because I spoke to Naboth the Jezreelite and said to him, Give me your vineyard for money; or if you prefer, I will give you another vineyard for it. And he answered, I will not give you my vineyard" (1 Ki. 21:6).

He wasn't getting what he wanted, so he threw a fit like a spoiled child. Jezebel then devised a scheme to have Naboth and his heirs murdered so that her childish husband could have his selfish desire.

How many times have you witnessed someone or some ministry, devise harm to a brother or sister Christian, or another minister or ministry, in order to position themselves in the place that the other possesses? This jockeying for position and place is far outside of the love of God.

Fulfil ye my joy, that ye be like minded, having the same love, being of one accord, of one mind. Let nothing be done through strife or vainglory; but in lowliness of mind let each esteem other better than themselves. Look not every man on his own things, but every man also on the things of others. Philippians 2:2-4 (KJV)

October 11 - Love Is Not Into Itself

Charity suffereth long, and is kind; charity envieth not; charity vaunteth not itself, is not puffed up,
1 Corinthians 13:4 (KJV)

Have you ever been around someone who is so focused on themselves that they never shut up about who they are and what they are doing? Fortunately, I tend to be a listener and so am able to gratify this type of personality. There are times, though, that I wish someone would show some interest in what the Lord is doing with me and the ministry that has been entrusted to me. Have you ever felt that way?

This word, vaunteth, *perpereuomai*, allows us to see the problem of self-centeredness. It comes from *perperos*, which means braggart. So, to vaunt oneself is to boast about one's self and to display self while employing rhetorical embellishments in extolling one's self excessively.

Self is the center of sin's attention. Another way to say this is: Sin is at the center of self's attention. All sin is self-centered, self-gratifying and self-aggrandizing.

As the old song goes, "It's all abut Me, Me, Me, nothing else but Me, Me, Me . . ." This was the problem with Lucifer's character and what caused him to lose his place in the presence of God. "I will . . . , I will . . . , I will . . . , rolls from his lips in utter contempt of God as we read the record of Isaiah 14:13, 14.

On the other hand, God Who is Love is always focused on the need of His creation. Every decision, every plan, purpose and act was, is, and will be, made and carried out for the ultimate benefit of those He loves. The creation, the world, and all that are in it, are loved by God (Joh. 3:16). He is always giving at His own expense to and for those whom He loves.

The late Edwin Louis Cole said, "Love gives to the benefit of others at it's own expense. Lust takes at the expense of others to gratify itself." God is love (1 Joh. 4:8, 16) and therefore can do nothing but give to the benefit of others. What if our interest was in others and helping them do what they are called to do?

October 12 - Love Is Not Prideful

Charity suffereth long, and is kind; charity envieth not; charity vaunteth not itself, is not puffed up,
1 Corinthians 13:4 (KJV)

Vaunt and puffed up are very similar in their connotation. Both deal with a feeling of self-importance that is ungodly and devoid of the love of God.

Puffed up, *phusioo*, gives us a picture of blowing in order to inflate, to blow up, to cause to swell up. In the context of our verses it means to make proud (in a negative sense) and to bear one's self loftily. This is an attitude of exaggerated importance that stems from insecurity or a lack of understanding the grace and mercy of the Lord. He created us and made us what we are. It had nothing to do with our astuteness or acumen.

Know ye that the Lord he is God: it is he that hath made us, and not we ourselves; we are his people, and the sheep of his pasture. Psalm 100:3 (KJV)

There is no room to boast but in the Lord:

For by grace are ye saved through faith; and that not of yourselves: it is the gift of God: Not of works, lest any man should boast. For we are his workmanship, created in Christ Jesus . . . Ephesians 2:8-10 (KJV)

How can anyone be puffed up about how the Lord is using them when it all emanates from Him and is according to His plan and purpose. We were not even able to "get saved" until His Word came to us and our ears were opened to hear:

So then faith cometh by hearing, and hearing by the word of God. Romans 10:17 (KJV)

If we are going to boast, let us brag on the Lord. If we are going to "blow" then let us "inflate" the value, worth, magnificence, ability, love, mercy and kindness of the Lord in the minds of those who will listen. Let us magnify His name.

October 13 - Love Behaves Itself Well

Doth not behave itself unseemly, seeketh not her own,
is not easily provoked, thinketh no evil;
1 Corinthians 13:5 (KJV)

The Greek word for behave one's self unseemly, **aschemoneo**, or to act unbecomingly, helps us to understand what the God kind of love is not. It is never inappropriate.

How, then, does this love behave itself? It behaves itself well in all circumstances. It behaves itself like Jesus did.

Love operates within covenant understanding. It asks for nothing in return except total loyalty to the covenant agreement.

In marriage it acts solely for the benefit of one's spouse. It causes an individual to always act appropriately toward the one to whom they are wed; attentiveness to their needs, likes, and dislikes. It demands fidelity, ongoing faithfulness to the marriage contract (covenant) which can be summarized in the vow that states, "to have and to hold from this day forward, for better or for worse, for richer, for poorer, in sickness and in health, to love and to cherish; from this day forward until death do us part."

In the Christian context it is first pledged in the prayer of acceptance (the sinners prayer) when an individual pledges their life to Christ by inviting Him to be both Lord and Savior. It can also be seen in Galatians 2:20:

I am crucified with Christ: nevertheless I live; yet not I, but Christ liveth in me: and the life which I now live in the flesh I live by the faith of the Son of God, who loved me, and gave himself for me. Galatians 2:20 (KJV)

The Christian is expected to live a life that is one with Christ in word and deed. As in marriage, the two become one and behave as such. That, for us, it is a process goes without saying. Sanctification is a process as well as a state of being.

We walk in love toward one another even as He walked in love toward us and behave ourselves accordingly (Joh. 13:34; 15:12, 17; Rom.13:8; 1 Thes. 4:9; 1 Pet. 1:22; 1 Joh. 3:23; 4:7, 11-12; 2 John 1:5). If we do this we shall behave well.

October 14 - Love Is Not Self-Centered

> Doth not behave itself unseemly, seeketh not her own,
> is not easily provoked, thinketh no evil;
> 1 Corinthians 13:5 (KJV)

Again, it is brought to the fore front that, *agape*, love seeks only to benefit the object of its love. It is not consumed with demanding that it be gratified at the expense of another. It does not seek, *zeteo*, seek after, seek for, aim at, strive after ways to demand something from someone. Love never manipulates in order to satisfy the cravings of self, *heautou*.

God, who is Love, agape, operates in Covenant Love which is unbreakable and unending (eternal); "for he hath said, I will never leave thee, nor forsake thee" and "Love never fails" (Heb. 13:5 KJV; 1 Cor. 13:8 AMP).

He has made a decision to love and to bless the object of His love. His decision to love is unalterable and His covenant He will not break:

> My covenant will I not break, nor alter the thing that is gone out of my lips. Psalm 89:34 (KJV)

A covenant partner will never seek his own way. He is bound to be a blessing, a covering, a protection, a defense and a source of strength. The enemies of his covenant brother are his enemies and the friends of his covenant brother are his friends.

> And I will bless them that bless thee, and curse him that curseth thee: and in thee shall all families of the earth be blessed. Genesis 12:3 (KJV)

God in Christ is in covenant with every believer and will behave Himself as a covenant partner with those who will live in covenant relationship with Him. If the believer will not seek his own but will seek that which is the Lord's, the plan and the purpose of God will be accomplished and blessing will flow.

> But seek ye first the kingdom of God, and his righteousness; and all these things shall be added unto you. Matthew 6:33 (KJV)

October 15 - Love Cannot Be Provoked

Doth not behave itself unseemly, seeketh not her own,
is not easily provoked, thinketh no evil;
1 Corinthians 13:5 (KJV)

Today, let's look at the segment of the verse that is rendered "not easily provoked." The translators must have been so incredulous at the thought of never being provoked, *paroxuno*, that they felt compelled to add the word "easily." It does seem like an impossibly exacting rule of thought and emotion. We must remember that we are not here speaking of natural love, but are speaking of the very nature and character of God who is love and whose mercies are new every morning.

Nevertheless, the word used for not, *ou*, is an absolute negative that emphasizes that love cannot be provoked, *paroxuno*. It is like saying, no, love cannot be stimulated, spurred on, nor urged enough to become irritated or be aroused to anger. You cannot exasperate love enough to provoke someone enveloped in it to burn with anger.

Is this really possible? Of course it is. We learn to deal with those things that might provoke us to anger in the same day.

Be ye angry, and sin not: let not the sun go down upon
your wrath: Ephesians 4:26 (KJV)

Even more importantly, we learn to forgive them before they stir the need to be dealt with.

Take heed to yourselves: If thy brother trespass against
thee, rebuke him; and if he repent, forgive him. And if he
trespass against thee seven times in a day, and seven times
in a day turn again to thee, saying, I repent; thou shalt
forgive him. Luke 17:3-4 (KJV)

The Lord is just (righteous altogether) and must punish sin. This is not a side of God that the believer will ever see.

For God hath not appointed us to wrath, but to obtain
salvation by our Lord Jesus Christ,
1 Thessalonians 5:9 (KJV)

Unto us He is ready to forgive and He is filled with mercy.

For thou, Lord, art good, and ready to forgive; and
plenteous in mercy unto all them that call upon thee.
Psalm 86:5 (KJV)

He, Love, cannot be provoked where we are concerned.

October 16 - Love Does Not Think Evil Thoughts

Doth not behave itself unseemly, seeketh not her own, is not easily provoked, thinketh no evil;
1 Corinthians 13:5 (KJV)

What, exactly, does it mean, "thinketh no evil?" *Logizomai* is the Greek word used for "thinketh". It is used in banking and deals with reality. If I *"logizomai"* or reckon that my bank book has $25 in it, it has $25 in it. Otherwise I am deceiving myself. This word refers to facts not suppositions. It means to count up or weigh the reasons, to deliberate by reckoning up all the reasons, to gather, consider or infer and to meditate on.

Evil, *kakos*, includes that which is of a bad nature and that which is not such as it ought to be. It speaks of a mode of thinking, feeling and acting in a base, wrong, wicked, troublesome, injurious, pernicious, destructive, and baneful way.

Love demands that we cast down every thought that does not line up with the Word of God and set our minds upon those things that are true and of a high nature.

Casting down imaginations, and every high thing that exalteth itself against the knowledge of God, and bringing into captivity every thought to the obedience of Christ;
2 Corinthians 10:5 (KJV)

Finally, brethren, whatsoever things are true, whatsoever things are honest, whatsoever things are just, whatsoever things are pure, whatsoever things are lovely, whatsoever things are of good report; if there be any virtue, and if there be any praise, think on these things.
Philippians 4:8 (KJV)

The individual filled with the love of God has no room in their thinking for anything less than the reality that has been wrought for every true believer by Christ Jesus. It is written of such a believer, ". . . love your enemies, bless them that curse you, do good to them that hate you, and pray for them which despitefully use you, and persecute you; Matthew 5:44 (KJV)

The first thought of love is to forgive and bless.

October 17 - Love Is Saddened By Iniquity

Rejoiceth not in iniquity, but rejoiceth in the truth;
1 Corinthians 13:6 (KJV)

There are many in our society today who rejoice, *chairo*, in iniquity. They are eager to embrace lawlessness and devise unjust ways to manipulate others for gain. This is not the way the Love of God works.

God's love is always looking for ways to benefit the one loved. Blessing is in the heart and mind of God as He always seeks ways in which to bring increase to those with whom He is in covenant. His love is so all encompassing that He even blesses the unjust along with the just; "he maketh his sun to rise on the evil and on the good, and sendeth rain on the just and on the unjust" (Mat. 5:45 KJV).

Don't ever let tradition or the teaching of the legalist cause you to think that God is against you or unjust. You are the object of His affection and the apple of His eye (Deut. 32:10; Zech. 2:8). The wrath of His judgement will only be felt by those who have rejected His Son upon whom fell the judgement for sin. Jesus paid the full price for the true believer's sin (1 Thes. 5:9).

Iniquity, *adikia*, or the injustice of a judge, is the result of unrighteousness of heart and life. It is an act that violates the law and justice of God. You can see, then, why this kind of demeanor is never embraced or deemed acceptable within the context of the love of God.

God, who is love, is the only Righteous Judge:

[As to what remains] henceforth there is laid up for me the [victor's] crown of righteousness [for being right with God and doing right], which the Lord, the righteous Judge, will award to me and recompense me on that [great] day—and not to me only, but also to all those who have loved and yearned for and welcomed His appearing (His return). 2 Timothy 4:8 (AMP)

As such, iniquity will never be found near or around Him. Neither should it be found near or around those that are of Him.

October 18 - The Outraying of The Divine

God came from Teman and the Holy One from Mount Paran. Selah! His glory covered the heavens and the earth was full of His praise. And His brightness was like the sunlight; rays streamed from His hand, and there [in the sunlike splendor] was the hiding place of His power. Habakkuk 3:3-4 (AMP)

It was as though God opened my eyes to see Him! Jesus the outraying of the divine! He is the express image, the sole expression of God's glory emanating from His divine Person - exploding into every circumstance and situation - dispelling every dark thing arrayed against His own!

He is the sole expression of the glory of God - the Light-being, the out-raying of the divine - and He is the perfect imprint and very image of [God's] nature, upholding and maintaining and guiding and propelling the universe by His mighty word of power. Hebrews 1:3 (AMP)

Beloved, God is on the move! His Spirit is moving as fresh winds of revelation across the face of the earth! His Glory is being manifest in ever increasing measure that those who seek after Him will experience supernatural healing and joy like never before! Strength will be renewed and liberty will be realized!

But unto you who revere and worshipfully fear My name shall the Sun of Righteousness arise with healing in His wings and His beams, and you shall go forth and gambol like calves [released] from the stall and leap for joy. Malachi 4:3 (AMP)

This is an exciting time to be a servant of the Most High God! It is the hour when we will be endued with strength, efficiency and might, like never before, to herald His coming!

October 19 - Love Rejoices In The Truth

Rejoiceth not in iniquity, but rejoiceth in the truth;
1 Corinthians 13:6 (KJV)

Love, *agape*, always rejoices in the truth! The word translated "rejoiceth," in "rejoiceth in the truth," is a different word than that which is used in "rejoiceth not in iniquity." This word is, *sugchairo*, which means, to rejoice with by taking part in another's joy, to rejoice together and to congratulate.

So, *agape* love congratulates truth, *aletheia*.

Biblical truth is the Word of God: "Sanctify them through thy truth: thy word is truth" John 17:17 (KJV). Jesus is the Word of God; the Truth:

In the beginning [before all time] was the Word (Christ), and the Word was with God, and the Word was God Himself. John 1:1 (AMP)

Biblical truth is that which is in, modeled and taught by Jesus, the Christ of God:

Jesus saith unto him, I am the way, the truth, and the life: no man cometh unto the Father, but by me. John 14:6 (KJV)

It is the spirit that quickeneth; the flesh profiteth nothing: the words that I speak unto you, they are spirit, and they are life. John 6:63 (KJV)

Truth, *aletheia*, is that which is true in any matter under consideration. It is reality and unalterable fact. It is what is true in things appertaining to God and the duties of man as it deals with moral and religious truth. Truth as taught in the Christian religion, respecting God and the execution of his purposes through Christ, and respecting the duties of man, opposing alike to the superstitions of the Gentiles and the inventions of the Jews, and the corrupt opinions and precepts of false teachers even among Christians.

Psalm 138:2 says that love heralds and establishes truth even above His name:

I will worship . . . and praise thy name for . . . thy truth: for thou hast magnified thy word above all thy name.

October 20 - Love Bears All . . .

Beareth all things, believeth all things, hopeth all things, endureth all things. 1 Corinthians 13:7 (KJV)

Love beareth, *stego*, can forbear, protects or keep by covering over with silence, hides and conceals, the errors and faults of others. It covers in order to keep off something which threatens, to bear up against or hold out against what or who would destroy, and so endure with.

"All things," *pas*, could also be understood to mean "all men." Just as the Lord opens salvation to whosoever will, so He who is love acts as a covering for whosoever are His own. The "all" mentioned here does not include the lost as well as the saved. This can be readily seen in the remarks of C. H. Spurgeon in the record of his sermon, "Particular Redemption:."

"the whole world has gone after him" Did all the world go after Christ? "then went all Judea, and were baptized of him in Jordan." Was all Judea, or all Jerusalem, baptized in Jordan? "Ye are of God, little children," and the whole world lieth in the wicked one". Does the whole world there mean everybody? The words "world" and "all" are used in some seven or eight senses in Scripture, and it is very rarely the "all" means all persons, taken individually. The words are generally used to signify that Christ has redeemed some of all sorts --some Jews, some Gentiles, some rich, some poor, and has not restricted His redemption to either Jew or Gentile."

As believers in covenant with the Almighty God, Creator of heaven and earth, Father of the redeemed in Christ, we find Love to have the desire, will, and ability to bear with the weaknesses of those with whom He is in covenant. There is nothing outside of His purpose or power to forgive in the name of Jesus.

If we confess our sins, he is faithful and just to forgive us our sins, and to cleanse us from all unrighteousness. 1 John 1:9 (KJV)

He hides our weaknesses and vanquishes our foes in Love.

October 21 - Love Believes In All . . .

Beareth all things, believeth all things, hopeth all things, endureth all things. 1 Corinthians 13:7 (KJV)

Believeth, *pisteuo*, is word that conveys the idea of being committed to someone or something. It can mean to commit to one's trust or to be put in trust with. Believeth is to have credited and to have credit both now and in the future. This word is used to express in Jesus or God by believing them to be able to aid either in obtaining or in doing something. It also speaks of being entrusted with a thing.

Therefore, love, *agape*, puts itself in the hands of the one loved and expects a positive result. For instance: God sent His Son to declare and display the good news of the New Covenant (Testament). He (God the Father) put the future of mankind in the hands of His only begotten Son.

Jesus put Himself "in trust" with the Father. Although He (Jesus) could take up His own life, He yielded that ability to His Father and God, leaving the future of the world in His hands, awaiting the Word of resurrection to release Him from the bonds of death.

After the ascension of Jesus the Holy Spirit was sent to indwell the believers who, from then on, would declare and display the good news of the New Covenant. The Godhead put the glorious gospel "in trust" with born-again mankind.

Here again, the "all" is not meant to be understood in the all inclusive sense in every case. The use of "things" after "all" tends to draw the understanding of modern English speaking peoples toward only those things that are all inclusive, thus hiding the depth of understanding that is here available.

So, we can see that "all" does not mean "all" all the time. Where the believer and the things of God are concerned, however, "all" does mean "all" in the all inclusive sense.

Love has committed to your trust the salvation of the lost, the glorious sharing of the Good News; "all things."

October 22 - Love Hopes All Things

Beareth all things, believeth all things, hopeth all things, endureth all things. 1 Corinthians 13:7 (KJV)

As we further look at the glorious truths concerning love, agape, we come to the word hope. The King James uses "hopeth, *elpizo*," which means, in a religious sense, to wait for salvation with joy and full confidence. It also can be understood to mean, hopefully to trust in. We have the same word used for "all" that we have dealt with in the first two uses in this verse of scripture. Therefore, we can turn our attention to the prisoners of hope who are in the bonds of love, the blood bought, redeemed of the Lord and the Lord of redemption Himself.

Return to the stronghold [of security and prosperity], you prisoners of hope; even today do I declare that I will restore double your former prosperity to you.
Zechariah 9:12 (AMP)
Love looks at the redeemed with excitement and in anticipation of the day when salvation will have had its complete work and His children are gathered to receive their reward.

Those who are the objects of His love look forward to the full manifestation of "salvation with joy and full confidence."

Love also looks at the lost with eyes of compassion and waits for their "salvation with joy and full confidence."

Who will have all men to be saved, and to come unto the knowledge of the truth. 1 Timothy 2:4 (KJV)
Both God and His own desire that none would be lost and do everything possible to keep and protect those who are in covenant with Him.

Both also desire to win the hearts of them who have yet to know God in Christ and experience the gift of inexhaustible love so freely offered. This common purpose is the fuel and fire of the Great Commission.

Go ye therefore, and teach all nations, baptizing them in the name of the Father, and of the Son, and of the Holy Ghost: Matthew 28:19 (KJV) (also see Matthew 28:20)

October 23 - Love Endures All Things

Beareth all things, believeth all things, hopeth all things, endureth all things. 1 Corinthians 13:7 (KJV)

By now you know that "all" is not necessarily "all" and that words we are familiar with do not always convey the same thought that we might initially think. The word "endureth" is, perhaps, another one of those words.

Endureth is the translation for the Greek word, *hupomeno*. This word carries the idea of taking patiently, waiting behind, abiding, and patient suffering.

We could say, then, that Love, *agape*, remains after suffering wrong done to it. Love will not, can not withdraw or flee when grieved or injured. This put to rest the idea that the Holy Spirit is so fragile that He will flee away at the least rejection or harsh word spoken. Not so; love never fails because it is permanent and strong in every situation.

Love will stay behind to bind up and heal every wounded one who embraces Him in His covenant of love.

Love always preserves and perseveres under misfortunes and trials so that the covenant believer may hold fast to their faith in Christ. We must not give ourselves too much credit where our strength in God is concerned. It is His love working in and through us that makes it all possible. We remain faithful, abide under the shadow of His wings and stay in His word as He draws us with His strong, unfailing love. Oh, our will is the governor (or governess) of our "house," but love makes the impossible possible.

We are drawn forward, higher, in Him and will not flee, nor our love toward Him recede, because of covenant *agape*.

While enveloped in Him, in Love, we can not only endure hardship, but bravely and calmly bear any ill treatment that is sent against us or upon which we chance to stumble.

Here, Beloved, "all" does mean "all." "Love endureth all".

October 24 - Love Never Fails

Charity never faileth: but whether there be prophecies, they shall fail; whether there be tongues, they shall cease; whether there be knowledge, it shall vanish away.
1 Corinthians 13:8 (KJV)

"Love never fails." That simple statement brings a thrill to every heart touched by it. Can it really be that there is such a Person, such a thing, as unfailing love? Oh, Beloved, how I would that you and I not only know of a surety that it is so but would experience "the power and be strong to apprehend and grasp with all the saints [God's devoted people, the experience of that love] what is the breadth and length and height and depth [of it" (Eph. 3:18 AMP).

Never, *oudepote*, does mean "never." As we roll this word on our tongue and let it move through our minds we will enjoy the absoluteness of it. It is "never, neither at any time and nothing at any time."

"Never" is followed by "fails." This Greek word, *ekpipto*, assures us that love will never fail. It will never cast us off and never, never be of none effect. The power and fulness of love will not diminish nor disappear ever. God's love is so filled with ability and efficiency that it is unwilling and unable to fall from the one loved nor to lose it in the clamor of situation and circumstance.

This, *agape*, love is eternal and will never perish but will always position the one loved in the place that is otherwise impossible for him to stay in. Thus, we can understand:

For the which cause I also suffer these things: nevertheless I am not ashamed: for I know whom I have believed, and am persuaded that he is able to keep that which I have committed unto him against that day.
2 Timothy 1:12 (KJV)

This is the divine promise of salvation to which we hold until "he shall appear, we shall be like Him; for see Him as He is" (1 Joh. 3:2).

October 25 - The Value of Fire

That the trial of your faith, being much more precious than of gold that perisheth, though it be tried with fire, might be found unto praise and honour and glory at the appearing of Jesus Christ: 1 Peter 1:7 (KJV)

The trial, *dokimion*, the proving, or, test, of your faith, *pistis*, of your conviction of the truth that God exists and is the creator and ruler of all things, the provider and bestower of eternal salvation through Christ, and the supply of all that we have need of, is more precious than gold.

Earthly elements, such as gold, which man values so greatly are nothing compared with faith, *pistis*.

But without faith it is impossible to please him: for he that cometh to God must believe that he is, and that he is a rewarder of them that diligently seek him.
Hebrews 11:6 (KJV)

Faith is not faith until it has passed a trial (a test). Faith is tempered in the heat of battle and the fire of adversity. It will be found to stand through all circumstances and situations much like that of the Giant Sequoia trees of California.

These magnificent trees depend upon the flames of the forest fire to open its cones. If there is no fire, there will be no new trees. The seeds hidden and locked away in the cones will never be released to fulfill their destiny until fire provides the heat to open them.

If the seed were to drop on the normal bed of pine needles that is found in the forest, they would not take root and provide the next generation of trees. The Sequoia seed needs a bed of ash in which to germinate, root and grow.

So, too, faith. Faith that has grown strong through the fire, endured the flames of the enemy, gone through the rigors of life and found rest in the ashes of the past can rise as incense to God, the Creator and ruler of all things. Through its exercise brings "praise and honour and glory at the appearing of Jesus Christ". To Him be all the honor, all the glory and all the praise.

October 26 - Get Out!

Now the Lord had said unto Abram, Get thee out of thy country, and from thy kindred, and from thy father's house, unto a land that I will shew thee: Genesis 12:1 (KJV)

When you are settled in and comfortable with where you are, the last thing you want to hear is, "Its time to leave. Pack up what you have, leave everything and everyone you are used to."

If you are like me, you will ask, "Where are we going and why?" Even if we were to get a clear, reasonable answer, we would most likely still feel a bit undone about the prospect. Imagine what it must have been like for Abram when he was asked to leave all and go to "who knows where?". Imagine being his wife Sarai when he told here, "God spoke to me and told me to get out of here." "Where are we going?," she would ask. His answer to here was so reassuring, "I don't know, the Lord said He would show it to me."

This is a challenge that many Christians face; but face it they must. Without faith that comes from the Word of God there is no way to yield to the call of God to, "Get out of where you are!" But, Beloved, in faith all things are possible; even following the Holy Spirit to places that you have never seen and never heard of.

So then faith cometh by hearing, and hearing by the word of God. Romans 10:17 (KJV)

In the Word we come to realize that God is always good, always working out His plan and purpose for our lives, always drawing us toward "a land that" He will show us, a land flowing with milk and honey, a land where He can bless us abundantly.

Certain relationships will have to be forsaken and there will be places that we must never return to. We are new creatures in Christ with a new direction for our lives. We are in covenant with the Creator of heaven and earth and no longer our own. We were bought with a price and that price was the Lamb of God, slain from the foundation of the earth. We are going with Him.

October 27 - Over Fifty Years!

Over Fifty-three years ago I married the most wonderful woman on earth! She is definitely a "Proverbs 31 Woman."

Proverbs 31:1-31 (NKJV) 10 Who can find a virtuous wife? For her worth is far above rubies. 11 The heart of her husband safely trusts her; So he will have no lack of gain. 12 She does him good and not evil All the days of her life. 13 She seeks wool and flax, And willingly works with her hands. 14 She is like the merchant ships, She brings her food from afar. 15 She also rises while it is yet night, And provides food for her household, And a portion for her maidservants. 16 She considers a field and buys it; From her profits she plants a vineyard. 17 She girds herself with strength, And strengthens her arms. 18 She perceives that her merchandise is good, And her lamp does not go out by night. 19 She stretches out her hands to the distaff, And her hand holds the spindle. 20 She extends her hand to the poor, Yes, she reaches out her hands to the needy. 21 She is not afraid of snow for her household, For all her household is clothed with scarlet. 22 She makes tapestry for herself; Her clothing is fine linen and purple. 23 Her husband is known in the gates, When he sits among the elders of the land. 24 She makes linen garments and sells them, And supplies sashes for the merchants. 25 Strength and honor are her clothing; She shall rejoice in time to come. 26 She opens her mouth with wisdom, And on her tongue is the law of kindness. 27 She watches over the ways of her household, And does not eat the bread of idleness. 28 Her children rise up and call her blessed; Her husband also, and he praises her:29 "Many daughters have done well, But you excel them all."

I'm more in love with her today than I was when we first met at 16. I'm more in love with her today than I was when we married. It is a true saying:

He who finds a wife finds a good thing, And obtains favor from the LORD. Proverbs 18:22 (NKJV)

Thank you Lord!

This is what God has in mind for each person that desires to be married.

October 28 - The Greatest Of Three

And now abideth faith, hope, charity, these three; but the greatest of these is charity. 1 Corinthians 13:13 (KJV)

King David had "Three Mighty Men" who were unlike all others. They were knit to him in covenant love since the cave Adullam.

Next to him among the three mighty men was Eleazar son of Dodo, son of Ahohi. He was with David when they defied the Philistines assembled there for battle, and the men of Israel had departed. 2 Samuel 23:9 (AMP)

And the three mighty men broke through the army of the Philistines and drew water out of the well of Bethlehem by the gate and brought it to David. But he would not drink it, but poured it out to the Lord. 2 Samuel 23:16 (AMP)

The three that abideth, *meno*, are seen to be faith, *pistis*, hope, *elpis*, and love, *agape*. So, those which will remain, never to depart are the "three mighty" attributes of covenant relationship. They will continue to be present as they are so valued as to be held and kept continually so as to last, endure and continue eternally.

This word, abideth, *meno*, also means to remain as one, not to become another or different. When one abides, they await one's arrival so as to be able to move on together with.

The greatest, *meizon*, strongest, elder of the three is love, *agape*. Love existed before faith and hope and is, therefore their elder. God is "the King eternal, immortal, invisible, the only wise God, and He is love (1 Tim. 1:17 KJV).

His God kind of love is what empowers and exercises faith and gives meaning and strength to the spiritual gifts (1 Cor. 13:1,2). Love is the fruit of the Spirit that gives hope its joy and peace during times of longsuffering (Gal. 5:22; Jam. 1:3).

There is no doubt: Love is chiefest of the "three mighty."

October 29 - I Will Bless You

And I will make of thee a great nation, and I will bless thee, and make thy name great; and thou shalt be a blessing: Genesis 12:2 (KJV)

The great promise of God in our text today was given to Abraham and his Seed. It is important for us to note that the promise was repeated to his natural descendants but was specifically spoken regarding the One which was to come, the Christ of God.

Now the promises (covenants, agreements) were decreed and made to Abraham and his Seed (his Offspring, his Heir). He [God] does not say, And to seeds (descendants, heirs), as if referring to many persons, but, And to your Seed (your Descendant, your Heir), obviously referring to one individual, Who is [none other than] Christ (the Messiah). Galatians 3:16 (AMP)

This is extremely important for you and I to understand because this is what gives us the authority to be bold when we appropriate the promises for ourselves.

To the end that through [their receiving] Christ Jesus, the blessing [promised] to Abraham might come upon the Gentiles, so that we through faith might [all] receive [the realization of] the promise of the [Holy] Spirit. Galatians 3:14 (AMP)

We who live by faith have every right to expect to be blessed with our father Abraham in Christ. It was in Him, Christ Jesus, that we were redeemed from the curse of the law and thrust in to a New Covenant relationship with God which allows His blessings to flow to and through us.

And I will make of thee a great nation, and I will bless thee, and make thy name great; and thou shalt be a blessing: Genesis 12:2 (KJV)

Beloved, you and I are blessed to be a blessing. Let us give as freely as we have received.

Heal the sick, cleanse the lepers, raise the dead, cast out devils: freely ye have received, freely give. Matthew 10:8 (KJV)

October 30 - Blessing & Cursing

And I will bless them that bless thee, and curse him that curseth thee: and in thee shall all families of the earth be blessed. Genesis 12:3 (KJV)

As Christians we understand that the "Seed" of Abraham is Christ and that in Him shall all families of the earth be blessed. We should also understand that though we see this prophetic blessing that flows to and through the Messiah, the natural seed of Abraham are also meant to be the recipients of the face value of the promise of God.

"I will bless them that bless thee, and curse him that curseth thee" is a real promise to the Israel of today and to the Church of the Living God.

The Church does not replace the Israel of God. The Church and those who call themselves Jews are both in covenant with God. Only the covenant agreements are different. Jews can, and must, become born-again by accepting Jesus as their Messiah but they are still in covenant with their God who swore by Himself.

For when God made promise to Abraham, because he could swear by no greater, he sware by himself, Saying, Surely blessing I will bless thee, and multiplying I will multiply thee. Hebrews 6:13-14 (KJV)

God has an agreement with three groups of people as listed in the book of 1 Corinthians:

Give none offence, neither to the Jews, nor to the Gentiles, nor to the church of God: 1 Corinthians 10:32 (KJV)

God has agreed to open salvation to whosoever will come to Christ. The lost must respond to His extension of love in Christ Jesus or spend eternity in torment. He has covenanted with the Jews to keep them as a people and bring them face to face with their Messiah. He has covenanted with the church to make her one with Himself.

Christianity is of the Jews, the Jews are not of Christianity, so consider taking a stand with Israel in these days of world wide terrorism if only to show the love of God in Christ: "I will bless them that bless thee, and curse him that curseth thee."

October 31 - After Lot Was Gone

And the Lord said unto Abram, after that Lot was separated from him, Lift up now thine eyes, and look from the place where thou art northward, and southward, and eastward, and westward: For all the land which thou seest, to thee will I give it, and to thy seed for ever.
Genesis 13:14-15 (KJV)

Just as an earthly father makes promises to his children and makes provision to fulfill those promises, our heavenly Father has made provision for us to walk in all that He has planned and promised to us. His Word is full of His loving provision for our time on this earth and for our eternal divine destiny.

Too often, we Christians begin to believe that God will never give us what He has promised. We see others receiving what the Word describes but we always seem to come short of what He has spoken to us. Prophecies seem to go unfulfilled and the Word of God does not seem to apply. Discouragement, flagging hope, and struggling faith creep in to emotions and thoughts to the point that doubt and unbelief become the demons of the night. Excuses and a twisting of the Word to fit our experience can become common place in our lives if we are not careful.

Don't let anything sway you from the sure promise of God!

Like father Abram, there just may be a Lot that needs to be separated from your life. There was certainly a lot that needed to leave my life before I could appropriate my Father's promises. When I thought myself to be mature in the faith, I was yet but a spiritual child in so many ways. This hindered the extent to which God could give me all He had laid up in store for me and the ministry which He had entrusted to me. I finally came to realize the principle found in the following verse.

Now I say, That the heir, as long as he is a child, differeth nothing from a servant, though he be lord of all; But is under tutors and governors until the time appointed of the father. Galatians 4:1-2 (KJV)

The quicker we mature in the faith, the sooner He can give us those things that belong to full grown, mature sons. The secret is to yield our lives, trusting Him to complete all that pertains to us.

NOVEMBER

November 01 - I Will Give It To You

And I will make thy seed as the dust of the earth: so that if a man can number the dust of the earth, then shall thy seed also be numbered. Arise, walk through the land in the length of it and in the breadth of it; for I will give it unto thee. Genesis 13:16-17 (KJV)

When your heart is to multiply, when your heart is to expand the Kingdom, when your heart is to see the birth of spiritual children into the society of God; the Lord will give it to you. There is a principle that underlies all principles in the plan and purpose of God:

Give, and it shall be given unto you; good measure, pressed down, and shaken together, and running over, shall men give into your bosom. For with the same measure that ye mete withal it shall be measured to you again.
Luke 6:38 (KJV)

Give of yourself. Give of your resources. Give love with joy and peace. Give longsuffering with gentleness, goodness and faith. Give in meekness with temperance (Gal. 5:22-23 KJV).

As we freely give of that which has been freely given us of God we find ourselves totally enmeshed in His plan and purpose, fully furnished by all of who He is. There is no lack in Him.

But seek ye first the kingdom of God, and his righteousness; and all these things shall be added unto you. Matthew 6:33 (KJV)

The Lord will never withhold any good thing from you when your heart is set on bringing in the harvest of lost souls and caring for them. His love has been shed abroad in our hearts so that we have an overflow to give and He will see to it that we have to give. Ask, believe and receive the land and its produce.

Let them shout for joy, and be glad, that favour my righteous cause: yea, let them say continually, Let the Lord be magnified, which hath pleasure in the prosperity of his servant. Psalm 35:27 (KJV)

November 02 - An Altar of Earth

An altar of earth thou shalt make unto me, and shalt sacrifice thereon thy burnt offerings, and thy peace offerings, thy sheep, and thine oxen: in all places where I record my name I will come unto thee, and I will bless thee. Exodus 20:24 (KJV)

The Creator of Heaven and Earth is Omnipresent. This simply means that He is everywhere at once. He does not dwell in a house made with the hands of man; and yet, He records His name in certain places and promises to meet with us there.

The first place He records His name is in an "altar of earth."

But we have this treasure in earthen vessels, that the excellency of the power may be of God, and not of us. 2 Corinthians 4:7 (KJV)

We are to make of ourselves "an altar of earth."

Know ye not that ye are the temple of God, and that the Spirit of God dwelleth in you? 1 Corinthians 3:16 (KJV)

We have been ". . . sealed with that holy Spirit of promise" (Ephes. 1:13 KJV), and God has written His name in the foreheads of His servants.

And they shall see his face; and his name shall be in their foreheads. Revelation 22:4 (KJV)

It is from this "place" that we "offer up spiritual sacrifices, acceptable to God by Jesus Christ" (1 Pet. 2:5 KJV). It is out of this "place" that give support to our spiritual leaders: "an odour of a sweet smell, a sacrifice acceptable, well pleasing to God" (Philip. 4:18 KJV).

The "altar of earth," our body, is one of the "places" which God has chosen to come to and to bless us. This "altar of earth" that burns with the flame of passion toward his God and yearns for the moving of His Spirit within is the one of which "God hath said, I will dwell in them, and walk in them; and I will be their God, and they shall be my people" (2 Cor. 6:16 KJV).

November 03 - Where I Record My Name

An altar of earth thou shalt make unto me, and shalt sacrifice thereon thy burnt offerings, and thy peace offerings, thy sheep, and thine oxen: in all places where I record my name I will come unto thee, and I will bless thee. Exodus 20:24 (KJV)

Because of the great truth that we considered yesterday, many have lost sight of the corporate church, the *ekklhsia*. Because of our societal propensity to be self-focused, many "Christians" have rejected the idea of a company of Christians, or of those who, hoping for eternal salvation through Jesus Christ, observe their own religious rites, hold their own religious meetings, and manage their own affairs, according to regulations prescribed for the body for order's sake. This word, *ekklesia*, denotes those who anywhere, in a city or village, constitute such a company and are united into one body for the purpose of establishing the rules and regulations of that society and who decide what is proper and what is improper within its jurisdiction and what the economy will be. Jesus said that He would build such a church:

And I say also unto thee, That thou art Peter, and upon this rock I will build my church; and the gates of hell shall not prevail against it. Matthew 16:18 (KJV)

This gathering of the church (assembly of Christ's followers) would take place in various "places" during established times. This can be seen from the following verses: (Acts 7:38; 11:22; 13:1; 14:23; 15:22, etc.). We are strongly encouraged to meet together as "the church," especially as we see the return of the Lord drawing near.

Not forsaking or neglecting to assemble together [as believers], as is the habit of some people, but admonishing (warning, urging, and encouraging) one another, and all the more faithfully as you see the day approaching. Hebrews 10:25 (AMP)

This is yet another "place" where God will meet with you and bless you. This is also a place where He records His name.

November 04 - I Will Come . . .

An altar of earth thou shalt make unto me, and shalt sacrifice thereon thy burnt offerings, and thy peace offerings, thy sheep, and thine oxen: in all places where I record my name I will come unto thee, and I will bless thee. Exodus 20:24 (KJV)

Genesis 3:8 records that "the Voice of the Lord God" was heard "walking in the garden in the cool of the day." Our God desires daily fellowship with those who are created in His image and likeness. How we receive His invitation to "walk" with Him, and how much we pay attention to and yield to what the "Voice" speaks to us, determines the measure with which He can bless us.

He records His name in us individually and with us corporately and promises to come and bless us.

One of the things that takes place when He comes and we walk together is that we are kept from disease.

And said, If thou wilt diligently hearken to the voice of the Lord thy God, and wilt do that which is right in his sight, and wilt give ear to his commandments, and keep all his statutes, I will put none of these diseases upon thee, which I have brought upon the Egyptians: for I am the Lord that healeth thee. Exodus 15:26 (KJV)

As we receive Him and obey the speaking of the Voice we are positioned to be blessed with every spiritual, and natural, blessing.

And it shall come to pass, if thou shalt hearken diligently unto the voice of the Lord thy God, to observe and to do all his commandments which I command thee this day, that the Lord thy God will set thee on high above all nations of the earth: And all these blessings shall come on thee, and overtake thee, if thou shalt hearken unto the voice of the Lord thy God. Deuteronomy 28:1-2 (KJV)

It is the desire of our heavenly Father to establish us as leaders of the nations, blessed and whole, walking in covenant with Him day by day. He is a rewarder of those who diligently seek Him (Heb. 11:6).

November 05 - Cry Unto God

I will cry unto God most high; unto God that performeth all things for me. Psalm 57:2 (KJV)

I find this verse intriguing in it's literal translation. The word "cry" is the Hebrew word, *qara'*, which speaks of one accosting another in order to proclaim with a loud voice. This, then, is a cry that proclaims our need for help and a summons, or invitation, to God to come into our present situation or circumstance and handle it as He sees fit.

The "cry" is unto God, *'elohiym*, The Godhead Most High, *'elyown*. It draws upon all of Who God is. The proclaimed invitation is for the Omnipresent, Omnipotent, Omniscient God who, as the Holy Trinity consisting of Father, Son and Holy Ghost, is the one and only Creator and Maintainer of all things.

'Elohiym is the word used to denote One God in three Persons (an inseparable plurality). The verse then uses, *'El* for "God," which can mean, "a sacrificial Ram named 'God His Praise,' or 'Immanuel,' God with us." It is indicative of "God, the one true God, Jehovah."

This proclamation of faith in the ability of Jehovah to come and perform should encourage us to do the same as the Psalmist.

This "God that performeth" is our God, Who in and through the Person of our Lord and Savior, Jesus the Christ, "performeth," *gamar.* This word simply states, "He will perfect, perform, and bring to an end, in order to complete, all that pertains to the one who speaks boldly to Him. This idea is ably captured in Psalm 138:8:

The Lord will perfect that which concerneth me: thy mercy, O Lord, endureth for ever: forsake not the works of thine own hands. Psalm 138:8 (KJV)

Here is found both the "cry" of faith and the "cry" of covenant mercy, *checed*, for the moment. Such a "cry" is always answered with God intervening magnificently.

November 06 - None Other Commandment

And Jesus answered him, The first of all the commandments is, Hear, O Israel; The Lord our God is one Lord: And thou shalt love the Lord thy God with all thy heart, and with all thy soul, and with all thy mind, and with all thy strength: this is the first commandment. And the second is like, namely this, Thou shalt love thy neighbour as thyself. There is none other commandment greater than these. Mark 12:29-31 (KJV)

Protos is the Greek word translated as "the first" of "all," *pas*, or, the primary and most important of the "commandments," *entole*. I marvel at how most "Christians" consider "commandments" to be suggestions when the very word, "commandment," is an injunction. This means that it is an authoritative and compelling, even unalterable, rule. When this unalterable rule is given as a dictum of God one would think that it should be adhered to with the highest degree of respect.

This first of all commandments establishes the passion of covenant relationship that God requires of those who would join themselves to Him. "Thou shalt love, *agapao*," the Lord thy God unconditionally, without end. We have spoken of this eternal covenant love before and so need not labor here.

This "love, *agapao*," is to emanate from, and literally, *olov holos*, consume, the believers' heart, *kardia*, soul, *psuche*, mind, *dianoia*, and strength, *ischus*. Every fiber of the believers' being, physically, emotionally, intellectually and all of one's ability and energy should be involved in developing the covenant relationship that this kind of love requires.

The second, *deuteros*, commandment, or, the other of two, demands the same intensity of love, *agapao*, toward all who are "near neighbor's," *plesion*. This "near neighbor" is anyone who is also in covenant with the "one Lord," the "Lord our God," who gave commandment.

November 07 - A Better Name

For thus saith the Lord unto the eunuchs that keep my sabbaths, and choose the things that please me, and take hold of my covenant; Even unto them will I give in mine house and within my walls a place and a name better than of sons and of daughters: I will give them an everlasting name, that shall not be cut off. Isaiah 56:4-5 (KJV)

The Lord does not overlook even one individual who trusts in Him. He has a plan and a promised blessing for all who look to Him for their hope. Our verses today begin with "For thus saith the Lord." This literally states, *'amar Yehovah,* "*YHWH* promises.*" He who cannot lie promises to the enuchs, *cariyc,* castrated chamberlains or officers, that, if they will choose those things that please the Lord, *chaphets bachar,* they would receive an everlasting name. The reception of an everlasting name suggests that their lives will be extremely fruitful throughout eternity.

Here is an eternal promise to mortal men. Here is a promise of eternal glory, honor and station to those who have set aside natural fruitfulness during their life on earth. This promise of blessing positions the servant hearted as better than sons and daughters of the Most High. The servant will be served.

Thus shall it be that even the most hidden from public view faithful servant becomes an heir of God and is rewarded:

Wherefore thou art no more a servant, but a son; and if a son, then an heir of God through Christ.
Galatians 4:7 (KJV)

And if children, then heirs; heirs of God, and joint-heirs with Christ; if so be that we suffer with him, that we may be also glorified together. Romans 8:17 (KJV)

And if ye be Christ's, then are ye Abraham's seed, and heirs according to the promise. Galatians 3:29 (KJV)

Hearken, my beloved brethren, Hath not God chosen the poor of this world rich in faith, and heirs of the kingdom which he hath promised to them that love him?
James 2:5 (KJV)

November 08 - Take Hold Of The Covenant

> Also the sons of the stranger, that join themselves to the Lord, to serve him, and to love the name of the Lord, to be his servants, every one that keepeth the sabbath from polluting it, and taketh hold of my covenant;
> Isaiah 56:6 (KJV)

The glorious truth of the Gospel that Isaiah saw in a figure is that "the sons of the stranger" are called into covenant relationship with the Lord. What was once open only to the physical sons of Abraham, Isaac and Jacob, has become available to whosoever will "love the name of the Lord, to be his servants."

The servants, *'ebed*, bond slaves, who choose to love, *'ahab*, to be a friend who loves the name, *shem*, Jesus, His reputation, fame and glory, and is willing to serve, *sharath*, minister to, Him by honoring Him on the sabbath. What was important to God was not so much the day but that each day wherein there is covenant atonement, should not be polluted, *chalal*.

A day is considered to be polluted when profane things are done in it. When a man or woman prostitutes themselves to any manner of carnal pursuit, when "the Lord's Day" is seen as "just any other day," when the day is used for "common things," the day is seen by God as "polluted" and "profane." A polluted day is a day wherein God is dishonored by one honoring other things rather than, or more than, Him.

This word, polluted, *chalal*, also carries the idea of "piercing," "wounding" and "killing." Could we then say that when an individual uses "the Lord's Day" improperly that he would "crucify to themselves the Son of God afresh?"

> For it is impossible for those who were once enlightened, and have tasted of the heavenly gift, and were made partakers of the Holy Ghost, And have tasted the good word of God, and the powers of the world to come, If they shall fall away, to renew them again unto repentance; seeing they crucify to themselves the Son of God afresh, and put him to an open shame. Hebrews 6:4-6 (KJV)

Keep His day Holy. Go to church, honor and worship God on "the Day of the Lord." Take hold of the covenant.

November 09 - Make Glad the City of God

There is a river, the streams whereof shall make glad the city of God, the holy place of the tabernacles of the most High. Psalm 46:4 (KJV)

What a picture is conveyed to us as we read of the river that flows from the right side of the altar in the temple of God. We see it bringing life and healing provision everywhere it goes.

In the midst of the street of it, and on either side of the river, was there the tree of life, which bare twelve manner of fruits, and yielded her fruit every month: and the leaves of the tree were for the healing of the nations. Revelation 22:2 (KJV)

This river, *nahar*, we are told, has, "*peleg*," or "channels" which make glad, *samach*, that is, causes the city of God to rejoice and be glad. This river begins at the right hand of God where we can look "unto Jesus the author and finisher of our faith; who for the joy that was set before him endured the cross, despising the shame, and is set down at the right hand of the throne of God" (Heb. 12:2 KJV). It is there we see the hole in the "Rock" from which the river flows.

But one of the soldiers with a spear pierced his side, and forthwith came there out blood and water. John 19:34 (KJV)

The risen Christ is the Rock that followed Israel in the wilderness and gave water at Moses command. This eternal "Rock" is the source of that water which flows through the City of God and carries leaves of healing for the Nations.

In the midst of the street of it, and on either side of the river, was there the tree of life, which bare twelve manner of fruits, and yielded her fruit every month: and the leaves of the tree were for the healing of the nations. Revelation 22:2 (KJV)

Today, this same water bubbles out of the lips of those who will yield their lips to utter divine words of healing.

He that believeth on me, as the scripture hath said, out of his belly shall flow rivers of living water. John 7:38 (KJV)

Make glad the City of God. Let the river of healing flow.

November 10 - Every One's Bands Were Loosed

And at midnight Paul and Silas prayed, and sang praises unto God: and the prisoners heard them. And suddenly there was a great earthquake, so that the foundations of the prison were shaken: and immediately all the doors were opened, and every one's bands were loosed.
Acts 16:25-26 (KJV)

When praise pierces through the moment of hardship; when a song cuts through the season of anguish, when the sun has long since set and morning is yet far distant and the midnight hour is shaken with words of faith, God opens every locked door as the chains of restraint fall away.

How can this be? Beloved, your Omnipotent God and Father loves to respond to and reward faith for those whose joy is based in their unswerving trust in Him. This is what is revealed to us as we read:

But without faith it is impossible to please him: for he that cometh to God must believe that he is, and that he is a rewarder of them that diligently seek him.
Hebrews 11:6 (KJV)

The Rewarder of faith recompenses those who, *ekzeteo*, worshipfully enquire after Him by seeking Him carefully and diligently. He responds to and rewards those who crave His presence in whatever circumstance or situation they may find themselves.

Praise, especially the sacrifice of praise, makes a demand upon Him to come into any given situation as one who takes our place. He inhabits, *yashab*, our praise. This means that He comes and sits down with us to judge our cause. He will settle whatever issue is at hand by joining Himself to us as One who is joined with us in a marriage covenant relationship.

But thou art holy, O thou that inhabitest the praises of Israel. Psalm 22:3 (KJV)

You and I are never alone in anything. He has promised, "I am with you alway, even unto the end of the world" and "I will never leave thee, nor forsake thee" (Mat. 28:20: Heb. 13:5 KJV).

November 11 - Spiritual Blessings

Blessed be the God and Father of our Lord Jesus Christ, who hath blessed us with all spiritual blessings in heavenly places in Christ: Ephesians 1:3 (KJV)

God, our Father and the Father of our Lord and Savior Jesus Christ, has blessed, *eulogeo*, you and I. He has celebrated our lives and shown His favor by invoking blessings upon us by pronouncement.

This decree brings the full weight of His Word to bear, causing a release of all, *pas*, all things, each and every thing, all manner of spiritual blessings, *pneumatikos*.

Let's look at this word translated, spiritual, *pneumatikos*. What is it telling us? A casual look would imply that what is in heaven's storehouse is going to be used to bless us. Oh, but it is more than that, Beloved. It is saying that God, Himself, is going to bless us with all of who He is! Think about it. Isn't that what He has done? He has filled us with Himself, God the Holy Spirit. That, dear one, is abundantly above and beyond all that we might ask or think.

And, what about the word, blessings? The use of the Greek word, *eulogia*, reveals that this is to the praise and laudation of Christ and of God; a concrete benefit that is like a benediction upon our lives that brings Him glory, honor and praise. His impartation of Himself in the person of the Holy Spirit is His supreme gift of salvation.

What, then, of the term, heavenly places? The two words are, in fact, one Greek word, *epouranios*, which could be stated specifically as, existing in the heavenly temple or sanctuary. Thus, we see that what is being referred to is He who is in the heavenly holy of holies, the Christ of 2 Corinthians 3:17 (KJV): "Now the Lord is that Spirit: . . .", and He that is spoken of in 1 John 4:4 (KJV): ". . . greater is he that is in you, than he that is in the world." This is heavenly spiritual blessings.
Selah.

November 12 - Not Against Flesh

For we wrestle not against flesh and blood, but against principalities, against powers, against the rulers of the darkness of this world, against spiritual wickedness in high places. Ephesians 6:12 (KJV)

Have you ever been kicked to the wall by a minister of the gospel? God forbid, but all men and women who are "Ordained" are not necessarily that sweet spirited.

We know that all are in the process of sanctification. Doctrinally, we were sanctified at our moment of salvation, we are being sanctified as we walk our salvation with fear and trembling and, when we stand before Him, we shall be sanctified.

It seems that the more wounded a person may have been, and the more unable to truly forgive those who wounded them they are, the more they wind up rending and wounding others. Nothing is more dangerous than a wounded wild animal. They become enemies to all they encounter.

Our "adversary the devil, as a roaring lion, walketh about, seeking whom he may devour:" 1 Peter 5:8 (KJV). Though, none of us wants to acknowledge that a devilish spirit (demon) can have any influence on us, it is a simple truth that to deny the possibility is the door of deception.

Knowing this should cause us to apply Matthew 5:44 (KJV) to those situations where we are met with a spirit that is other than Christ like. "But I say unto you, Love your enemies, bless them that curse you, do good to them that hate you, and pray for them which despitefully use you, and persecute you."

Ever be mindful that "we wrestle not against flesh and blood, but against principalities, against powers, against the rulers of the darkness of this world, against spiritual wickedness in high places." Our battle is not with people or personalities. Keeping this in mind will always cause the love and grace of God to modify any fleshly behavior that we may be tempted to display.

November 13 - The Whole Armor

Wherefore take unto you the whole armour of God, that ye may be able to withstand in the evil day, and having done all, to stand. Ephesians 6:13 (KJV)

The importance of "the whole armor of God" cannot be over emphasized. It is with these that the Christian is "able to withstand in the evil day." Our verse is preceded by the admonition to "put on the whole armor of God" so that we are made "able to stand against the wiles of the devil" (Eph. 6:11).

To many, the only warfare they face on a daily basis is the one they can see. The simple truth is, though, that the true warfare of the whole human race is one against "principalities, against powers, against the rulers of the darkness of this world, against spiritual wickedness in high places" (Eph. 6:12 KJV).

Even the seasoned veteran of the faith can lose sight of the forces behind what is going on in the seen realm. Busy-ness tends to cause spiritual blindness and lull an individual into a vulnerable spiritual state prone to defeat.

Truth is still absolute in spite of what contemporary "thinkers" think and say. Truth will always bring ultimate victory. Righteousness will guard the vital parts of the soul. The Gospel of peace adjusts the atmosphere of any society and faith will never fail to "quench all the fiery darts of the wicked" (v.16), while those who have made Jesus both Lord and Savior wear a well disciplined mind filled with power and love.

People who enjoy real integrity of character are those who wield the "sword of the Spirit, which is the word of God" and meet with its Teacher daily in prayer and supplication.

Those who have "done all" and are yet able "to stand" are those who walk in the equipping of the Most High, availing themselves of the Word, the Spirit and the enabling power of His anointing; the "armor of God."

Today, take what God has offered so freely and walk enabled and empowered by virtue of that which is His whole armor.

November 14 - Being Confident

Being confident of this very thing, that he which hath begun a good work in you will perform it until the day of Jesus Christ: Philippians 1:6 (KJV)

Early in my Christian life there was a song that said, "He didn't bring us this far to leave us. He didn't pick us up to let us down . . .". Nothing could be more sure in our relationship with the Lord. We can be "confident of this very thing." He who gave Himself for us said, " . . . I will never leave thee, nor forsake thee" (Heb 13:5 KJV).

We are assured that our Lord is not only going to stay the course with us but He is going to complete the thing that He has begun. God said that He has "begun a good work." The Greek word for good, *agathos*, speaks of, a gift which is truly a gift, pre-eminently of God, as consummately and essentially good.

So, then, this "work," *ergon*, that is in process and going to be completed, is the gift of God: "Christ in you the hope of glory" (Col. 1:27). The work, *ergon,* here referred to is "good," *agathos,* undertaking by God Himself.

Our verse states that, He will perform, *epiteleo*, this good work that He has begun. This simply means that He is going to perfect, accomplish and finish the performance that He has taken upon Himself to make an end of for Himself.

Be confident, *peitho*! Be fully persuaded, filled with belief and say what God has said about who you are and who you are becoming. These two words, "be confident," call us to continually persuade ourselves of God's plan for our lives by speaking His words as found in His Word. "So then faith cometh by hearing, and hearing by the word of God" (Rom. 10:17 KJV).

The final act and finished "performance of God" will be unveiled at "the day of Jesus Christ. We shall be like Him!

Till we all come in the unity of the faith, and of the knowledge of the Son of God, unto a perfect man, unto the measure of the stature of the fulness of Christ: Ephesians 4:13 (KJV)

November 15 - That Your Love May Abound

> And this I pray, that your love may abound yet more
> and more in knowledge and in all judgment;
> Philippians 1:9 (KJV)

"And this I pray," could be rendered, "and for this cause, *touto*, I offer prayers, *proseuchomai*, for you". The "cause" being that found in verse eight where we see "I long after," *epipotheo*, your well being, *humas*, or, for your sakes.

The request of this prayer is that love, *agape*: God's unconditional love) may exceed any fixed measure, *perisseuo*, and will continually exist and be at hand in abundance. This is the measure of God's love which is exceedingly, abundantly, above all that we may ever ask or think.

Our prayer for one another should always be of this sort. We should be so concerned for one another's well being that we pray for this love to be abounding in the same sense as that of a flower going from a bud to full bloom.

This love is not a feeling nor is it something that is the result of happenstance (a happening, circumstance, or situation). It is to be solidly rooted in knowledge and judgment.

We are here speaking of the knowledge, *epignosis*, the acknowledging of ethical and divine love, with precise and correct knowledge of such things. We are asking God to give supernatural quality and quantity to our love of one another in the Body of Christ.

This also deals with judgment, *aisthesis*, that is, perception, not only by the senses but by the intellect. It has to do with discernment and the moral discernment in ethical matters. Thus, I declare in prayer that you will excel in love by the supernatural working of the Holy Ghost. I declare in prayer that you will, today, receive a supernatural, divine, revelation of the love of God in all the knowledge and judgment that He has Himself.

November 16 - God Had Mercy

For indeed he was sick nigh unto death: but God had mercy on him; and not on him only, but on me also, lest I should have sorrow upon sorrow. Philippians 2:27 (KJV)

Epaphroditus, whose name means, " lovely," was sick, *astheneo*. That is to say, he was weak, feeble, without strength, powerless and about to die. He was sick unto death, *thanatos*. That doesn't sound to "lovely," does it?

Paul did not want to lose this friend and ministry partner and, unlike Job's comforters, sincerely cared about the well being of this man. Every Christian leader, whether a senior pastor or group leader should sincerely care for, and pray for, those God has placed along side them and in their care.

The love of God should flow freely between leaders and their charge. The weakness, infirmity, or sickness of a fellow saint should give us "sorrow upon sorrow." This word, *lupe*, which is translated, sorrow, also carries the meaning of that which is grievous and brings heaviness, even the grief and pain of one mourning. Oh, Beloved Saint, how God would have us bear one another's burdens. We so need one another in this walk of Christian warfare and service.

The healing of Epaphroditus was seen as the mercy of God, *eleeo*. This mercy is a picture of the same compassion Jesus showed for the multitudes. While He was on earth, Jesus displayed the compassion, or mercy, of God. It is help extended to the afflicted that can be seen and felt. This compassionate concern should call us to prayer and intercession of the most passionate kind. This is the heart of God expressed through His chosen and called out ones.

Wherefore also we pray always for you, that our God would count you worthy of this calling, and fulfil all the good pleasure of his goodness, and the work of faith with power: 2 Thessalonians 1:11 (KJV)

November 17 - Receiving Honor

How can ye believe, which receive honour one of another, and seek not the honour that cometh from God only? John 5:44 (KJV)

Nothing hinders the faith of a man more than the need to be accepted by other men. It is impossible to be a servant of Christ and seek to please men. The Lord who made us knows this weakness and so had Paul warn us about this danger.

For do I now persuade men, or God? or do I seek to please men? for if I yet pleased men, I should not be the servant of Christ. Galatians 1:10 (KJV)

We are asked in today's verse, "How can you believe . . . if you seek honor from other men?" To believe, *pisteuo*, is to commit to one's trust (in this case committing ourselves into God's trust). It is to have put our lives in trust with our Lord. We are persuaded and have absolute confidence in our God to lead us into our highest destiny according to His plan and purpose

To "receive" honor from one another carries the force of the Greek word, *lambano*, which means to take with the hand or to claim for one's self. It is not receiving honor earned from others because of an exemplary life of service so much as it is appropriating it for one's self from others.

Our focus in this life should be to seek, *zeteo*, to fulfill the pleasure, plan, and purpose of God. Our desire should be to seek in order to find, to aim at, and strive after the will of God.

There is an honor, *doxa*, a dignity, a glory that God gives to the faithful whose heart is toward Him. He clothes such a one with honor and a dignity by filling him with His own grace, splendor and excellence of spirit. This is a most glorious condition, a most exalted state that seats us with Christ at the right hand of the Father and ultimately draws us to that honored position for eternity in Christ.

But seek ye first the kingdom of God, and his righteousness; and all these things shall be added unto you. Matthew 6:33 (KJV)

November 18 - Armor Bearers

> And Jonathan said to the young man that bare his armour, Come, and let us go over unto the garrison of these uncircumcised: it may be that the Lord will work for us: for there is no restraint to the Lord to save by many or by few. And his armourbearer said unto him, Do all that is in thine heart: turn thee; behold, I am with thee according to thy heart. 1 Samuel 14:6-7 (KJV)

There is none in the Body of Christ more underestimated nor more overlooked than the armor bearer. Yet, there is no one of more worth, more value or more precious than such a person.

If you have ever been in a fight alone, you know how vulnerable you can become if your enemy outnumbers you. I learned early on that if you were going to fight more than one opponent at a time you had better find a corner to fight from. The walls keep your back covered.

On the other hand, if you have an armor bearer, someone to "watch your back," you have an even better chance of winning the fight; no matter how many are against you.

As Christians we have the Lord on our side and those that be with Him, therefore with us, are more than those that be against us. Elisha and his servant give us a picture of what the reality of that is like:

> And he answered, Fear not: for they that be with us are more than they that be with them. And Elisha prayed, and said, Lord, I pray thee, open his eyes, that he may see. And the Lord opened the eyes of the young man; and he saw: and, behold, the mountain was full of horses and chariots of fire round about Elisha. 2 Kings 6:16-17 (KJV)

Many times, however, the Lord will let us move into the fray much like Jonathan and his armor bearer. When we do, the presence of that one whose heart is knit with ours to win the skirmish is of inestimable worth.

My prayer today is that you will have one who, when faced with the good fight of faith, will say, "Do all that is in thine heart: . . . behold, I am with thee according to thy heart." One that will be unswerving in allegiance and whose love will that of Jonathan and David.

November 19 - No Restraint

And Jonathan said to the young man that bare his armour, Come, and let us go over unto the garrison of these uncircumcised: it may be that the Lord will work for us: for there is no restraint to the Lord to save by many or by few. 1 Samuel 14:6 (KJV)

There is no limit to what one man or woman can do in God. He doesn't need a great army to accomplish His plan and purpose. In fact, our verse today speaks of two men, joined in heart, believing in God, doing what an army was afraid to do: Attack the Philistines.

You always will always out smart, out maneuver, out wait, out fight, and over come every obstacle when the Lord is with you.

But no weapon that is formed against you shall prosper, and every tongue that shall rise against you in judgment you shall show to be in the wrong. This [peace, righteousness, security, triumph over opposition] is the heritage of the servants of the Lord [those in whom the ideal Servant of the Lord is reproduced]; this is the righteousness or the vindication which they obtain from Me [this is that which I impart to them as their justification], says the Lord. Isaiah 54:17 (AMP)

There is no weapon that can prevail against you! Believe it in your heart, speak it continually with your mouth and receive it by faith.

For verily I say unto you, That whosoever shall say unto this mountain, Be thou removed, and be thou cast into the sea; and shall not doubt in his heart, but shall believe that those things which he saith shall come to pass; he shall have whatsoever he saith. Therefore I say unto you, What things soever ye desire, when ye pray, believe that ye receive them, and ye shall have them. Mark 11:23-24 (KJV) Now!

Now faith is the substance of things hoped for, the evidence of things not seen. Hebrews 11:1 (KJV).

. . . there is no restraint to the Lord to save by many or by few. (1 Sam. 14:6 KJV)

November 20 - Scarlet Thread

Behold, when we come into the land, thou shalt bind this line of scarlet thread in the window which thou didst let us down by: and thou shalt bring thy father, and thy mother, and thy brethren, and all thy father's household, home unto thee. Joshua 2:18 (KJV)

The scarlet thread of this verse in Joshua is a type of the covenant blood of the Lamb for a house who is, as we now know, Jesus Christ.

And the blood shall be to you for a token upon the houses where ye are: and when I see the blood, I will pass over you, and the plague shall not be upon you to destroy you, when I smite the land of Egypt. Exodus 12:13 (KJV)

There is nothing more powerful than the shed blood of Jesus. It speaks of mercy, grace and the fulness of redemption. Both the blood on the door posts and lintels of the Hebrew houses and the scarlet thread of Rahab's house in the wall speak of a covenant promise to the whole family.

And ye shall take a bunch of hyssop, and dip it in the blood that is in the bason, and strike the lintel and the two side posts with the blood that is in the bason; and none of you shall go out at the door of his house until the morning. Exodus 12:22 (KJV)

All who remained inside the houses were spared by the Lord. Beloved, God wants your whole house saved.

Consider the house of Cornelius spoken of in Acts Chapter Ten. The whole household was saved, filled with the Spirit and water baptized. Another example would be the keeper of the prison in Acts, Chapter 16. We read in verse 34 that he, ". . . rejoiced, believing in God with all his house."

Just as the Hebrew spy's promised Rahab that her house would be saved, so God has promised that your household shall be saved.

The LORD shall increase you more and more, you and your children. Psalms 115:14 (KJV).
Selah!

November 21 - It Is Yours!

Every place that the sole of your foot shall tread upon, that have I given unto you, as I said unto Moses.
Joshua 1:3 (KJV)

How is your believer? Have you enough confidence in the Word of God, who cannot lie, to believe that wherever you set your foot becomes your rightful inheritance?

Too often, with the passing of time, we can be tempted to lose sight of this powerful promise. "Every place," simply put means, every place. Our Hebrew word, *maqowm*, or, *maqom*, includes such things as the place where you stand, the room you are in, the house you are in, whatever place you find yourself, and the region or land where you are. It also includes the post or office that you hold.

The words translated, sole, *kaph*, of your foot, *regel*, picture the power to grasp and possess the place where you set foot. As a believer, you are empowered to possess all that God has given you. Given, *nathan*, can be translated, bestowed upon, granted to, ascribed to, committed to, entrusted to, and given over to.

When the Lord decides to bless you, and tells you He is giving you something, you are blessed with the ownership of it! So, receive it! Surely, we have learned by now that we possess what God says we have before we see it? So much is left outside of our grasp because we have forgotten the basics of faith.

Remember Mark 11:23-24 (KJV)?:

For verily I say unto you, That whosoever shall say unto this mountain, Be thou removed, and be thou cast into the sea; and shall not doubt in his heart, but shall believe that those things which he saith shall come to pass; he shall have whatsoever he saith. Therefore I say unto you, What things soever ye desire, when ye pray, believe that ye receive them, and ye shall have them.

We believe, and continually say what we have been given. We receive by faith (Heb. 11:1) until we have what is promised.

November 22 - These Are Not Drunken

For these are not drunken, as ye suppose, seeing it is but the third hour of the day. Acts 2:15 (KJV)

There are a people who are so liberated, so joyful and so filled with life that our society thinks that "they must be on something." Quite frankly, that's what the world should think. We should be so glaringly different and so exuberant in our life-style that our drugged, drunken and sexually confused, still not satisfied or gratified, society would want to know what we're on.

I don't know about you, but I don't need a "happy hour" to make it through the weekend. "TGIF" doesn't mean, "Thank God It's Friday," it means "Thank God I'm Forgiven!" I'm forgiven and free from the bondage of sin seven days a week. Glory!

Being saved is enough to make a mummy shout; and being Baptized in the Holy Ghost too is just totally superabundantly, above and beyond anything that one could ask or think. The Spirit-filled believer is a walking fulfillment of prophecy.

But this is that which was spoken by the prophet Joel; And it shall come to pass in the last days, saith God, I will pour out of my Spirit upon all flesh: and your sons and your daughters shall prophesy, and your young men shall see visions, and your old men shall dream dreams: And on my servants and on my handmaidens I will pour out in those days of my Spirit; and they shall prophesy: Acts 2:16-18 (KJV)

"This is that." This is that which the prophet spoke of (Joel 2:28, 29). This is that which makes a people "drunk" in the spirit at nine in the morning (Acts 2:15). This is that which allows a person to "speak mysteries to God" (1 Cor. 14:2). This is that which will arrest the attention of the whole world (Acts 2:7-12, 17).

It is early in the day and we who have the same Spirit that raised Christ from the dead should be noising abroad the wonderful works of God in the midst of the city (Rom. 8:11: Acts 2:11).

November 23 - Do You Hear it?

1 Kings 18 reveals how the natural realm follows the realm of the Spirit where faith rules under the mighty hand of God.

One of the most important things that a Christian must do is learn to "hear" the voice of the Spirit of the Lord. It is by hearing that we are guided into a relationship with Truth Himself.

Jesus said to him, I am the Way and the Truth and the Life; no one comes to the Father except by (through) Me. John 14:6 (AMP)

It is by hearing that we receive faith:

So then faith cometh by hearing, and hearing by the word of God. Romans 10:17 (KJV)

It is by hearing that we come to know what the Father is speaking.

But when He, the Spirit of Truth (the Truth-giving Spirit) comes, He will guide you into all the Truth (the whole, full Truth). For He will not speak His own message [on His own authority]; but He will tell whatever He hears [from the Father; He will give the message that has been given to Him], and He will announce and declare to you the things that are to come [that will happen in the future]. John 16:13 (AMP)

It is by hearing that we can know what will happen in the future.

Do you hear what I hear? I hear the promise of God to me and those who are a part of this church concerning our place in the plan of God for the end time harvest of the world. I hear the cry of the heart of God to seek and save those which are lost.

I hear the Lord speaking concerning the importance of establishing this property as a center of salvation, healing, deliverance and miracle producing revival. Do you hear it?

I hear the Spirit of Resurrection calling us higher in the things of God so that we can walk in the limitless Love of God and demonstrate the unstoppable power of God to this community.

November 24 - Thanksgiving

And let the peace (soul harmony which comes) from Christ rule (act as umpire continually) in your hearts [deciding and settling with finality all questions that arise in your minds, in that peaceful state] to which as [members of Christ's] one body you were also called [to live]. And be thankful (appreciative), [giving praise to God always]. Colossians 3:15 (AMP)

We are admonished to be thankful always. Always? Yes, always, even in the "mean time." My Pastor, Bill Sharp, used to say, "In the mean time, it's a mean time." When Jesus is our joy, our love, our life and our purpose for living, difficult times are quite insignificant.

During the good times it is easy to be thankful; albeit many forget who gives them times of refreshing and abundance. It is the "mean times," the time between the promise and the provision, the time between the crisis and the answer when the giving of thanks is most precious. This is when a sacrifice of thanksgiving issues from just knowing that God is God (Psa. 107:22; 116:17 KJV).

The thankless find themselves going spiritually blind (Rom. 1:21) because an unappreciative, thankless heart is a hardened heart with no revelation of God. This eventually brings about what the Bible calls senseless, darkened minds.

The thankful, on the other hand, find themselves in the very presence of God (Psalm 95:2; 100:4 KJV), and experiencing abundant increase and provision on every hand (Mat. 15:36; Joh. 6:23).

This is faith, which pleases God (Heb. 11:6) working. We give thanks that He is our Father, our God, and that He loves us. We give thanks that our provision is in Him now (Heb. 11:1).

We give thanks with our voice and in our actions and the result is always found in our God (Mar. 11:23-24).

As you prepare to have a wonderful Thanksgiving Day, stop to consider the goodness of God (Psa. 136)

November 25 - Do You See it?

Not only do I hear the sound of an abundance of rain but I see a cloud the size of a man's hand that is moving swiftly across the sky, growing ever larger, to bring harvest rain. This is the former and latter rain that is a result of the Spirit of Supplication working in the intercessors of the Lord's harvest.

It is important that we hear and see what the Spirit is speaking and what the Spirit is showing us concerning our future.

He that hath an ear, let him hear what the Spirit saith unto the churches. Revelation 2:29 (KJV)

Seven times the book of Revelation tells us to "hear what the Spirit saith." Each time that we hear and heed what is spoken, there is instruction and promise.

We must also be able to see impending judgement so that we can be warned and repent.

Then the angel that talked with me went forth, and said unto me, Lift up now thine eyes, and see what is this that goeth forth. Zechariah 5:5 (KJV)

Without a redemptive revelation of the plan and purpose of God we will find ourselves and those who follow us wandering aimlessly and ineffectively rather than moving ahead with purpose and strength. We must be able to see in the realm of the Spirit's dreams and visions:

Where there is no vision [no redemptive revelation of God], the people perish; but he who keeps the law [of God, which includes that of man]—blessed (happy, fortunate, and enviable) is he. Proverbs 29:18 (AMP)

We must be able to see spiritual truth in order to know the hidden mystery of God as revealed in Christ:

And to make all men see what is the fellowship of the mystery, which from the beginning of the world hath been hid in God, who created all things by Jesus Christ: Ephesians 3:9 (KJV)

Let us, you and me, be a people who both hear and see -
Selah

November 26 - The Word . . .

And they overcame him by the blood of the Lamb, and by the word of their testimony; and they loved not their lives unto the death. Revelation 12:11 (KJV)

There is nothing more important than the word you and I speak. Yes, the Word you and I speak. Our words should be those of the Word of the living God.

Our God, Jehovah Himself, is a speaking Spirit.

God is a Spirit: and they that worship him must worship him in spirit and in truth. John 4:24 (KJV)

He is the Voice that walked in the Garden of Eden:

And they heard the voice of the Lord God walking in the garden . . . Genesis 3:8 (KJV)

When He breathed Himself into man, He created man to be a speaking spirit after His own image and likeness.

You and I, Beloved, are to be people who speak the Word with assurance [faith], knowing that what ever we speak will accomplish what it was sent to do.

Then said the Lord to me, . . . , for I am alert and active, watching over My word to perform it.
Jeremiah 1:12 (AMP)

When we learn to speak what He speaks with the assurance [faith] that He backs His word when it comes out of our mouth, we will see the results of our speaking like we never though possible.

Remember, God has been in covenant with you and I from the moment that we accepted Jesus as our Lord and Savior. He will do whatever we say when we do whatever He says.

. . . whosoever shall say . . . and shall not doubt in his heart, but shall believe that those things which he saith shall come to pass; he shall have whatsoever he saith.
Mark 11:23 (KJV)

November 27 - The Blood . . .

And they overcame him by the blood of the Lamb, and by the word of their testimony; and they loved not their lives unto the death. Revelation 12:11 (KJV)

Once born-again, you and I were transformed into a new creation by the power of God. We are now the sons of God.

But as many as received him, to them gave he power to become the sons of God, even to them that believe on his name: John 1:12 (KJV)

We are now witnesses of His grace. We have experienced and benefitted from His unconditional, supernatural agape love. As we yield to His command to be endued with power from on high (the Baptism in the Holy Spirit) we can be witness to His resurrection power.

But ye shall receive power, after that the Holy Ghost is come upon you: and ye shall be witnesses unto me both in Jerusalem, and in all Judea, and in Samaria, and unto the uttermost part of the earth. Acts 1:8 (KJV)

He said that we, "shall be witnesses unto me." This means we shall be witnesses to Him in resurrection power.

But if the Spirit of him that raised up Jesus from the dead dwell in you, he that raised up Christ from the dead shall also quicken your mortal bodies by his Spirit that dwelleth in you. Romans 8:11 (KJV)

When we witness, or speak what we have seen and what we have known of Him, we are joined with the supernatural speaking of the precious Blood of "the Lamb Slain from the foundation of the world" (Rev. 13:8).

The Blood speaks and The Voice speaks as our testimony [our witness] speaks. In other words, when we speak of what we have seen and heard of Him, what we have experienced in Him, there is a supernatural empowerment that God Himself backs and attests to with signs, wonders and miracles.

November 28 - Know the Love of Christ

And to know the love of Christ, which passeth knowledge, that ye might be filled with all the fulness of God. Ephesians 3:19 (KJV)

We are encouraged to know, *ginosko*, the love of Christ. The Greek word used here is that of an intimate knowing that is shared by a husband and wife. Their innermost secrets are shared and their physical bodies are shared in their bed.

This is how familiar the true believer is to be with the, *agape*, covenant love found only in Christ (the Anointed One and His anointing). The knowledge of this love is pursued with more passion than can be found in the pursuit of anything or anyone else.

This is supernatural love "which passeth, *huperballo*, knowledge, *gnosis.*" It is covenant love that transcends, exceeds, and excels beyond general intelligence, knowing the difference between right and wrong, education or science.

The call to know this kind of supernatural love is so that we can be "filled, *pleroo*, with all the fulness, *pleroma*, of God.." To be "filled" is to be liberally supplied and rendered perfect. It is to be saturated, as when all the air is wrung out of a sponge and every pore is filled with liquid. It is to be filled to the top so that nothing shall be wanting to full measure. The Lord's desire is to bring us to the place where we experience the "fulness of God" Himself. The word "fulness," *pleroma*, gives us the idea of being a ship filled, or manned, with sailors and soldiers and laden with valuable cargo.

The Word of God is telling us that we are to seek that *agape* covenant love which allows us to be filled with the presence, power, agency, efficiency, ability, and riches of God and of Christ that the natural man will never know.

Such is the will and pleasure of our Father and our God. This is what Christ Jesus has provided to those who will seek to know.

November 29 - He Is Able

Wherefore he is able also to save them to the uttermost that come unto God by him, seeing he ever liveth to make intercession for them. Hebrews 7:25 (KJV)

Dunamai is the Greek word used here for "he is able."

This means that Jesus has power by virtue of His own ability and resources. We see that He is in a state of mind by permission of the law and character of Almighty God to do something for those that come to God by Him. He is not only of a mind to save us but He is capable, strong and powerfully able to do so.

This salvation, *soteria*, rescues the perishing from danger, makes whole and sound, heals from disease of all kinds, and restores to health while preserving that one until they safely arrive at their intended destination. It the arms of such a salvation one finds themselves perfected and/or completed, *panteles*, by means of its effectiveness.

When we come to, *theos*, the Godhead: God the Father, God the Son and God the Holy Spirit by, *dia*, by means of, through, or perhaps better rendered, by reason of, or on account of, Jesus the Christ, we enter into a salvation that is eternal and cannot be denied.

This is because He ever, *pantote*, lives, *zao*. He is eternally living, breathing, active, blessed and endless in the kingdom of God. In that position He is strong and efficient, powerful and efficacious (effective and competent) in a work particular to keeping those who come to God by Him.

He "ever liveth" to make intercession, *entugchano*. By His spirit He lights upon the saved, meeting them with the purpose of conversing with them and giving them counsel that will help them along the way. His eternal ministry to them is to pray for them.

You see, Beloved, Jesus is praying for you at this moment. He is available to speak with you and guide you every inch of the way with divine competence and effectiveness.

November 30 - Peace is Deaf & Dumb

But I, like a deaf man, hear not; and I am like a dumb man who opens not his mouth.   Psalm 38:13 (AMP)

There is one thing that will help you to have the peace of God and that is to not give place to what is said about you. Yes, that's right. Pay no attention to what others say when others are seeking your hurt. Our verse for today tells us to be like a deaf man who cannot hear, *shama*. We are to refuse to hearken to, or obey what is being said. We won't repeat it and so will not give it access into our life.

Yes, I have become like a man who hears not, in whose mouth are no arguments or replies. Psalm 38:14 (KJV)

Not only are we deaf to what is said but we are dumb regarding it. The word, opens, *pathach*, carries the idea of engraving what was said by repeating it. We must not open ourselves up to the destruction that the words spoken against us were designed to inflict. In other words: Whose report will you believe and, therefore, speak?

Yet we have the same spirit of faith as he had who wrote, I have believed, and therefore have I spoken. We too believe, and therefore we speak, 2 Corinthians 4:13 (AMP)

We must not give ear to anything that is contrary to the Word of God nor are we to speak anything but what aligns with the Word of God. That begins with what God says about who, and what, we are.

Our hope and trust is in the Lord and He will answer those who speak against Him and His anointed children. As it is written:

For in You, O Lord, do I hope; You will answer, O Lord my God. Psalm 38:14-15 (AMP)

Keep your peace, the peace of God that passes all understanding, by refusing to listen to, or speak, words that do not agree with what God has said. His Word is Truth (Joh. 17:17) and will never fail you.

So shall My word be that goes forth out of My mouth: it shall not return to Me void [without producing any effect, useless], but it shall accomplish that which I please and purpose, and it shall prosper in the thing for which I sent it. Isaiah 55:11 (AMP)

DECEMBER

December 01 - Speak With Boldness

And now, Lord, behold their threatenings: and grant unto thy servants, that with all boldness they may speak thy word, Acts 4:29 (KJV)

The right of Christians to speak out concerning their faith is being eroded by the liberal thinkers of our day. The propaganda efforts of a liberal press, secularized church and "politically correct" educational system is bringing our great nation to a time of crisis equaling that preceding the fall of the Roman Empire. In fact, even the seat of modern day Rome is reeling under the onslaught. "And now, Lord, behold their threatenings," is a prayer that surely must be voiced to God in this hour.

This time in which we live is a time of great darkness and great light. The light, in fact, seems all the more bright as it is contrasted with the gross darkness that rules the hearts of so many the world over. But, Beloved, we are the light of the world.

You are the light of the world. A city set on a hill cannot be hidden. Matthew 5:14 (AMP)

The light of the world must not be hidden. The light of the world must "with all boldness . . . speak thy word."

When the Holy Ghost was poured out upon the followers of Christ in the Upper Room on Pentecost, the Church who received Him was endued with power. Power to become witnesses. Power to move with love and a sound mind. The Holy Ghost came to indwell and empower each believer for the task of telling the people of the world about the resurrected Savior, Jesus the Christ of God. They were to be fearless witnesses of what Christ Jesus had done in their lives and proclaimers of what He will do for whosoever will come to Him.

Our prayer in these great and glorious days before the coming of the Lord should be, "grant unto thy servants, that with all boldness [we] may speak thy word." It is even more important now when we are set upon by "their threatenings."

December 02 - Signs And Wonders Follow

By stretching forth thine hand to heal; and that signs and wonders may be done by the name of thy holy child Jesus. Acts 4:30 (KJV)

This prayer for God the Father to reach out and heal holds some interesting words. The word for hand, *cheir*, is one of those words. *Cheir*, symbolizes the might, activity and power of God in creation and in upholding and preserving (God is ever present protecting and aiding us collectively and as individuals).

Another word of interest is, *iasis*, "to heal." Our Father God, as Creator is more than able to heal, *iasis*, or bring about a cure that can only come about supernaturally. Recognizing this, the individual believer can draw upon His eternal omnipotence (great might, activity, and power), and allow it to flow through him. As it is written:

And these signs shall follow them that believe; In my name shall they cast out devils; they shall speak with new tongues; They shall take up serpents [that old serpent, the devil]; and if they drink any deadly thing, it shall not hurt them; they shall lay hands on the sick, and they shall recover. Mark 16:17-18 (KJV)

Signs, wonders and miracles are done by virtue of delegated authority exercised by the name of the only begotten Son, Jesus. His name, *onoma*, the name is used for everything which the name covers, everything the thought or feeling of which is aroused in the mind by mentioning, hearing, remembering, the name, i.e. for one's rank, authority, interests, pleasure, command, excellences, deeds etc.. We use His name (presenting all that He is) as covenant partners with full authority and power of that name.

He gives all the power, we receive all the benefit. He gets all the glory, we receive His blessing. We stretch forth our hand and God stretches forth His hand to affect the cure.

December 03 - The Place Was Shaken

And when they had prayed, the place was shaken where they were assembled together; and they were all filled with the Holy Ghost, and they spake the word of God with boldness. Acts 4:31 (KJV)

The verse says, when, not, if, they had prayed. This word "they," *autos,* is intriguing in that it does not just speak of a physical person, or group of persons, praying but it speaks of those who are praying out of their spirit (a baffling wind). There is no prayer like that which arises out of one's spirit man and there is no prayer like the prayer of agreement.

We see believers gathered together, or assembled together, *sunago,* as was the practice of the early church. This gathering was one to which they were drawn by the Holy Ghost for the purpose of God. The assembling of God's people always serves a divine purpose.

This kind of gathering and this kind of prayer repeatedly shakes something. The place where they were gathered "was shaken," *saleuo,* as though waves, a mighty wind or storm had shaken even what cannot be shaken. This was no small event. It was as though a tsunami had hit the building.

They all were then filled with the characteristics of God and were separated to Him by His Spirit, the third person of the triune God. They were filled, *pletho*, furnished and fulfilled by Him so that they would be witnesses; "they spake the word of God with boldness," *parrhesia.*

This speaking was now with supernatural confidence and cheerful courage and assurance.

But ye shall receive power, after that the Holy Ghost is come upon you: and ye shall be witnesses unto me both in Jerusalem, and in all Judea, and in Samaria, and unto the uttermost part of the earth. Acts 1:8 (KJV)

For God hath not given us the spirit of fear; but of power, and of love, and of a sound mind. 2 Timothy 1:7 (KJV)

December 04 - Potential

Much food is in the tillage of the poor: but there is that is destroyed for want of judgment.
Proverbs 13:23 (KJV)

How many opportunities have passed us by? How many open doors have we not walked through because we did not see them as places we could go? God sees our full potential and calls us to press past our fears in order to find our rightful place in His plan and purpose for our lives.

The problem most people have is that they have poor judgment, *mishpat*. Their sense of right, order, fashion and custom is lacking. They are unable to make good decisions and to follow the process or procedure necessary to bring their decision to fruition. Wanting for "judgment" is also not knowing one's right or privilege in God.

There is "much," *rob*, a multitude, abundance, plenty, and greatness within each individual. It was put there by the Almighty Himself. Man was created after the image and likeness of God.

"Tillage," *niyr*, is fallow ground, ground that is tillable, plant able and potentially productive. If you ever put the seed in, the seed will grow and produce a harvest. Proverbs 12:23 is showing us that there is potential within us but we can realize no benefit from it if we are devoid of good judgment.

The Word of God will make the "poor" (head of the poor man), *var ro'sh*, wise. The two Hebrew words together speak of the mentality of a poor man, a spiritually and mentally slack man; a man whose head is limited by his thought process. His thoughts must become the thoughts of God.

For as he thinketh in his heart, so is he . . .
Proverbs 23:7 (KJV)

A man can impoverish himself by the way he thinks. But, if he begins to think properly, it is written of him: ". . . If thou canst believe, all things are possible to him that believeth" Mark 9:23 (KJV). This is the mind of Christ.

December 05 - Magnified

I will worship toward thy holy temple, and praise thy name for thy lovingkindness and for thy truth: for thou hast magnified thy word above all thy name.
Psalm 138:2 (KJV)

God has given us so much. As believers we must realize it and believe it. You and I, Beloved, are joint-heirs with Christ and the sooner we accept that fact the sooner we will enjoy our inheritance.

Our approach to God should be that of a worshiper. After all, God has extended to us His lovingkindness, *checed*. This is His mercy, kindness, goodness and favor. He sent Jesus as an act of mercy, kindness, and goodness so that He could show us favor.

He has sent His Word which He has magnified, *gadal*, that is, made greater and more powerful than His name. When we believe His Word and speak it we release something greater and more powerful that the name of Almighty God Himself.

He is *Jehovah Rapha*, the God that Heals. We speak verses of scripture that deal with healing and those words become greater and more powerful than the name of God.

He is *Jehovah Jireh*, the God that Supplies. When we speak verses of scripture that deal with provision and supply those words become greater and more powerful than the name of God.

Don't you see, the Word of God was given by God so that we could manifest His glory and power here on earth? He has given us His Word so that the dominion authority, Jesus, the Christ of God, lived, died, and was raised from the dead to give us can be exercised.

It is the silence of the Church that gives the devil the ability to steal, kill and destroy. We are given the right to take dominion over what is allowed to go on across the planet. This is done by submitted words.

Submit yourselves therefore to God. Resist the devil, and he will flee from you. James 4:6-7 (KJV)

December 06 - Delivered and Fearless

I sought the LORD, and he heard me, and delivered me from all my fears.   Psalm 34:4 (KJV)

Seeking the Lord is the answer to everything. He has promised that if we will seek Him, we will find Him and He will hear us. Seeking the Lord is to read, and meditate on, His word until we fix our minds upon Him. This will lead us to seek Him according to His Word and therefore according to His will. Effectual prayer is brought forth by the one walking in faith by the Word of God.

When we are in the will of God we are surrounded by His perfect peace no matter what the situation or circumstance. We are settled and secure in the knowledge that He is going before us to order our steps and light our path. Too many people are wishing and hoping but are not in faith because they are not in the Word.

When our mind is fixed upon Him and His ways there is no room for fear. Fear cannot exist in a vessel filled with faith.

There is no fear in love; but perfect love casteth out fear: because fear hath torment. He that feareth is not made perfect in love. 1 John 4:18 (KJV)

Thou wilt keep him in perfect peace, whose mind is stayed on thee: because he trusteth in thee. Isaiah 26:3 (KJV)

So, faith brings confidence and peace. Faith comes by hearing the Word of God. Remember, God spoke the Word so that it could be written. He made sure that it was written so that you and I could read it. We read it so that we can speak it.

So then faith cometh by hearing, and hearing by the word of God. Romans 10:17 (KJV)

We are assured God hears us when we seek Him. This tells us that we must speak (in order to be heard). Speak the Word of God back to God and your faith will soar and fear will flee.

December 07 - The Blood Speaks

And to Jesus the mediator of the new covenant, and to the blood of sprinkling, that speaketh better things than that of Abel. Hebrews 12:24 (KJV)

Night before last, there was a "theologian" showing his views as regarding the Virgin Birth. After explaining that the only reason Christians used the concept of the virgin birth was that the people of that day believed that Caesar was a god born of the union of a god or goddess and a mortal woman or man. He said, "everyone understood the metaphor when they spoke of Jesus Christ being born of a virgin. Everyone knew he was Joseph and Mary's son. The language used was simply to convey that Jesus was the Christ of God to those who believed in Caesar's deity. We Christians have no problem with such thinking"

Excuse me? I, for one, am a Christian that has a "problem with such thinking." If Joseph was the father of Jesus the Christ then Jesus had the blood of sin stained mortal man in his veins. Such blood could never cleans away the sin of the world. The blood of a child is established by the father. Joseph's blood could never atone for sin.

I might note here that "theologian" is a word that implies that a person is an expert in the study of theology but actually means that a person is qualified to speak God things. This gentleman, however well educated, was certainly not speaking the things of God. We must understand that what is important about education is that what is learned is taught by those who know truth verses falsehood and fact verses theory. It is also noted that a person can be educated beyond their level of intelligence and common sense.

The blood of Jesus "speaks" with the authority of a holy Father and a sinless life. Only the spotless, sinless blood of the "Lamb slain from the foundation of the world" can meet the requirement of God for the salvation of man (1 Pet. 1:18-20 KJV).

December 08 - A Pre-Christmas Blessing

Dearly Beloved,

I pray that your calling is sure, that the work entrusted to you is flourishing, and that you and your family are prospering and in good health.

You are being blessed to be a blessing and you are to me and to all those who know you I am sure.

Draw near to God to know His ways and do exploits for Him with great boldness.

As we prepare to celebrate His birth this Christmas season, may we have a Divine impartation that will gestate within our inner man and bring forth a new thing birthed in the power of the Holy Ghost.

Yes, the Holy Spirit will hover over you and impregnate you with that which the Lord wishes to bring forth in this next season of harvest.

Speak to it, prophesy, and it shall come into being full of the Divine purpose for which it was given.

Even as the Wise Men came with gifts for the Christ Child, so too will men bring unto you to provide for the years ahead. This is so that the vision will be hastened to arrive on time and that there will be no lack during the journey.

Take heart, for the Lord your God is with you and the prayers of the Saints under gird you and commission the angels to surround you with protection and provision as led by the Holy Ghost and the direction of the Lord of hosts.

You are chosen, called and sent with the mandate of the Most High to be fruitful and multiply, to have dominion and to be a possessor of heaven and earth in the authority of the name of Jesus.

Be strong and of a good courage for the Lord will make your way prosperous and you shall have good success (Josh. 1:6, 7, 8).

December 09 - To Speak or Not To Speak?

And to him they agreed: and when they had called the apostles, and beaten them, they commanded that they should not speak in the name of Jesus, and let them go. Acts 5:40 (KJV)

Nothing upsets a corrupt, self-righteous, society quite like an individual, or group, that remind them of their wicked bent. You and I both know that nothing upsets such as the mention of the name of Jesus.

Where I live the County and City still invite "ministers" to bring an invocation prior to their business deliberations. This, in and of itself, is a good thing. In fact it can be a great thing if done with sincerity of heart and a recognition of the need of Divine guidance.

I put the word "ministers" in quotes above because the word has come to mean, Buddhist Monks, Islamic Imams, Mormon Bishops, and a whole host of New Age Practitioners besides the traditional Christian understanding of the word and office. There is a politely written note to the "minister" to keep the prayer generic so as to not offend anyone and include as many understandings of deity as possible.

Beloved, who is it that we are to invoke the blessings of if not the Almighty God, Creator of heaven and earth, our Father, in the name (authority vested in the name) of Jesus? For a Christian to offer a prayer without recognizing that the only right and means of access is in the name of Jesus and His shed blood is unthinkable.

It would be a gross breach of integrity for a Christian, whether a "minister" or not, to pray in a public venue and not utter boldly the only name by which they were saved.

To do less is to deny the only One who can bring a revelation of, what to the world is, "the unknown God," and He who, by Himself, cleansed us of our sin and filled us with righteousness, peace and joy in the Holy Ghost.

Why, who knows, one so bold might even dare to greet all with a hearty "Merry Christmas" rather than an insipid Happy Holidays. After all, Jesus is the only real reason for the season.

December 10 - Relationship is Everything

I would know the words which he would answer me, and understand what he would say unto me. Will he plead against me with his great power? No; but he would put strength in me. Job 23:5-6 (KJV)

No matter in what manner of situation or circumstance you find yourself, never think that God is against you.

For God hath not appointed us to wrath, but to obtain salvation by our Lord Jesus Christ,
1 Thessalonians 5:9 (KJV)

He is on your side. He chose you and called you unto Himself. Revelation 17:14 (KJV) says, that, ". . . they that are with him are called, and chosen, and faithful." Our part is to remain faithful to our covenant relationship with Him.

We are like a watchman at our post. It is critical that we stay awake and alert during our time of service. When our Commander in Chief shows up we should be open to instruction and guidance so that we can better serve Him. If there are weaknesses in our character or demeanor, we need be open to correction. After all, we represent Him.

I will stand upon my watch, and set me upon the tower, and will watch to see what he will say unto me, and what I shall answer when I am reproved. Habakkuk 2:1 (KJV)

Our Lord is always working to perfect all that pertains unto us and doing only that which is beneficial to our eternal destiny. How, then, can we say in times of distress and perplexity as some do, that He is pleading "against me with his great power?"

"No; but he would put strength in me." This is what our God does. He comes to us in our times of doubting, distress, consternation, and pain, and says, ". . . lo, I am with you alway, even unto the end of the world," and ". . . I will never leave thee, nor forsake thee" (Mat. 28:20; Heb. 13:5 - KJV).

In the midst of every situation and circumstance the Word gives joy, and "the joy of the Lord is your strength" (Neh. 8:10).

December 11 - Fulness of Joy

Thou wilt shew me the path of life: in thy presence is fulness of joy; at thy right hand there are pleasures for evermore. Psalm 16:11 (KJV)

As the song says, "This joy I have, the world didn't give it to me. The world didn't give it and the world can't take it away!" Joy, not to be confused with happiness that comes from enjoyable happenstance, comes from the presence of the Lord. Praise draws the Presence and the Presence brings "joy unspeakable and full of glory."

Whom having not seen, ye love; in whom, though now ye see him not, yet believing, ye rejoice with joy unspeakable and full of glory: 1 Peter 1:8 (KJV)

When you love someone, you cannot say enough good about them. You "praise" them and all they are and do. You tell everyone how much you love them. So should our love and praise be for our God who daily shows us "the path of life."

The right hand is a place of honor and delegated authority. To be at the right hand of God in Christ, which is where every true believer dwells, is to be surrounded by "pleasures for evermore." Our problem, in too many Christians, is that we cannot see ourselves seated in heavenly places with Christ at the right hand of God. Yet, Beloved, this is your rightful place of blessing and rest.

Blessed be the God and Father of our Lord Jesus Christ, who hath blessed us with all spiritual blessings in heavenly places in Christ: Ephesians 1:3 (KJV)

Which he wrought in Christ, when he raised him from the dead, and set him at his own right hand in the heavenly places, Ephesians 1:20 (KJV)

Take your place and don't apologize for it:

Who, being in the form of God, thought it not robbery to be equal (*isos* = agreeing together in thought and deed) with God: Philippians 2:6 (KJV)

December 12 - It Is Not Robbery

Who, being in the form of God, thought it not robbery to be equal with God: Philippians 2:6 (KJV)

Jesus the Christ of God, the Anointed One did not think it was wrong to be equal with God. What was really being spoken of here? How does that apply to those who are "in Christ."

If you have ever said that you are after the God kind and have the fulness of God in you, you have probably seen eyes roll and heard something like, "You know that we're supposed to be humble," or, "That kind of pride goes before a fall."

Well, people are destroyed due to a lack of knowledge (Hos. 4:6). Tradition and wrong teaching has left the Body of Christ weak, anemic, and without their God-given stature and authority.

Let's take a look at this often misunderstood verse. Form, *morphe*, is a word of great interest. It means, primarily, the form by which a person or thing strikes the vision. It can also mean, external appearance, but that is not the case here. Jesus, and every believer, is in the form that "strikes the vision" of God on the earth (causes the vision of God to come suddenly in the natural realm). God is seen in Him, and in us, as we are led by His Spirit who indwells us.

We as being found in Him are not to think, *hegeomai ou*, count ourselves as the leader or governor of being equal, *isos*, with God, but, by the Holy Spirit, are agreeing together in thought and deed with God. This is the essence of active righteousness; agreeing with and acting upon His will.

You see, Jesus was not, nor are we, saying that we are the same in physical form with God (God is a Spirit - John. 4:24). We are created in the image and likeness of God (Gen. 1:26; 5:3). We are speaking spirits, like God Himself. His word spoken through our mouths has the same power as if it were spoken through His mouth (1 Pet. 4:11).

We are the demonstration of resurrection on earth; the manifested sons of God in spirit and truth.

December 13 - The Word of God will Keep You

Concerning the words of men, by the word of thy lips I have kept me from the paths of the destroyer.
Psalm 17:4 (AMP)

The words of men, however profound sounding they may be, are lifeless. They are the utterances of dead men walking; "dead in trespasses and sins" (Eph. 2:1 KJV). You may say, "I have heard great wisdom from the lips of men." That may well be so, but those concepts and words of wisdom are simply the words of God plagiarized by those who refuse to defer to Him. This holds true of the reward or gain of the efforts of man without God.

There is nothing more important than the Word of God. It is, "alive and full of power [making it active, operative, energizing, and effective] . . ." Heb. 4:12 (AMP). His words are eternally established and, "profitable for instruction, for reproof and conviction of sin, for correction of error and discipline in obedience, [and] for training in righteousness (in holy living, in conformity to God's will in thought, purpose, and action)"
2 Tim. 3:16 (AMP).

No wonder, then, that the Psalmist said that the word spoken by God is what had kept him safe from destruction. "The word used in this case is, *dabar*, and can mean chronicles, sayings, speech, commandments, business, occupation, acts, or manner, which guides and protects.

It is by the Word of God that we are led away, and kept, from the paths, *'orach*, or mannerisms, ways, or way of living of the destroyer, *pariyts*, the robber, murderer, or violent one.

Scripture teaches us that the devil is a thief and a destroyer. "The thief cometh not, but for to steal, and to kill, and to destroy" John 10:10a. It also reveals to us that the Word, the , *logos*, Jesus, has, "come that [we] might have life, and that [we] might have it more abundantly" Jn 10:10 (KJV).

The Psalmist also confesses: "Thy word have I hid in mine heart, that I might not sin against thee" (Psa. 119:11 KJV).

December 14 - In Whom do You Trust?

There is a song that issues from the heart when once we are delivered from our enemies. Our love for God is easily expressed during these times and we can joyfully speak of the strength of our Lord.

The voice of faith sings the song before the deliverance comes and we see our enemies placed beneath our feet. Faith sees the victory before it is manifest and speaks of it as a thing already done. Faith grabs hold of the promised deliverance and victory when it still seems a long way off. Hebrews 11:1 (KJV) says that, "Now faith is the substance of things hoped for, the evidence of things not seen."

Faith knows that the Lord is my Rock, and my Fortress, and my Deliverer; my God, my Strength, my Buckler, the Horn of my salvation, and my High Tower, when circumstance and situation are arguing that God has forgotten His covenant.

Faith sings, "I will call upon the Lord, Who is worthy to be praised: so shall I be saved from mine enemies! The Lord reigneth, and blessed is my Rock, and blessed is the God of my salvation," while the prisoner of hope is standing in darkness.

It is good to sing praises to the Lord in the day of deliverance, but it is far better to sing the sacrifice of praise in the face of the enemy when the battle looks lost. God cannot resist coming to those on the road of faith. Hebrews 11:6b (KJV) says that, "He is a rewarder of them that diligently seek him."

December 15 - His Word

> In God will I praise his word: in the Lord will I praise his word. Psalm 56:10 (KJV)

In God, *'elohiym*, the Father, the Son, and the Holy Ghost (plural intensive-singular meaning), and His works and possessions, will I praise, llh halal, boasting of Him, will I glory in Him, will I celebrate with a wild spinning dance. The "I will" along with the word, **halal**, carries the idea that this praise was begun in the past and is being done, and will continue again and again. In other words, it is an extended action of great exuberance as a result of great joy and thankfulness.

The Word of God is what is being praised. His word, **dabar**, refers not only to what He says, but embraces what He has done by means of His speaking. This includes, for instance, His business, His manner, and His acts. When He speaks there is a creative result. In Psalms 33:9 (KJV), the Psalmist said it this way, "For he spake, and it was done; he commanded, and it stood fast." The New Testament makes reference to the fact that all things were made by the Word, **logos**: John 1:3 (KJV) "All things were made by him; and without him was not any thing made that was made."

This brings us to the apparent repetitive phrase, "in the Lord will I praise his word." Here, however, the One in whom praise is expressed is none other than Jehovah, **YHWH**, the Existing One.

This repetition emphasizes the act of praise being an act of the will. "In God will I," and "In **YHWH** will I" act like, what to some would be, a mad man. Remember King David as he wildly danced with all of his might and focus before the Ark of the Covenant as it entered the City (2 Sam. 6:14). He was dancing and praising in wild abandon (like a madman) because he was so over joyed at the thoughts of the Presence being near.

He was praising "in the face of God" or, as our verse for today reads, "In God."

December 16 - The Man of Integrity

> LORD, who shall abide in thy tabernacle? who shall dwell in thy holy hill? Psalms 15:1 (KJV)

The man of integrity is the man who will find a continual abode in which to rest in the tabernacle of God that is upon His holy hill.

If this is so, then, what kind of man is a man of integrity? The beginning of the answer to this question can be found in Psalm One:

> Blessed is the man that walketh not in the counsel of the ungodly, nor standeth in the way of sinners, nor sitteth in the seat of the scornful. But his delight is in the law of the LORD; and in his law doth he meditate day and night. And he shall be like a tree planted by the rivers of water, that bringeth forth his fruit in his season; his leaf also shall not wither; and whatsoever he doeth shall prosper. Psalms 1:1-3 (KJV)

The man of integrity does not need the affirmation of the ungodly because he is affirmed by his covenant with God Almighty in Christ Jesus. He loves the Word of God and holds it as the absolute rule and guide for life. He will be found searching the scripture and thinking about its precepts day and night.

Because of his love for the Word of God, he will be stable in all his ways and will not be uprooted by the storms of life. He will have the wisdom, knowledge, and understanding to navigate through seasons of slow business climates as well as those times of great plenty. As a consequence, he will prosper at all times and will not suffer lack.

The man of integrity is one who recognizes that all he has belongs to God and that he is only a steward of the riches of the kingdom of God. As such, he receives great reward for being a good steward of his Master's goods. He abides in the Master's house and is fed at His table. There is no lack to the faithful.

> Moreover it is required in stewards, that a man be found faithful. 1 Corinthians 4:2 (KJV)

> The young lions do lack, and suffer hunger: but they that seek the LORD shall not want any good thing. Psalms 34:10 (KJV)

December 17 - His Name is Great

To the chief Musician on Neginoth, A Psalm or Song of Asaph. In Judah is God known: his name is great in Israel. Psalm 76:1 (KJV)

This Psalm, or melody, is written to the natsach, chief overseer of the singers and musicians, on, *negiynah*, or *negiynath*, stringed instruments.

The interesting thing is that the words, *negiynah*, or *negiynath*, also infer a taunting or mocking song. It could just be that the chief musician might have let talent and skillful excellence become mechanical to the place where they replaced or clouded the anointing and heartfelt praise.

As the rest of this verse states, God is known in, *Yahuwdah*, praising Him. When circumstance or situation make our praise a sacrifice, He receives it as a sweet smelling sacrifice and runs to our aid. He is always pleased with the adoration, thanksgiving, worship, and praise that flows from a sincere heart. As worshipers, we must be ever watchful that our service to Him never becomes rote and lifeless.

God is known, *yada'*, means that we can perceive and understand Him in praise. Praise brings us into an intimate knowlege of Him where we become more than acquainted with Him but are allowed close enough to find out and discern His ways. In other words, He reveals Himself to us as we praise Him. We are drawn ever closer to Him and there can be instructed and made to know the things unknowable by the natural mind.

His name is great in Israel but not only in Israel. He has shown Himself mighty on behalf of His people Israel time and time again. But He is not just the God of the Jews. He is the God of the whole earth and the Creator of all things.

His name is great throughout the whole earth. He is the King of kings, the Lord of lords, the Alpha and Omega, the Aleph and the Tov.

Far above all principality, and power, and might, and dominion, and every name that is named, not only in this world, but also in that which is to come:
Ephesians 1:21 (KJV)

December 18 - The Mighty God Man

For unto us a child is born, unto us a son is given: and the government shall be upon his shoulder: and his name shall be called Wonderful, Counsellor, The mighty God, The everlasting Father, The Prince of Peace.
Isaiah 9:6 (KJV)

One of the names of the Child is the Mighty God Man. This can be seen in the word, mighty, *gibbowr*, which means: mighty man, valiant man, strong man, upright man, champion and chief, and the word, God, *'el*, God, god-like one, mighty one, mighty men, men of rank, mighty heroes and God, the one true God, Jehovah.

Gibbowr is used again in the book of Zephaniah as we read, "The, *Yehovah*, the existing One, thy, *'elohiym*, the (true) God in the midst of thee is, *gibbowr*, the Mighty God Man. It is this Mighty God Man who will save and who will, *suws*, greatly rejoice of thee with great rejoicing.

The LORD thy God in the midst of thee is mighty; he will save, he will rejoice over thee with joy; he will rest in his love, he will joy over thee with singing.
Zephaniah 3:17 (KJV)

Verse 17 goes on to say that this Mighty God Man will, *charash*, rest and be silent in the engraving or ploughing because of His great love.

Have you not read in Isaiah 50:6 (KJV) where it reads, "I gave my back to the smiters, . ." or in Isaiah 53:7 (KJV) where it is recorded that, " He was oppressed, and he was afflicted, yet he opened not his mouth: he is brought as a lamb to the slaughter, and as a sheep before her shearers is dumb, so he openeth not his mouth." It was His great love that caused Him to yield to the cruel mocking, even the mockery of a trial that lead to the whipping post where they ploughed His sinless back.

Yes, even in His suffering and silence He prepared His heart to joy over thee with, *rinnah*, a song of triumphal proclamation sung with shouting, joy, gladness, and, yes, even tears. With a ringing cry it began with, "It is Finished!".

Every enemy of our soul was vanquished by the Mighty God Man at Calvary's Tree!

December 19 - Pray For The Peace of Jerusalem

Pray for the peace of Jerusalem: they shall prosper that love thee. Psalms 122:6 (KJV)

I am a born-again Gentile. As far as I know, I have no Jewish blood in me. Even if I did, I would still be Christian first and foremost. That being said, I am a solidly pro-Israel Zionist.

Oh, I know, this is not an especially popular position. Anti-Semitism is rampant in the world today. The City of God is divided and in constant turmoil. If Islam could have its way there would be no Israel and no Jews on the earth. Oh, did I mention that there would not be any Christians either?

Biblically, I only see three people groups that God recognizes. According to 1 Corinthians 10, He recognizes Jews, Gentiles, and the Church. Scripture also teaches us that He has a covenant with the Jews (Israel), a covenant with the Church and that He will deal with the Gentiles (Nations).

Give none offence, neither to the Jews, nor to the Gentiles, nor to the church of God:
1 Corinthians 10:32 (KJV)

Beloved, don't get duped into thinking that all the problems of the world are because of the Jews. Don't buy into the lie that the Holocaust never happened. Don't let the devil deceive you into believing that God doesn't care what happens to Israel and the remnant of His "chosen people."

I'm totally against Christians being Judaized (taken back into bondage to the law - We are saved by grace . . .). But I am totally for Israel and the Jewish people. God must be too or He would not promise to prosper all that love Jerusalem the rightful Capital of Israel.

Let's not forget that Israel is one of our staunchest allies and of great benefit to our nation.

Take some time to pray for Israel today. God will be pleased.

December 20 - Wonderful!

What a marvelous word. "Wonderful". It has a ring of expectancy, of excitement. It was one of the words used to describe Jesus the Messiah in Isaiah.

> For unto us a child is born, unto us a son is given: and the government shall be upon his shoulder: and his name shall be called WONDERFUL, Counselor, The mighty God, The everlasting Father, The Prince of Peace Isaiah 9:6 (KJV)

The synonyms of "Wonderful" are intriguing. They are: fantastic, magnificent, marvelous, splendid, amazing, incredible, miraculous, remarkable, and spectacular.

Jesus is Fantastic! He is the Magnificent Counselor as well as a Marvelous Brother. A most Splendid Friend Who is simply Amazing in His ability to understand our every need. His unconditional love is as Incredible as His Miraculous intervention in the affairs of our lives. It is positively Remarkable how He fulfilled all prophecy that concerned Him. This feat is more than the human mind can comprehend. When He comes for His bride it will be a Spectacular event surpassed only by His return, for the second time, with Her to reign on the earth....

Wonderful! All He has done for you and I! How can we but praise Him!

> O LORD, thou art my God; I will exalt thee, I will praise thy name; for thou hast done WONDERFUL things; thy counsels of old are faithfulness and truth. Isaiah 25:1 (KJV)

Take time, as you celebrate His virgin birth, to consider all that Jesus is. Ponder His workings in your life. Savor His Presence. Give a gift to Him! A gift to further His work. A gift to the house of God.

Better yet - The gift of yourself.

December 21 - As Concerns You

As I was reading 1 Chronicles 28 one evening I felt that wonderful quickening of the Word as concerns you.

King David was speaking to his son Solomon; giving direction and encouragement concerning the building of the temple. He revealed that every detail had been given by the direction of the Holy Spirit[1]

You are the son of the King; one of the precious builders of that temple not made with hands.[2]

Take heed now; for the Lord has chosen you to build a house for the sanctuary. Be strong and do it![3]

This is the hour of the setting up of the pillars and the crowning of their heads with a covering of glory. The Spirit of the Living God is moving with great decisiveness across the face of the earth. He is gathering His people and sounding the trumpet call to assemble His tribes as He sets the battle in array.

Leaders are needed in great number. As you minister to, train, equip, anoint, and release them into this great field of conflict, in the midst of overwhelming odds, the Lord will crown them with His wisdom and empower them with His own glorious anointing. They shall be strong and do exploits for they shall know their God.[4]

Be strong and courageous, and do it. Fear not, nor be dismayed: for the Lord God, my God, is with you. He will not fail or forsake you until you have finished all the work for the service of the house of the Lord.[5]

1) 1Chronicles 28:12: 2) 1 Corinthians 3:16; 2 Corinthians 6:16: 3) 1 Chronicles 28:10: 4) Daniel 11:32: 5) 1 Chronicles 28:20

December 22 - Have A Blessed Christmas!

Can you believe it? Christmas and the Year's end already!

Time, as we know it, is moving by so very quickly. God is doing "His act, His strange act." The world is racing toward it's end time fulfillment. All is unfolding as it should.

Do you feel the same stirring within that I do; that thrilling sense of urgency that permeates everything that we are about? What an hour in which to live!

Dear One, the year ahead is going to be one of the most difficult and yet one of the most fruitful of worldwide harvest times for the Church. I'm not just talking about opportunities for ministry overseas, in the "mission fields" (although these opportunities will be great!) but right where you live. Even if schools, government agencies, sections of cities, clubs, Conventions, groups and individuals continue to close their doors to Christianity you will find that individual hearts will begin to change. God is turning it around!

Your city is one of the greatest harvest fields in the world! The nations have moved next door and are looking for a hand of welcome and encouragement. Jesus would be found moving in their midst, speaking their language, offering hope, pointing them toward the Living God; and such is our calling.

Be strong and very courageous . . . turn not from (your calling) to the right hand or to the left, that you may prosper where ever you go. Do exploits for God in this hour and see them prosper like never before! [Joshua 1:7; Daniel 11:32b].

Have a blessed Christmas and a Prosperous New Year!

December 23 - Follow

Saying, Where is he that is born King of the Jews? for we have seen his star in the east, and are come to worship him. Matthew 2:2 (KJV)

When they had heard the king, they departed; and, lo, the star, which they saw in the east, went before them, till it came and stood over where the young child was.
Matthew 2:9 (KJV)
You cannot lead until you learn to follow. The Wise Men were the leaders of their day because they knew how, and were willing, to follow the star.

What we follow shapes our lives: The Wise Men were made to be worshipers.

What we follow gives direction to our lives: They traveled to Bethlehem to meet their destiny.

What we follow sets (establishes) the goal of our lives: Their goal was to see the Christ Child and provide for Him with gifts (Gold for the King, Frankincense for the Priest, and Myrrh for the Sacrifice).

What we follow will determine who we meet on our way to our destination: They, no doubt, met marauders and thieves along the way. Herod the Tetrarch hosted their arrival. An angel warned them of impending danger and they met Joseph and Mary who allowed them to see the Lord of Glory.

Who we follow will determine our destiny: The Wise Men were never the same after they saw Him.

Who we follow defines all we are and all we do: Jesus said, And he saith unto them, Follow me, and I will make you fishers of men. Matthew 4:19 (KJV)

He will make us: 1) Our nature is changed. 2) our purpose is changed. 3) Sometimes our vocation is changed.

He will define us: 1) Now we are "fishers of men." 2) Now we are "Sons of God" (Rom. 8:14). 3) Now we are "Heirs of the World" (Psa. 2:8).

The Christmas season is a time to recommit our lives to follow Him.

If we do, God will make us like Him (1 Joh. 3;2).
Selah.

December 24 - The Mystery

Now to him that is of power to stablish you according to my gospel, and the preaching of Jesus Christ, according to the revelation of the mystery, which was kept secret since the world began, Romans 16:25 (KJV)

The Christmas season is designed to lure the inquisitive into a revelation of the mystery of the ages: God Incarnate. The historical story of He who always was, is and will be, contained and constrained in the womb of a virgin birthed upon the earth.

For unto us a child is born, unto us a son is given: and the government shall be upon his shoulder: and his name shall be called Wonderful, Counsellor, The mighty God, The everlasting Father, The Prince of Peace.
Isaiah 9:6 (KJV)

The Mystery, *musterion*, the hidden thing, secret, mystery of God and His plan that was set in motion in the secret counsels which govern God in dealing with the righteous, which are hidden from ungodly and wicked men but plain to the godly.

It's no wonder, then, that Satan wants to eliminate every mention or semblance of Christmas from our minds. Isn't it wonderful to know that there is nothing he can do to remove the wonder of the birth of Christ from the believer's heart?

Who shall separate us from the love of Christ? shall tribulation, or distress, or persecution, or famine, or nakedness, or peril, or sword? For I am persuaded, that neither death, nor life, nor angels, nor principalities, nor powers, nor things present, nor things to come, Nor height, nor depth, nor any other creature, shall be able to separate us from the love of God, which is in Christ Jesus our Lord. Romans 8:35, 38-39 (KJV)

It was the good pleasure of God to reveal the mystery of His Son and redemptions plan to us and nothing can steal that from us!

Having made known unto us the mystery of his will, according to his good pleasure which he hath purposed in himself: Ephesians 1:9 (KJV). And to make all men see what is the fellowship of the mystery, which from the beginning of the world hath been hid in God, who created all things by Jesus Christ: Ephesians 3:9 (KJV).

December 25 - Family

God instituted "family." Family consists of one man and one woman along with their offspring. The extended family includes relatives (both in-laws and out-laws). We are taught by the Lord to honor our mothers and our fathers. We are also taught to protect, nurture and guide our children in those gifts which God has placed within them and to raise them in the fear and admonition of the Lord. The family is meant to be a ministry unit in Christ.

What better way to minister as a family on Christmas day than to attend church as a family. A family should gather with the church family to minister to them and the Lord as they worship together.

Our society is drifting away from esteeming the Lord's Day as a holy day set apart for the pursuit of God and the establishment of His Kingdom on earth.

If we're not careful our busy life-styles leave no time for the church family and corporate worship. The most important things are set aside for the important and the important things are lost in the pressing things.

How do we know what is really important? I believe that the Bible can help us here. Listen to what Jesus said when His family wanted to take Him away from His "family."

And he looked round about on them which sat about him, and said, Behold my mother and my brethren! For whosoever shall do the will of God, the same is my brother, and my sister, and mother. Mark 3:34-35 (KJV)

Then came to him his mother and his brethren, and could not come at him for the press. And it was told him by certain which said, Thy mother and thy brethren stand without, desiring to see thee. And he answered and said unto them, My mother and my brethren are these which hear the word of God, and do it. Luke 8:19-21 (KJV)

Was this disrespectful of Jesus Mother, brothers, and sisters? No, not one bit. Remember, Jesus cared for His mother and family and made sure that John would take care of her after His death, burial and resurrection. It is just keeping first things first.

December 26 - Perfecting You

The Lord will perfect that which concerneth me: thy mercy, O Lord, endureth for ever: forsake not the works of thine own hands. Psalm 138:8 (KJV)

The Lord will not only perfect those things that concern you, He will perfect you.

Yes, His work to bring the environment around you into a garden like state begins with you. From the moment that you yield to the Person of Jesus the Christ, repent of, and confess your sins, ask Him to come into your heart and life as Lord and Savior, God begins to make you like His Son.

For whom he did foreknow, he also did predestinate to be conformed to the image of his Son, that he might be the firstborn among many brethren. Romans 8:29 (KJV)

But we all, with open face beholding as in a glass the glory of the Lord, are changed into the same image from glory to glory, even as by the Spirit of the Lord. 2 Corinthians 3:18 (KJV)

This powerful promise is also borne out in 1 Corinthians 15:49 where it reads, "And as we have borne the image of the earthy, we shall also bear the image of the heavenly."

That, "The Lord will perfect that which concerneth me," uses the Hebrew word, **gamar**, for "perfect" brings emphasis to the promise. He will bring to completion by performing the promised act Himself. He will not fail to accomplish what He has promised concerning you!

This has nothing to do with your efforts whatsoever. It has everything to do with His eternally enduring mercy. His, **checed**, that is, His merciful favor, goodness, and lovingkindness is what is at work in our lives to complete His plan and purpose for our lives.

As it is written:

For I know the thoughts that I think toward you, saith the LORD, thoughts of peace, and not of evil, to give you an expected end. Jeremiah 29:11 (KJV)

December 27 - The Sum of the Matter

How precious also are thy thoughts unto me, O God!
how great is the sum of them! Psalm 139:17 (KJV)

Of how much worth do we count the thoughts of God?
Do we, *yaqar*, esteem them, appraise them to be something
prized, highly valued and costly? Do they hold such importance
to us that we search them out and ponder the fulness of their
meaning?

Solomon was said to be the wisest man that ever lived on
earth (1 Ki. 3:12) and he is recorded as saying that the sum of the
activity of life is to "Fear God, and keep his commandments."

Let us hear the conclusion of the whole matter: Fear
God, and keep his commandments: for this is the whole
duty of man. Ecclesiastes 12:13 (KJV)

To, "fear God," is to be filled with reverential awe of Him
with whom we have to do. His commandments are the concepts,
precepts, and commands, of God Almighty. These are recorded
in His Word, the Bible.

Solomon counted the thoughts of God to be foundational
and indispensable to every facet of human existence. Jesus had
this same regard for the thoughts and words of God the Father,
if not more. He knew that the thoughts, *rea'*, of God revealed the
wisdom, knowledge, purpose and aim of God.

The Hebrew word used for "great" is the word, *'atsam*, and
carries with it the idea of increased mighty strength. The, sum,
ro'sh, or, the beginning or first, the principal part of, the chapter,
choicest, and best, or the chief of a band.

It seems that the "thoughts of God" are the choicest, best,
and principal part of the wisdom, knowledge, purpose and aim
of, the "sum" of, His ever increasing might and strength. From
this, it would appear that He who is omnipotent (all powerful) is
ever increasing in His display of might and strength. This display
of His ability and power is like the chapter is to the column.
It crowns the structural pillar with stately beauty and finishes
the joint between the column and lintel. These "thoughts" are,
therefore, "precious" to the appraiser.

December 28 - I Will Make Them

>   And I will make them and the places round about my hill a blessing; and I will cause the shower to come down in his season; there shall be showers of blessing.
>   Ezekiel 34:26 (KJV)

The Lord said, "I will make them . . .". I will make, *nathan*, bestow upon, deliver to, yield to, cause, entrust to, produce in, or extend to them a blessing. The word used for blessing is, *barakah*, which includes in its meaning, source of blessing, prosperity, a gift, a praise of God, and a treaty of peace.

The Prince of Peace is giving us a treaty of peace and offering to make us a source of blessing and prosperity. This gift will make our lives a praise of God.

The Lord also promises to make the places round about, *cabiyb*, that is, round about us on every side, to be places of blessing and prosperity. His "hill" is simply a poetic word used for mountain, *gib'ah*. The idea being that anywhere around His Presence is a place of blessing.

The shower, *geshem*, is a allusion to the natural showers that bring fruitfulness to the earth. The Lord will cause the shower to come down "in His season." Ecclesiastes 3:1 (KJV) tells us that, "To every thing there is a season, and a time to every purpose under the heaven." The Book of Genesis 8:22 (KJV) reminds us that, "While the earth remaineth, seedtime and harvest, and cold and heat, and summer and winter, and day and night shall not cease."

There are "seasons" set by God Almighty Himself and He will maintain their integrity. Just as there are natural seasons that bring showers of blessing to the earth, so we see the promise of showers of blessings flowing from the spiritual realm that will bring prosperity to those He has made to be a blessing.

You and I, Beloved, are blessed to be a blessing and, "Every good gift and every perfect gift is from above, and cometh down from the Father of lights, with whom is no variableness, neither shadow of turning." James 1:17 (KJV)

402

December 29 - Compact Together

Jerusalem is builded as a city that is compact together: Psalm 122:3 (KJV)

There is the natural and there is the spiritual. According to 1 Corinthians 15:44 (KJV), the body of man is sown a natural body and then is raised a spiritual body. "There is a natural body, and there is a spiritual body."

We are told that the enemies we face are not natural but spiritual: Ephesians 6:12 says,

For we wrestle not against flesh and blood, but against principalities, against powers, against the rulers of the darkness of this world, against spiritual wickedness in high places. Ephesians 6:12 (KJV)

There is a city in Israel named Jerusalem, the City of Peace, or the Teaching of Peace. Its name speaks of a plurality: Jerusalem, *yerûshālaim*, a dual (in allusion to its two main hills or, possibly, its natural and spiritual foundation. It also means, founded peaceful. The words, compact, and, together, also reinforce this idea. *Chabar*, the word translated, compact, means coupled, or joined together. It gives the sense of being united, or in league together with. Together, *yachad*, also means, together, in fact, altogether, and lends more to the idea of, unitedness or being alike.

Tradition holds that the heavenly Jerusalem is located just above, or, better said, is superimposed over, the natural Jerusalem. One might even consider it more of a dimensional superimposition rather than a spatial proximity.

If we consider this possibility we might better be able to comprehend how Jacob could see the top of the ladder at Bethel or why Jesus would walk through the wall into the room where His disciples were assembled in fear of the Romans. This, too, might help explain how one can "see" angels or demons or the Lord, high and lifted up from a natural location on earth.

The day is coming, perhaps soon, when the heavenly will appear and descend

And I John saw the holy city, new Jerusalem, coming down from God out of heaven, prepared as a bride adorned for her husband. Revelation 21:2 (KJV)

December 30 - An Even Balance

> Let me be weighed in an even balance, that God may know mine integrity. Job 31:6 (KJV)

I have always been intrigued with the revelation of the Christ of God that some of the early Old Testament believers had. It was Job that said, "For I know that my redeemer liveth, and that he shall stand at the latter day upon the earth:" (Job 19:25 KJV)

Our verse today gives us a look at how deep this revelation was imbedded in his heart. He knew by the Spirit that his own righteousness was not enough to tip the scale in his favor. You see, the righteousness of God is the balanced scale.

Job asked the Lord to be weighed in an "even" balance. This word, even, is the Hebrew, *tsedeq*, which means, besides righteousness, the righteousness of the Davidic king, Messiah, Jesus the Christ. This righteous scale, or balance, is known as an attribute of God as covenant-keeping in redemption.

Beloved, you and I live in the day in which the Davidic King, Messiah, Jesus the Christ of God has been revealed to us and indwells us. He is known by born-again believers as no Old Testament believer ever could know Him. We are most blessed as we allow the finished work of Christ to be our righteousness through faith.

> For he hath made him to be sin for us, who knew no sin; that we might be made the righteousness of God in him. 2 Corinthians 5:21 (KJV)

How can this be? Speaking to and of Abraham, it is written: "And he believed in the LORD; and he counted it to him for righteousness" (Gen.15:6 KJV). "But to him that worketh not, but believeth on him that justifieth the ungodly, his faith is counted for righteousness" (Rom. 4:5 KJV).

Job understood that his righteousness was by faith in his coming Messiah, Jesus the Christ of God, not his own works.

He said, that "God may know, *yada,* may touch upon and reveal so all will know mine integrity, *tummah*. He knew that he would be justified by faith in his eternal Redeemer who would surely stand upon the earth at the latter day.

May we have such assurance in this day in which we live. *Selah!*

December 31 - God's Plan For You

For I know the thoughts that I think toward you, saith the LORD, thoughts of peace, and not of evil, to give you an expected end. Jeremiah 29:11 (KJV)

Jeremiah 29:11 is one of the most quoted verses in our church and with good reason. The assurance that God has a plan for each of us brings a sense of Divine destiny to our lives as well as a strengthening of our hope and faith for the future.

The Hebrew word used for thoughts is, *machashabah,* which not only means, thought, but device, devise, plan, purpose, means and imaginations.

Hold that and consider what the Lord means when He says, "the thoughts that I think." The word think is, *chashab,* (you can see it in *machashabah*) which, though it has much of the same interpretation, also carries the idea of cunning, reckoning, purpose, esteem, prophetic prediction, imputation and conception.

In other words, the thoughts that God has for you are prophetic and shall come to pass. He will conceive, cause to be birthed and matured in your life those things that He has planned for you.

No wonder that "all things" work in our lives to bring us into the fulness of His master plan.

And we know that all things work together for good to them that love God, to them who are the called according to his purpose. Romans 8:28 (KJV)

These thoughts are thoughts of peace, *shalowm,* which brings completeness (wholeness), prosperity, safety, and health which are the benefits of a covenant relationship with Him.

Knowing this should give every believer a sense of well-being and a revelation of the love of God that can only come from being positive that He will bring to pass what He has purposed and said. Our end, *'achariyth,* prophetic destiny and reward is one that is expected, *tiqvah,* the very thing that I long for.

The dream and plan for your life is that you will receive, as a gift from Him, the very thing that you have longed for!
Selah!

RESOURCES

OTHER BOOKS BY THE AUTHOR

$15.00

ISBN 978-0-9855128-1-1

51500>

9 780985 512811

411

www.ingramcontent.com/pod-product-compliance
Lightning Source LLC
Chambersburg PA
CBHW051937090426

42741CB00008B/1177